BRAIN DAMAGE:

A Juror's Tale

By

Paul Sanders

The 13th Juror

Third Edition: 2022

Library of Congress Control Number: 2017900671
CreateSpace Independent Publishing Platform, North Charleston, SC

Dedicated to the memory of Dale Harrell and all the people he touched in his life.

With special acknowledgements to:

- ❖ Mindi Harrell
- ❖ Judge Roland Steinle III
- ❖ Eric Basta
- ❖ Michelle Arino
- ❖ Mike Bishop
- ❖ Alan Tavasoli
- ❖ Andrew Clemency
- ❖ Laura Rivers
- ❖ My fellow 15 Jurors
- ❖ The State of Arizona Jury Commissioner's Office
- ❖ KC Wuraftic
- ❖ Jennifer Wood

*There can be no good ending in a
murder trial...
only lessons.*

September 6, 2014

CONTENTS

PROLOGUE

FORENSICALLY SPEAKING

Gilbert, Arizona Police Department

Evidence I.D. Number: 168537-3

Computer Forensic Investigator: Detective Scott Zuberbuehler.

Document Name: "Something Odd Going On."

Built-In Properties Containing Metadata: 3

Title: Something Odd Going On

Author: Dr. Allen Flores

Creation Date: 12/13/08 @ 9:52:00 AM

Last Save Time: 12/13/08 @11:18 AM

Last Saved By: Dr. Allen Flores

Total Edit Time (Minutes): 86 Minutes

(One month before the attack on Dale Harrell)

"Something Odd Going On:

I am writing this as I am in a state of confusion and turmoil with regards to my relationship with Reese (Marissa-Suzanne DeVault).

We have been dating since March of 2007 and things were initially wonderful. We became quite close and our families effectively merged. However, around the time she moved to her new house, things became strained, starting with the time Rhiannon ran away and came here.

The last few months have been odd with missed appointments, temporarily lost phones and other strange things. I discovered last weekend that Dale (Reese's ex-husband) has been living at Reese's house for at least a few months now. I knew that Dale had been constantly abusive but Reese has been trying to work things out...for the good of the girls. She wants him to be a part of the girl's lives but he uses that as a lever to stay involved with Reese's life as well. A couple of months ago, Dale injured Reese sufficiently to get himself arrested but Reese went to the prosecutor and requested that he not be charged with a felony (otherwise he would not be able to keep his job and pay child support).

As I understand from Reese, this arrangement cleared by the court last week so Dale is now back at work. She and I are hoping that this will be a new beginning for him. (Hopefully), this will be a new beginning for him and he will turn this around for himself and become a better father for the girls and (be) more respectful of Reese having her own, separate life.

The initial story from Reese when I discovered that Dale was living at her house illegally (has a restraining order against him) was that since he was not working while he was in jail and the plea bargain was being arranged, Dale lost his apartment. She said that he played on her emotions...and allowed him to stay on the stipulation that he be back in his own place by February. However, when I checked with Rhiannon and then I told Reese that I knew this had been going on much longer, she said that he has, in fact, been living with her off and on for many months, even though all of the times he had been out on bail and had various restraining orders against him. She has said that he would terrorize her, using the kids as pawns, and often hit her if he stood up for himself.

Sadly, this is her call to make for her life.

I have discussed battered women support groups with her; I have read up on Arizona laws pertaining to domestic violence and harassment...I have tried to give her the encouragement and strength to stand up to him. I believe that has worked and she seems more confident than she has in a while. I would like to think that my compassion and understanding of her situation...has contributed to her increased sense of self-worth. Reese has said she needs to conceal much of that around Dale, though, to avoid getting hit.

Reese said that she was going to allow Dale to stay until the beginning of February, which would allow him time to get some paychecks together to get an apartment as well as allow him time to spend the holidays with the girls. I argued that that seemed like a generous timeframe, but she said that was what she had agreed and she would stick to it. I am skeptical that Dale will actually leave in February but Reese's relationship with Dale is hers to deal with, not mine. I offered to loan Reese money to get Dale his own apartment but initially she rejected that idea. I think she hoped that this would give him time to get himself together.

Reese has just now asked for a sizable loan for Dale, though. She hasn't exactly said how much yet, so I am assuming she is either looking at apartments and/or is talking with Dale about how much it will take to basically "buy him out of the house". I have cautioned that the money should go directly to the apartment complex with, perhaps, some pocket money for Dale. We both know that any agreement with Dale that he not come back into Reese's life (except for visitation with the girls), will only last as long as the money does.

Hopefully, money will not be an issue for Reese much longer. I have been loaning her money for the last year or so for living expenses, rent in her previous house, medical expenses for her and the girls and (for) much of the down payment for her new house. She is due a payout from an insurance policy from The Hartford which was tied up for quite a while with her grandmother's trust. She is represented by Platt & Westby in the suit and she says that The Hartford has agreed to pay within a matter of a month or so, after more than a year of legal machinations. The amount due is $1.8 million. The plan is that Reese will use those funds to pay me back, pay off the mortgage on her house and set up trust funds for the girls' futures. I am hoping that, with financial security in her life, Reese will have the personal fortitude and resources to be completely herself and not fall back into the pattern of giving into the fear of Dale, with the rationalization that it's for the sake of the girls.

I am writing this to myself as there are still a number of things which make me quite uneasy. Reese has admitted to concealing that Dale was living at her house. I suspect there are a number of other things which are not as she has told me. She is involved in a case filed against her and others for her house; she doesn't act as if she is about to come into a lot of money (perhaps it's just a "don't count your chickens before they are hatched" feeling"). Is she being completely honest about the relationship with Dale?

I just have the sense that there are some odd things going on in her life and she isn't being completely honest with me about them. Whatever they are, and whatever the real stories are, I hope they get resolved between now and February, if not sooner. If not, although I will miss her and the girls, I'm going to have to break things off."

***

Gilbert, Arizona Police Department

Evidence I.D. Number: 168537-3 (Part 2)

Computer Forensic Investigator: Detective Scott Zuberbuehler.

Document Name: "Something Odd Going On."

Built-In Properties Containing Metadata: 6

Title: Something Odd Going On

Author: Dr. Allen Flores

Creation Date: 12/20/08 @ 6:12:00 AM

Last Save Time: 12/20/08 @7:23 AM

Last Saved By: Dr. Allen Flores

Total Edit Time (Minutes): 58 Minutes

(Twenty Five days before the attack on Dale Harrell)

"Something Odd Going On, Continued Part 2:

{It is now 6:30 AM, Sunday morning, 12/20/08}

Even more odd things going on...

I met with Reese on Wednesday and Thursday this week...We talked about her going with Dale to the Harrah's Ak-Chin Casino as a birthday celebration Thursday evening and she asked to borrow more money so she could gamble and have a good time. The plan was for her to have a nice time with him and then broach the subject of him moving out sooner than the agreed February 1st.

Well, when I met with Reese on Thursday, and I mentioned that something odd seemed to be going on, she confided in me that the money I had given her was not for Dale to get an apartment but she was using it to take out a hit on him! According to her, she has given the money to an old friend named, Travis Tatro who lives at {redacted} who was in a relationship with an old stripper friend of hers, Mistie Robbins. Apparently, Reese and Travis had a relationship when Reese was stripping a number of years ago.

Reese also told me that contrary to what she has told everyone, her father is not dead. He just decided that he wanted nothing to do with her many years ago and made her swear to have no contact with him.

She also said that none of her three girls are Dale's. In fact, she has said that her youngest, Diahnon, is actually Travis Tatro's daughter!

It took me awhile to recover from the series of admissions. When I did, I explained that there are a variety of legal ways to deal with Dale. She said she had to be done with him and she saw taking out the hit on him as the only way. She explained that that was the real reason she had allowed him to come back into her house, so she could "keep an eye" on him while she made her plans to kill him herself which she was planning to do in early February on a trip to the dunes with their friends.

Rather than doing that, she went on to say that she had gotten in touch with Travis who agreed to do the hit on Dale...

So, Reese borrowed $4000 from me on 12/14 and another $3000 on 12/16 to prepay Travis half of the cost of the hit. She went into some detail that Travis had to purchase an unregistered car plus a completely clean handgun with no history...

She detailed the plan that on Thursday evening; she would take Dale to Harrah's for his birthday. She would hide money in a couple places in the car in advance. They would have dinner and begin to gamble. At various points, when they were running out of money or Reese needed cigarettes, she would send Dale out to the car to get cigarettes or for another stash of the money. On one of those trips, Travis was supposed to surprise Dale and kill him, making it look like a botched robbery attempt. The backup plan if Travis didn't show up was to let Dale get drunk, stay over at the casino that night, wait until Dale was asleep and then kill him, claiming that he was being abusive and she was defending herself, or even claiming that he was attempting to rape her.

Well, I had a horrible night Thursday night, worrying about what might happen and what I should do, if anything. Friday, about noon, I text messaged Reese to ask if she was home yet. She called me back and said the plan did not come off on Thursday night but she and Dale were staying at the casino for another night which would give Travis additional opportunities. As usual lately with Reese, things sounded odd.

Last night, just before midnight, I picked up David, my son, from his school dance. I had mentioned to him about the decorations Reese had done on her house for Christmas. We drove over to her house so he could see the decorations. However, when David and I drove past, the Expedition was in the driveway and all the lights were out in the house. This is quite unusual as Stan (her roommate) usually stays up playing video games during the night, and his window is in the front of the house, and other house lights are usually on all of the time. Clearly, the house was vacant.

So, what are the possible explanations? My best guess at this point is that Reese lied to me and she and Dale took the girls on vacation, and there was no trip to the casino. So, rather than using the money for an apartment for Dale, and rather than using the money for a hit on him, she used the money to plan a trip with Dale and the girls. As upset as I would be for being played a sucker, that would be preferable to the alternate scenario I am imagining.

Is it possible that Reese took out a hit, not on Dale, but on me?

If I were killed, Reese wouldn't have to worry about paying me back the nearly three hundred thousand which she owes me at this point. If the fact that her down payment on the house came from me were known, it could create problems with her current lawsuit with National Tax. I am assuming there are numerous other lies which will eventually come to light – perhaps there is no Hartford insurance payout coming, nor a trust fund settlement – so perhaps she is figuring I will be upset and put a lien on the house, or possibly even take the house, for the money owed me. It would also prevent me from reporting that Dale has been living at the house illegally; that Reese has allowed herself to be abused by Dale, sometimes in front of the girls; that Dale has been abusive to the girls occasionally also; and that Dale should be in prison and the girls taken away from Reese.

Up until a week ago, I would never have thought Reese would be capable of taking out a hit on someone, much less me, but at this point I believe it's possible. If she and Dale took the kids on vacation somewhere, now would be the opportune time for Travis (or whoever she may have actually hired), as Reese would have an alibi for herself.

I pray nothing happens and everything resolves peacefully for everyone concerned. If not, though, I hope this document helps answer questions about what really happened.

I have attached the most recent printout of the monies owed me by Reese and an old copy of her promissory note. The most recent promissory note is in the safe in my office. The combination is {redacted}."

***

Gilbert, Arizona Police Department

Evidence I.D. Number: 168537-3

Computer Forensic Investigator: Detective Scott Zuberbuehler.

Document Name: "Something Odd Going On. Part 3"

Built-In Properties Containing Metadata: 6

Title: Something Odd Going On

Author: Dr. Allen Flores

Creation Date: 1/13/08 @ 10:35:00 PM

Last Save Time: 12/14/08 @12:43 AM

Last Saved By: Dr. Allen Flores

Total Edit Time (Minutes): 11 Minutes

(Fifty-four minutes before the attack on Dale Harrell)

"Something Odd Going On, Part 3 Continued:

It is now Ten PM on Tuesday, 1/13/09. I am now more convinced that Reese has been lying all along and has, quite possibly, taken out a hit on me.

She told me that, last Thursday, January 8, she took Dale to dinner and told him that he is no longer welcome in their home. When they got home, they had a big fight and he had her on the ground and was hitting her presumably trying to kill her. She said that Stan, Dale's brother, called 911, threw down the phone, and grabbed a tire iron from the garage. He then hit Dale in the head repeatedly. When the police arrived shortly thereafter, Dale was taken to the hospital with massive head injuries and he died forty-five minutes later. Since then, Reese has told me about family from both sides coming to visit, making funeral arrangements, being questioned by the police about the incident and a host of other things.

These were all lies! I went to Reese's house this evening when she said she was at work and Dale's truck was there. The kids and Stan said that Reese was out with Dale.

After I returned home, I conversed with Reese online and via text, and she was still lying about being at work (I don't believe she's actually worked at Macy's for at least three months now). In a most unusual request, she asked that I come pick her up at work. Even on its face, this seems quite odd. She claims that she has Stan drop her off at work, thinking that I might come pick her up, which I have never done before...Stan did not drop her off at work and Reese and Dale have the Expedition with them. My guess is that they are at a club since Reese left here today in club wear. Dale's truck is still at home. So, why would Reese want me to come pick her up?

The only conclusion I can come to is that she and Dale are planning for me to come to the Macy's parking lot....and they have arranged for something to happen to me.

I have just texted her that I will not be picking her up..."

***

We were sitting outside in the courthouse courtyard at a table at "The Change of Venue". I had just finished reading the evidence that, we, the jury had not been allowed to see.

"What do you think?" Jen asked me. She was a court reporter for an internet trial news channel. She and I had struck it off right after the sentencing of Marissa DeVault.

My involvement in the trial had begun on January 23, 2014 and sentencing had been on June 6, 2014. As most trials go, this was considered one of the longer term trials and had been high profile with cameras and reporters in the courtroom every day.

I was happy that I could finally talk about it once the admonishment had been released.

"This isn't what happened," I said in reference to the computer forensic documents I had just read.

"What's your opinion of the trial," she asked.

I reached into my briefcase and pulled out a thick manuscript and laid it on the table in front of her. "This is what I think happened," I said. I pushed it toward her.

Jen flipped though the document while being careful to keep hold of it due to the hot breeze blowing.

"I kept a journal of everyday that we were in court on this case," I said. "I want you to read it. Keep in mind that it is not a court record. It is a journal of what I heard and interpreted at the trial. The quotes may not be exact and only represent what I remembered daily. I also changed all the Juror's names."

"Wow," she said holding the thick manuscript.

"This is what I think really happened, as it was given to us by the trial."

DAY 1

THE LOTTERY

I first received my notice in the fall of 2013 for jury duty in the State of Arizona. It was an innocuous three by five post card stating that I was due to appear on the 23rd of October, 2013. It was about 10 days before I was to appear that I realized I had a schedule conflict. I called the courthouse, I told them I had a conflict and they changed the date to January 23rd, 2014.

It was a simple twist of fate.

I had been called for jury duty in a multiplicity of other states that I have lived in such as Michigan, Florida, Utah and California. It was usually the same routine. I would hurry downtown for the designated time, check-in and stand around for eight hours never really leaving the lobby of whatever courthouse I had appeared in. Usually, it was another few years before I received another notice and it was always the same routine. Wait and wait all day for apparently nothing.

When I received my second notice to appear for my rescheduled date, I planned on the same thing. This time however, I wanted to make productive use of the day and brought a briefcase with all my receipts for the year so that I could prepare the groundwork for my taxes. I wouldn't be standing around doing nothing for eight hours. I would make value of the day.

It was a beautiful and crisp morning when I left for downtown Phoenix. Living in the upper west side of the Valley, I thought I had allowed plenty of time to get there. Unfortunately, being that it was now eight in the morning, I had to break the law to get there on time, using the carpool lane to make it down the 51 Freeway. I thought it ironic that I had broken the law in order to make the law, as it were. In a panic, I found the juror parking garage, showed my notice and parked the car in the first parking spot I saw; which I couldn't find until I was on the eighth floor, a level shy of the roof.

I grabbed my briefcase and ran to the courthouse, not wanting to wait for the juror bus, and run the risk of being late. Checking in through security, they confiscated my Swiss Army penknife and told me to pick it up later.

I was directed toward a kiosk area with machines lined up like ATMs. I made my way to one and checked myself in. There was a short questionnaire to verify my jury card information. I was asked my occupation and checked in as an author/ bartender. The machine spit out a sticker that I was to place on my shirt for identification. I found a seat in a packed jury assembly area, looked for my name on a display screen and, not seeing it, began to work on my receipts.

"Hey, do you know what we're getting paid?" he asked.

I looked up from what I was doing. Ironically, I had looked up that question online before setting out for the day. "We're paid twelve dollars a day," I answered.

"Well," he said as he picked up his newspaper, "it's better than Jersey. We got paid five bucks a day. The first day doesn't count out there."

"It isn't much better than California," I offered. "Jury duty is fifteen a day out there and they make you wait nine hours before they release you. Did you know that the IRS taxes you on top of it?"

"It's ridiculous," he said as he turned a page in his newspaper. "Somebody should do something about it."

"Uh-huh," I answered closing the matter.

I sat in the jury assembly room with about five or six hundred other recipients of jury notices. Most people seemed to busy themselves with their iPhones and tablets. I saw a chessboard sitting with its pieces lined up waiting for someone to play although no one did. I pulled out my briefcase and began lining up my receipts on the floor, in piles by the month. I had no sooner organized them by date and time, when I looked on the screen and saw my name listed along with hundreds of other individuals. It is similar to watching designated flights on a computer display screen at an airport. It figures! The moment I had plans, I would finally be called. Not knowing what to expect, I gathered my belongings and jumped into the gathering queue. We assembled in an alcove area.

"I am going to give each of you a laminated card," a somewhat portly lady called out to the group of us. "I will call your name and after I give you a number, you will no longer be known by your name but rather your assigned number. You are to keep your card with you at all times and you are to wear your juror badge. You will give your numbered card back to me by the end of your day," she instructed. "My name is Sydney and I will be your coordinator throughout the process."

One by one, our names were called and each of us was given a laminated sign with a number on it. My card was green with a large "B-198" on it. I remember thinking that it sure seemed like a lot of people to be called for a jury, but was content knowing that the day would complete itself rather quickly compared to my previous jury duty experiences. The best that I could tell was that the numbers went up to three hundred.

Once all the people had their cards and were lined up numerically, they led us into a room that opened into a large courtroom.

We were filing in and the moving queue split at the entrance of the courtroom. I remember seeing three people facing us as we walked in. The person in the center had long, dark wavy hair and was smiling at us as we were filing in. I had no idea that I was looking at Marissa DeVault, the defendant. I thought she was either an attorney or a court official.

They sat us down and I saw that the courtroom was filled to capacity. There was a defense team lined up on one side, while a prosecuting team was lined up on the opposing side. They watched the potential jurors get settled and not a word was spoken.

I put my briefcase at my feet and the Judge began speaking into a microphone from his bench.

"First," he said, "I want to thank all of you for taking your time out of the day to be here. Our system cannot work without your valued service as a potential jury member. My name is Judge Roland Steinle. We are here today to begin the jury selection process for the defendant, Marissa Suzanne DeVault. The defendant is being charged with first-degree murder. This trial carries a maximum penalty of death. This trial is expected to last through May 26th of 2014 and will require an immense amount of your time and consideration. This trial will be televised and cameras will be in the courtroom," the Judge said, as a matter of business.

I was stunned. This was the last thing in the world that I expected to hear. I had surmised that if I was ever on a jury, it would be a simple assault or robbery case. I never imagined a first-degree murder trial. The Judge had certainly gotten my undivided attention.

"The first thing we want to establish is your position on the death penalty, and is this something that you can consider given the facts of the case in conjunction with the laws of Arizona?" the judge continued. "In that, we are going to pass a microphone throughout the room and I need you to tell me if you can pass a death penalty sentence in accordance with the laws of Arizona..."

Certainly, much more was said but that was it in a nutshell. Personally, the death penalty is not something I have thought a lot about. It is my belief that for whatever state one chooses to live in, he or she inherits the laws of that state in an unwritten contract. In other words, if I choose to kill someone, I would know that this state has the death penalty and that may very well be the sentence I could expect. If it was a law I didn't agree with, then there are about forty-five other states I could reside in instead. If I were picked for a jury that had the death penalty, the same would apply. I could expect that a jury may, if circumstances are correct, impose the death penalty. Although it's easier contemplated than done, I was feeling right down the middle of the road. I could go either way depending upon the circumstance involved. It is not something I would wish upon anybody but as a citizen of Arizona, I believed in my heart that the law would lay the path and when the decision came to it, I could.

The microphone was passed throughout the room and the morning was spent not picking a jury but rather dismissing jurors.

"Juror Number B-17," the judge said, "could you vote for the death penalty given the correct circumstances?"

"No, your Honor, I cannot vote for religious reasons," a lady said passing the microphone to the person next to her. Her response caught on quickly, with easily two out of every three potential jurors repeating that they could not vote for religious reasons.

It seemed like no time at all had passed before the microphone came to me. I raised the cordless microphone to my mouth and said, "Juror B-198, I can" and then passed the microphone to the gentleman next to me.

I remember thinking that my odds of getting on a jury were infinitesimally small. I didn't really feel the need to get into the thought process of what that meant, unless push came to shove and I was seated on this jury. So, as much as I said I could vote for the death penalty, it was not something I was overly concerned about since my odds of being on a jury were so small. However, I would take the process seriously.

"I cannot do it because I cannot survive on twelve dollars a day," a man said when the microphone came to him.

"If I may address that issue," the Judge said, taking off his glasses. "This trial will draw jury funds from Arizona Lengthy Trial Fund account and is different from standard jury service. The court recognizes that this trial may have a financial impact on some jurors. You will provide financial information to the Jury Commissioner's Office and you will be compensated for lost pay on a daily basis. This fund allows for up to $350 per day of jury service," he explained.

The man with the microphone simply responded with his jury number and said that he could be on the jury.

The microphone had completed its journey around the room. "I need all the jurors who cannot do jury service to stand and meet Sydney at the back of the courtroom. You are dismissed and the court considers your service complete for a term of one year. Remember that those who have committed to doing jury service are needed for the next step of this process. You will not be selected today and jury selection will take approximately three weeks," the Judge said.

There was a flurry of activity as three-quarters of the room got up and met Sydney at the back of the courtroom.

Since there were going to be cameras in the courtroom, the Judge explained to the remainder of us that he expected publicity about this case and we were admonished not to speak with anyone about the case including media, family, friends, etc. Further, we were not to watch anything on the news or radio about the case. We were instructed to come back after lunch.

I followed the other remaining jurors down from the sixth floor. I think there were only twenty of us left after all the dismissals. Few of us said anything, but you could sense there was some excitement about this potential trial. I went out into the shade of the courtyard and found the smoking area. I was too nervous to eat and was excited about the next step. I smoked a few cigarettes and noticed how few people seemed to smoke nowadays.

An hour later, I made my way back through security and up to the sixth floor, showing my badge and laminated card to Sydney. Forty of us were gathered in a hallway. Sydney then led us to a conference room with a long table in the center. She handed each of us a packet and pointed to a basket of pens in the center of the table.

"Please don't steal the pens," she said. "If you use a pen, you will need to return it. I am going to give each of you a questionnaire. We are asking you to fill this out to the best of your ability. All we want is honesty," she said. "This information is strictly private and will not be shared by anyone except the attorneys in this case. If there are questions that you do not prefer to answer on the Voir Dire, also known as the questionnaire, you may write 'Private' in the answer area and you can meet the attorneys privately. Once the questionnaire is complete, you will return it to me and you will turn in your juror number. You are now scheduled to return one week from today for the next step in the jury selection process."

Somebody asked Sydney. "What's Voir Dire".

"It's the process by which attorneys pick fair and impartial jurors. It begins with your completion of the questionnaire," Sydney responded.

"What happens next week?" Cherie, another potential juror asked. "Can you give us an idea of what to expect?"

"It's nothing to worry about. You will sit in the jury box and the attorneys will ask you questions. The Judge may ask you questions, as well," she said as an afterthought.

Sydney was like a high school teacher of days long ago, with her demeanor and direction. One could also feel that she was like a mother hen moving strangers about in her work. She would gather us up and then direct us in a most pleasant but firm manner. At the same time, she was quite adept at being tight-lipped.

I took my questionnaire packet and sat down at the table. We were packed in the room with everyone busy filling out their packet. It was pretty thick and I would guess it to have had about one hundred questions and was approximately forty pages long.

I remember thinking of Jean Casarez, a reporter for the old Court TV channel on cable. She once said that attorneys do not want jurors who want to be jurors. At the time, I thought it was a strange statement. I looked at the questionnaire and remembered what she said and decided that I would approach it with simple answers, so as not to talk myself out of being a juror.

I approached each question honestly and tried to keep my comments to one-sentence answers. The Voir Dire was not difficult, although it did get very personal as to various aspects of my life, including who my roommates were; of which I had none.

The forty or so questions ranged from basic statistical facts to areas where one had to describe an experience on the lines provided. I almost expected it to ask if I had ever hurt small puppies as a child and, thankfully, didn't. It had the feel of searching for your competency level, as well as providing a psychological profile.

The basic questions covered such things as my fifty-two years of age and where I was born. It inquired how long I had lived in Maricopa County, and that was between three and four years. It pursued my current job position as well as those jobs worked in the past. I answered that I was currently a bartender, and also noted being a manager at the same restaurant prior to becoming a bartender. I briefly explained that I had chosen the position as my life goals had changed from being a manager to pursuing a writing career.

As if on cue, the question asked if I had ever published anything. I proudly answered that I had published a book on Hot Wheels collecting.

There was a question about law and whether I had studied law in the past. Although there was a time in college that I considered being a lawyer, I had never pursued the education mostly in part because I couldn't afford it. I had never studied law but I found it interesting.

The questionnaire asked if I had ever been convicted of any felonies or misdemeanors. I was truthful but embarrassed to say that I had pled guilty to a DUI in 2005, the badge of an alcoholic. I took my last drink on January 3, 2010 and wasn't as worried about that question as I would have been were I still drinking.

29

I had to think about the question regarding my religious beliefs. I answered that I had no real religious belief except that I was spiritual in a Celestine Prophecy type of way and I believed in God. James Redfield's book is not a religion but does serve to explain in my mind the coincidences that show up throughout our lives, and those coincidences should be recognized as signposts throughout life. I realize that I'm minimizing the book, but it is the lesson I took from it and how I look at our life experience.

As far as religion, I had lived in Utah for some time and became familiar with the term 'Jack Mormon', those Mormons who had fallen away from the church after being raised Mormon. I suppose I was a 'Jack Catholic' in the same sense after being alienated by the church at a young age.

There was another question that asked if I had experienced violence in my household. Quickly, I marked the box with a "No", as I don't like violence and work to stay away from it at all costs. Later in the questionnaire, it asked what profession my parents were in along with any of my direct family. I answered that my father was a doctor while my mother was a nurse. I wrote in my brother's name saying he was a pilot and then froze, as I was about to write in the occupation of my sister. Simply enough, after not seeing or hearing from her in over thirty years, I didn't know what she did for a living. The last I knew, she was in a sanitarium.

This opened up the first can of worms, as I had to go back into the questionnaire and re-answer the question that asked about violence in my family.

"Have you experienced, directly or indirectly, violence in your direct family or household?" I struggled with that question. It was a long time ago, in my early teens that I had experienced it. I remember thinking that nobody really knew about it and why would I want to bring that up? I remember squirming in my seat and twisting the hairs on my head. I could leave the answer as it was. There was no reason to open up an old wound that never really went away. But, I remembered that I was under oath to tell the truth. I could let it go and feign being normal or I could tell the truth and hope for the best. I decided to tell the truth and wrote, "Yes, I took my parents to court when I was fourteen for child abuse."

It was a strange thing to put in writing. It had been the 1970's and things were different then. It was acceptable that parents could be "heavy-handed". It was a time that we saw a President leave office because he was caught lying. It was a time when gas prices went up and the economy went down. It was also a time when it was okay to hit your children without fear of reprisal. But, where did one draw the line the line between discipline and abuse?

The voir dire pursued what television programs I liked to watch. I explained that I don't watch a lot of television (in part because I detest commercials) but when I do, my preference is movies and HBO Series things. I also enjoyed the show Forensic Files. It asked whether I watched the news, and responded that I favor CNN and HLN. I like to leave it on in the mornings when I'm getting ready for the day. Who reads newspapers anymore?

Here and there were odd questions, interspersed between the same questions repeated but worded differently. I just answered the truth as best I knew it. One particular question asked, "Have you ever called a "We-Tip" hotline anonymously?"

This was another can of worms, but from the 1980's. It involved a situation of which I was neither proud nor ashamed, but it was still an ugly piece of my past. Vowing to tell the truth, I wrote "Yes, I turned in a former employer for forging death certificates." This was certainly something I really didn't want to talk about and I knew by writing it, I was exposing myself to relive that part of my past.

I knew I couldn't go wrong if I was honest. I also expected that someone would be checking into our backgrounds and they would probably find that I was on the front page of the L.A. Times in November of 1987 for exposing my employer. There is no glamour in being a whistleblower.

Later, the questionnaire asked if I was familiar with any trials. Well, after having lived in Arizona the last few years, one could not ignore the snippets of the Jodi Arias trial. It was everywhere for about a year. It didn't matter whether you went to a Starbucks for a cup of coffee or you were grocery shopping, there was always something about the Jodi Arias trial permeating our lives on a television somewhere. I remember seeing a court scene where Jodi was on the stand saying everything got "foggy" when the incident happened. There was another court scene about a bunch of gas cans and her trip to Arizona to kill her ex-boyfriend, Travis Alexander. I remember thinking what pain the roommates and family went through in this horrible tragedy.

Mostly, I remember her showcasing those t-shirts at her trial with the word 'survivor' and wondering how she had the gumption to do that. I knew enough to know that what she had committed was first-degree murder and the punishment should have been death. However, the jury had hung on that issue so her trial was still incomplete.

Ironically, when I had requested the day off from work for jury duty, I had written Jodi Arias as the reason for my request. I was just being silly when I wrote that down, which only goes to show how surprised I was to be considered for this trial.

The voir dire questionnaire asked if I had ever heard of Marissa DeVault and the hammer killing death of her husband, Dale Harrell, which took place in the fall of 2009. I answered honestly that I had never heard of her, the victim, Dale Harrell or any such killing.

I put down the questionnaire without really reviewing it. I had been honest and knew I was probably too honest in some spots but felt that the chips would fall as they may.

I picked up my briefcase, handed the questionnaire to Sydney and was told to come back in a week. I left the building and walked back to my car, a short eight blocks down the road. If the trial had been in July instead of January, I would probably have taken the nice air-conditioned jury bus.

The moment I got in the car and turned it on, the sounds of KTAR came on, a local Phoenix news station.

"Jury selection has begun in the Hammer Killing Trial of Marissa DeVault..." the voice said. I quickly changed channels to a local classic rock station called KLSX. REO Speedwagon sang about riding a storm out.

I left the car in idle as I thought about the events of the day. It was hard to get my head wrapped around it. I realized that this was a potentially great opportunity. I didn't want to get excited about it but I could not help it. This could be the new book that I had been looking for.

I can vividly remember that day in 1996 when the verdict was announced for O.J. Simpson. My girlfriend lay on the bed next to me as we both guessed what the verdict might be. Although the verdict surprised us like everyone else, I remember mostly thinking about the jury in that case. The most vivid thing I remember saying out loud was that if I were ever on a jury of that magnitude, I would write a book about it. She thought I was crazy.

It would not be the first time in my life that I would do something crazy.

The next visit to court couldn't come soon enough in my mind.

I spent the week revisiting my answers on the voir dire questionnaire in my head over and over again. There was a solid realization that some of my answers would preclude me from being on the jury.

I studied French for six years. The best I can see is that "Voir Dire" means, "To see to speak". It sure made me say a lot and see a lot.

It occurred to me that I had a very little chance of being on this jury...

SKELETONS

I spent the entire week distracted by the potential trial. I worked like a robot on constant autopilot. I mulled over the answers to my questionnaire wondering if I would be selected or if my answers had taken me out of the picture. It was strange to have ghosts from the past resurface in such an unexpected way. I found myself wondering if I should defend my actions or accept my past as a reality that I could do nothing about. I could only guess as to what would happen on my return visit to the courtroom. I spent a lot of time rehearsing in my head how I would answer questions presented by either of the attorneys. I was certain I would be approached and had to somehow encapsulate the events of the 1970's in a short and concise way.

It was intimidating to think that we, as potential jurors were on trial when we returned.

I was sure why I wanted to be on this jury. I could list a good number of reasons the least of which was the opportunity to be a part of something that very few people get to experience. At the same time, I knew that each of us bears a responsibility in trade for the great freedoms we have in this country.

In 1976, I was fourteen years old and remember that year as if it were yesterday. This was the year that I found myself taking my parents to court for child abuse. This was also the year that marked the loss of my family. I did not understand at the time the fallout or damage that my actions would cause. I should not have been surprised to find myself dropped off at the bus station at age seventeen, the day after I graduated from high school. I would never see my parents again.

In 1987, I learned my father was dying of colon cancer. I wrote a letter to my mother asking for her forgiveness and told her I was ashamed for everything I had done. I asked her to let me come home to make peace with my father.

On the day I was to leave on a plane to see my father, I received a reply from my mother. I was no longer welcome home. I was not to contact anyone in the family. My sister, Louise was in a sanitarium and had 'just gone crazy'.

My anger over the years had been replaced by an undeniable shame. I had done a bad thing and paid the price for it.

Ten years later, I wrote my first book, aptly called "Mortician" after the experience of working for a mortuary. I wanted to take the reader into the back rooms of a mortuary and see things the way I did. The book was resoundingly rejected as being something that the public was not ready for. But, I learned how to write a book from beginning to end and enjoyed the experience of seeing one of my girlfriends reading it for the first time. Her crying as she read through the pages made me proud. She was crying over a fictionalized character that had been created from my imagination and I realized the power in that.

It was not long after surviving those rejections that I dove into a book I called, "Hell is for Children", the story of taking my parents to court seen through the eyes of a fourteen year-old. I began the book with the protagonist killing his mother with a knife, then waking up and not remembering it. He then sees his psychiatrist and they have to journey back in time to learn why his memory is being blocked. They end up running away from the law together as the protagonist revisits parts of his childhood throughout the book.

I searched out an agent who made me rewrite it ten times before we went to auction with it in New York City attended by the ten largest publishers in the world. Needless to say over those ten years, I came to understand a blue pencil edit as well as I understood my own name.

On a fall day in 1996, months after the O.J. trial, my writing career collapsed as all ten publishers summarily rejected the piece at auction. They recognized the talent but didn't feel the story held true. I think I headed in the wrong direction by taking a story of child abuse and turning it into an adventure story. I also think my psychiatrist character wasn't as real as she could have been; I didn't even know a psychiatrist. I felt like Miles in Sideways. I always had a book but could never cross the bridge.

It was on that note that I quit writing and decided to pursue a real career with real results and dove into the restaurant industry with fervor. I opened restaurants all over the country and then worked up through the ranks of restaurant management. I felt that despite all my hard work, writing had betrayed me and that I had victimized myself by revisiting that dreadful story from 1976, again.

It was late in 2009 that I learned my only brother had attempted suicide by hanging and it crushed my world. He did not want me to know and did not want to be contacted. My life had become one of three states: work, being drunk or being hung over. One day, I woke up and realized that I was slowly committing suicide by drinking. I also realized that I missed my writing and that feeling resonated deep in my soul.

I quit drinking on January 3, 2010 because I was killing myself and I wasn't doing what I wanted to in my life, and that was to write. It took two years of learning how to be sober before I could consider my plan and direction.

I met Dean Koontz a number of years back at a book signing and someone asked him what the trick was to writing a new book. He responded, "Just write and write what you love."

I gave my thirty-day notice at work and resigned as manager in order to write a book and get it published. I surprised myself by doing exactly what I set out to do and then lost everything. I couldn't survive on EBay and book sales alone and found myself hitting rock bottom. This was strange because I was sober and trying to do the right thing and yet, it only served to bring me financial destruction as I sold everything just to stay alive and pay the bills.

One day, I woke up to the power being shut off and the reconnect fees were far beyond what I had. I was forced to go to Arizona Family Services and ask for their help in paying my bills. It was one of the hardest days I have ever experienced, realizing just how much trouble I was in after gambling on a dream. Out of desperation, I went back to my old job where I had been a manager and got a job bartending. It was a lot harder than I thought it would be, returning to the role of worker instead of being the boss.

Even so, it was good to be working again and great being able to say that I had published something, so the journey really hadn't been as bad as I'd thought.

I remember telling the state worker, Grace, who had facilitated this financial fix that I would somehow pay this debt back even though I had no direct responsibility to do so. Coincidentally, her name was the same as my long departed grandmother. I was grateful and I was serious. When the opportunity of jury duty arrived, I felt that the State Of Arizona was asking for my help and this would be a way to pay it back.

The jury notice showed up in my mailbox and everything changed.

I couldn't help thinking that this was a great coincidence. It looked like a Celestine Prophecy type of coincidence. I couldn't help thinking that God had put me here for a reason.

I've heard that God never puts more on your plate than you can handle. I had to wonder why this situation, at the particular time was being served on my plate. It was intriguing to be sure but I wasn't confident about being the right man for the job. I calmed myself knowing that God presented the opportunity, and would pave the way if it were meant to be.

I remember trying to anticipate the questions the attorneys might ask me and at the top of the list was, "Why had I taken my parents to court?"

"Juror B-198," an attorney would ask, "can you explain in detail why you said that you took your parents to court when you were fourteen?"

"If it's okay with the court, it may take me a few minutes to explain what happened," I would answer.

The Judge would nod in the affirmative and allow me to speak.

"The 1970's were a completely different clamshell than we live in now. We didn't have the advantage of instant information at our fingertips. We looked at the world differently and we looked at situations differently. Consider the issue of child abuse. People knew of it but it wasn't talked about. I think that what people did under the roof of their homes was their business and not to be shared with anyone. How people raised and disciplined their children was kept behind closed doors," I would say knowingly.

"My parents had the best intentions. They wanted to raise their children to be successful. I believed they loved their children. Unfortunately, things went south due to financial problems. My father was a well-respected doctor in the area where I was raised. As a matter of fact, he was the only doctor of his kind covering over 400 square miles of territory. This meant he was always busy and was comfortably supporting his family of six."

The judge would nod in understanding, allowing me to continue.

"My mother was a full-time housewife after having worked as a certified RN for many years. Her side of the family, however, lived 800 miles away and she missed her family terribly. My father had always promised that once we were comfortable financially, we would move closer to her side of the family. So, in the early 1970's, my father felt that we could move to where she desired. To that end, he had a multi-million dollar home designed from the ground up for the family and we moved."

I would pause and look at the judge before I spoke. "The move was devastating. Where my father previously had thousands of patients, he now had only a scant few patients because in the city, practitioners could be found on every other block. Consequently, the money stopped coming in creating an immense amount of pressure on him. There was no intent on what happened next. Discipline somehow crossed a bridge and became abuse..."

"Do you want to explain what you mean?" the attorney would ask.

"Well, for example, I remember having issues at school. I can't remember whether it had been a bad grade or I was causing trouble, but my father came home and he was mad. Typically, one could expect getting the belt if one didn't live up to the standards set. This wasn't uncommon. Maybe we weren't the best kids, but I don't think it was anything out of the ordinary from what other kids did."

"I remember my father sending me to the basement to get the belt. You can bet we were always scared of the belt. I went to the basement and waited for my father to come in. When he came into the basement, he locked the door behind him. I remember hearing the click and somehow thought that it seemed different than times past. I didn't ever remember him locking the door. I waited, bent over a washing machine as he took his wide belt off and folded it in half. You could expect a solid, well-whipped crack of the belt for ten times. In the screams of pain, you always counted. Then, this time became different as the cracks reached eleven and then fifteen and then I lost track. I remember screaming and crying as the torrent of cracks hit me harder and harder. I can't remember at what point I finally heard my mother pounding on the locked door telling my father to stop. She was pounding harder and harder as he whipped the belt harder and harder. I couldn't tell you when it stopped but it was the worst beating I had ever had. I remember my mother yelling at him saying that he had to control his temper."

I would let that sit in their heads a moment before I continued. "They say anger is fear turned outward. My father was afraid of losing everything he had built and took it out on his kids. I won't bore you with every story but the next four years saw his anger flare more and more often and it happened with all the kids."

"I turned to running away from home. I was not only scared for me but I was becoming scared for my brother and sister. I always ended up back at home and things only seemed to get worse."

I would take a deep breath and tell the story that I had rewritten a hundred times in "Hell is for Children."

"The problem reached a new level when my mother got involved. One night, my brother and sister were roughhousing in the laundry room and my mother lost control. I was in another room clenching my fists and crying as my mother began beating the daylights out of my brother and sister for being kids. She grabbed a 'Spray 'N Wash' can (which used to be an aerosol can) and hit my sister over the head. The hollow-sound crack it made and the moment of silence before my sister started screaming in pain was the most heart-wrenching sound I've ever heard. My mother started screaming to the other kids, "Get me towels! Get me towels!"

They ran out of the laundry room scrambling to get towels from the linen closet. I was frozen in fear in the adjacent study. I remember seeing the flowered wallpaper sprayed in blood.

She made all of us clean up the bloody mess before we left the house to go to the hospital. Even though she had been trained as a nurse, the wound that my sister received was beyond her capabilities to fix.

My father wasn't home that evening as he had been called to the emergency room earlier. Knowing that, my mother made the decision to drive sixty miles to another hospital, in order to avoid running into my father. Because of that deception, I firmly realized that what was happening was wrong.

I remember my sister receiving over twenty stitches for the wound in her head. I remember driving home and taking my sister's hand in the silent car to calm her. There was no talking and only our thoughts running around in our heads.

It was just before we pulled into the driveway that my mother drove the car over to the side of the road and got out. She opened the back door where my sister was and removed the gauze that was surrounding my sister's head. She got back in the car saying, "If any of you mention a word of this to your father, you will regret it!"

We never did mention it to our father.

The most important thing I learned is that no one listens to a kid.

The final time I ran away, it was to the house of a former baby sitter. She used to watch us whenever my parents would go on vacation to Europe or some other state or country. As it turned out, she was a director with the Department of Social Services. She took pictures of my wounds and pursued taking my parents to court.

I remember walking into court only to be escorted back to the Judge's Chambers. It seemed like seconds later, two policemen put me in handcuffs and I was sent to a juvenile delinquency home.

It was not until 2010 when I stopped drinking that I finally put down the cross that I had been carrying for so many years. I paid a high price for my actions and lost my complete family for the action. At the end of the day, though, I feel that I did the right thing given the circumstances I was in."

I realized that everything I had just rehearsed was hogwash. The stories were true but the court wouldn't want to hear a lecture on my life.

It would be best if they asked about it to admit to being abused and to show remorse for taking my parents to court.

The tiny voice inside me told me I was still ashamed.

The day for phase two of jury selection arrived. I dressed in a Ralph Lauren collared shirt with a Jerry Garcia tie. My pants were pressed and shoes were shined.

When I arrived, I recognized some of the twenty remaining jurors standing in the hallway waiting to be called into the courtroom. We were each given the same numbers as we had been given the week prior on the same eight and a half by ten laminated cards. I noticed that none of us really made conversation except for some small talk as we lined up chronologically by our original but remaining numbers. It was as if no one wanted to commit to any sort of relationship knowing we could be easily dismissed, so there was no real point in getting to know each other.

The double doors opened as we slowly filed in. Standing in front of us was the prosecution team of three and we walked past the defense team. As we sat in our seats, it was the first time that I really looked at the defendant, Marissa DeVault. She was a slight girl and might even be considered good looking by most male standards. She was dressed smartly in a black suit with a white blouse. She had long dark curly hair and almost looked affable. It was immediately hard to believe that this could have been the girl being readied for a first-degree murder trial.

The courtroom was different than the large expansive courtroom we had been in during the first phase of jury selection. I could see that the jury box was on the left side instead of the right side. We were led to the jury box.

The only thing that seemed out of place was the defendant smiling and watching us as we sat. If I were in that position, I could hardly picture myself smiling. It may have been out of politeness or it may have been out of nervousness but that smile seemed very out of place. I spent the rest of the day taking furtive glances over at the defense table but made an attempt not to look at her until these proceedings became more official.

"My name is Eric Basta and I am the prosecutor in this case," he said to us while a court reporter took notes on a computer machine. "You will see Michelle Arino seated to my left who is the assistant and next to her is Detective Mike Bishop, the lead detective in this case."

Eric Basta was dressed in a gray suit with a white shirt and red tie. He had a flair about him that told me he was experienced and comfortable in the courtroom. He looked almost like Jim Carrey with the wave of his hair and his front teeth. I wondered why he had a bump over his left eye.

"We promise not to keep you here too long and we respect your attendance," he said sitting down at the prosecution table.

The lead defense attorney got up next and spoke to us. "Thank you for being here," he said. "My name is Alan Tavasoli and the attorney seated next to me is Andrew Clemency who will be assisting the defendant, Marissa DeVault. The lady seated next to her is a mitigation specialist, Pamela Mudryj, who will be here throughout the trial for the defendant."

I noticed something else although it seemed minor. The prosecution had introduced Marissa DeVault pronouncing her last name as it is spelled. The defense, however, presented the defendant pronouncing her name as "De-Vwah". I wondered why there were two different pronunciations.

Mr. Tavasoli sat down and the interrogation of the potential jury began. It was as if we were targets on a shooting range as each attorney got up and started asking questions of jurors.

The day was spent watching potential jurors being dismissed one by one. The first juror dismissed was the guy who arrived in tennis shoes and a hoodie. He was an hour late and it was clear the Judge was displeased and almost angry that one would not take such a process seriously.

The attorneys stood in front of the jury with a stack of questionnaires that each of us had completed the week before. Randomly, they would call on potential jurors by number and question their answers. They were looking for inconsistencies. There was almost a heated discussion between the prosecution and one potential male juror.

"So," the prosecutor asked, "are you saying that it is okay for a woman to hit you but you won't hit a woman?"

"My wife can hit me forty times a day but I will never hit her," the juror responded.

"Isn't that a double standard?" the prosecutor asked.

"That may be," the juror answered. "It is what it is. I will never hit a woman."

"Thank you," the prosecutor responded. "Please dismiss Juror B-199."

The juror got up with his laminated card, walked to the back of the courtroom where Sydney was waiting, turned in his card and disappeared beyond the double doors never to be seen again.

At another point, Mr. Tavasoli got into a discussion with a juror concerning his statement regarding punishment when the juror had written, "Don't do the crime if you can't do the time."

"Can you explain that a little further?" he asked.

"If a person knows they are committing murder, then they should know that it carries the death penalty. So, if you don't want to die, then don't murder," he answered confidently.

"Thank you, juror B-69. You are dismissed."

Throughout the morning, the Judge continued dismissing potential jurors one by one. Some were dismissed for technical reasons such as not being able to get the time off for pre-planned trips or for being the sole supporter of a family who could not afford the length of the trial.

"I have just a couple questions for you, Juror number two hundred and forty," Mr. Basta continued as he zeroed in on a tan and mature lady who sat a few seats down from me. "It says that you get heart palpitations when you have anxiety. Is this a medical condition that we should know about?"

"Yes, Sir," she answered nervously. "I mean, no, sir. It's not a medical condition. I just get nervous and my heart flutters sometimes."

"Okay," he answered. "I want to make sure you can make it through a trial. Do you think this condition will prevent you from being here?"

"No, Sir," she answered.

Mr. Basta went to the podium and looked at the questionnaire turning a few pages. He clicked the pen in his hand as he approached her again. "You wrote that you've lived in an abusive relationship and you have called the police and they would not come out to you?"

"That was thirty-five years ago," she said with a nervous laugh. "Things were different then. Since I had not applied for a divorce, the police would not come out."

"Are you still married to this person?" Mr. Basta asked.

"No," she answered. "I am remarried and live with a wonderful man."

"I'm glad to hear that," Mr. Basta said with a smile. "Things are okay now?"

"Yes, they are," she answered.

I was sure I would be called upon next but Mr. Basta went on to jurors around me.

I watched as jurors were dismissed for a variety of reasons, some clear and some not so clear. The Judge dismissed us for lunch. I was happy to have survived the first round of the shooting range without being asked a question.

We returned an hour later and we were directed to wait in the hallway. I would guess there were twenty-five of us seated outside the courtroom. We watched as jurors were called into the courtroom one by one. Someone asked Sydney what was going on and she said that this was the segment where jurors had written 'Private' on various answers of the Voir Dire questionnaire and each was going in to discuss those questions. It didn't take long to realize that most of those people were dismissed after their consultation with the court.

A person would go into the double doors and they would come out ten minutes later, hand Sydney their laminated number and then walk down the hallway.

I sat on a bench next to a tall and friendly African-American lady. She introduced herself as Cherie. She was a computer firm IT Manager. I noticed on the lapel of her blue business suit that her juror badge was in a clear plastic case with a clip hanging on her chest.

"Where did you get that?" I asked. My juror badge wasn't sticking to my shirt anymore and I had to keep pressing it down so I wouldn't lose it.

"I made it," she said. "I don't have to worry about losing it."

I thought it presumptuous to go through that effort at this early stage of the trial. However, I was jealous of it at the same time.

In the late afternoon, Sydney gathered the remainder of us and sent us back into the courtroom. We were led to the jury box on the left side of the room.

Judge Steinle was located in the center of the room at an equal height to the upper row of the jury box. He had gray tussled hair and wore steel-rimmed glasses. I did not expect that he was a tall man but one could not be sure with him behind his desk.

"Juror Number sixteen?" the Judge asked, looking toward us in the jury box.

A girl below me raised her hand. She had long hair with tinted blonde streaks in it. I had seen her in the hallway and she was a pretty girl that one could picture driving a Lexus. She carried herself well.

My hands started sweating again as it looked like the judge was shooting the gun in the gallery.

"It says that you are out of town the second week of April. Is that correct?"

"Yes, Sir," she answered. "My husband and I have a trip planned to Cabo San Lucas."

"Is this for business or pleasure," the Judge asked.

She paused.

"Or is it a little of both?" he asked.

"It's both, Your Honor," she answered with a little laugh.

"That's fine. I am not making any promises but we will see what we can do," he said putting her file aside on his desk. "Ladies and Gentlemen, thank you for your service," the Judge said. "We will be making final jury selection next week and we expect each of you to be here at 10:30 AM. Does anyone have any questions?"

I counted the people left in the jury box and saw there were only nine left. No one had any questions.

"Very good," the judge said. "We are adjourned until next week."

Somehow, no one asked me a question.

The Judge gave us a reminder that we were not to look up anything on the Internet, Twitter about it, watch news programs or discuss the trial in any way.

We were summarily dismissed and asked to come back a week later for final jury selection.

It meant another week of waiting on pins and needles. It meant another week of rehearsing a response.

It occurred to me, however, that our next meeting was slated to be only an hour and a half long. I think that meeting will be different from the prior two meetings because at some point, the teams will have to select jurors rather than dismiss them; suddenly my odds of my making the jury looked better. I couldn't understand why there were only nine of us when I thought a jury was twelve people. Maybe there were only six people needed on the jury and I didn't catch that part last week.

Something else bothered me, though. Why had neither side asked about my parents and what I had done?

I drove home with anticipation in my heart and excited that the odds looked good of being on this jury.

Dave Ramsey, the financial expert, was speaking on the radio. He made a random comment that, "Opportunity shows up at your doorstep dressed in work clothes." I do not know what context it was in but it was enough to tell me that I needed to start this book.

I do not think it was a coincidence that I was called for this jury. I think it was put on my plate for a reason and only God knew what that reason was.

I couldn't believe that I had made it through the second day without being dismissed.

DAY 3

TWO WORDS

It was exciting that our group was left with only nine but it was also nerve-racking that we had to wait another week. I remember someone saying that there was another group of potential jurors for the same trial but knew nothing more than that. I assumed that the number remaining had to be a low number like our group.

The week gave me time to think more about my responses on the questionnaire and I was still surprised that no one had pursued questions of me after all my preparation. I got to thinking about the other skeleton that this had pulled out of my past.

The question had read something to the effect of "Had I ever called "We-Tip" or some anonymous tip phone line that was similar. I had answered in the affirmative saying something to the effect that I had, and was responsible for reporting a past employer for the falsification and forgeries of death certificates.

This event took place in the mid 1980's after being a certified funeral director for a Los Angeles mortuary. I had taken the job offered as a mortuary assistant. It paid well, offered good benefits with a good opportunity for upward advancement. Plus, the job seemed as if it would offer challenges and was something different from a regular run of the mill job.

The job entailed such duties as picking up decedents from hospitals, homes and, often times, from the Coroner's Office. The job also involved picking up death certificates from various doctor's offices. In a sense, the mortuary assistant was a messenger for the mortuary handling small details after someone has passed away and necessary prior to a decedent being buried or cremated. A mortuary could not move forward on a burial until proper paperwork was in order.

Three years after my employment, I was promoted to a supervisor and worked the graveyard shift from five o'clock at night until eight o'clock in the morning every other day with every weekend off. Aside from being a night watchman, in a sense, the hours were great. One could also make an additional fifty dollars for every deceased person that I picked up after working my shift. I usually offered my services two or three times a week to make some extra money. I could make this extra money after I got off work at eight in the morning and be home to sleep by ten or eleven a.m. I would then return to work the next evening at five p.m. to take 'first calls" throughout the evening or morning for the five mortuaries that I was responsible for. There were nights where nothing would happen and there were nights that the phone rang off the wall.

It was not long after I became state certified as an actual funeral director that I began to notice some things amiss. It may have been as a result of my education in becoming a funeral director that brought a particular issue to life.

I was at the receptionist desk working on some paperwork when I mistakenly threw a piece of paper in the trash. I obtained the sheet out of the trash and noticed torn up death certificates in the trash. I recognized that a couple of those certificates were ones I had obtained the prior morning after my shift. It didn't make sense. Why were the original certificates tossed in the trash?

I began matching names on the certificates with those who were on the schedule to be buried. The files had what looked to be original death certificates but instead of manner and cause of death being hand-written by the doctor, they had been retyped with the doctor's signature.

It was upon closer inspection that I noticed the causes of death were typed in and the manner and cause of death was changed from what the doctor had written. If I compared the doctor's signature to that of what was being filed, it was clear that the signatures had been traced and was not an original signature.

Many years prior, I remember forging my father's signature on a report card that we were to return to school after our parents had looked at it. I had received a particularly poor grade in a subject that I no longer remember. I do remember forging the signature and returning it to school and was immediately busted by the teacher who called my parents to verify the signature. It is one of the few times that I remember the beating I received as well as the reason for the beating. I learned to never forge again especially given the fact that my father was a doctor.

To that point, when I started finding multiple torn up death certificates with forgeries being accepted by the State of California, I clearly knew that what was happening was wrong. I began re-assembling and taping those original certificates back together and started making a collection. That collection quickly grew to more than one hundred in a matter of less than six months. Given that I was now a certified funeral director, I was concerned that if anyone was caught, I would get trapped in the situation and might be personally accused of forging or be in trouble just for having knowledge and not doing anything about it.

I didn't know what to do, as this job was my livelihood. Yet, it seemed that every time I went to work, my collection of original documents would grow.

One night while I was at my girlfriend's mother's house, I asked to use a telephone in private and called "We-Tip" with this information in hand because the guilt was becoming overwhelming. I couldn't just walk away and ignore it. I had one hundred certificates lined up when I called this anonymous tip line. The tip line only took ten names of decedents saying it was enough to get them started and enough to verify my story.

I felt better after making the call, thinking I could finally stop worrying, as the authorities would step in after verifying my story.

Six months later, the pile of death certificates grew and nothing happened. I remember a body coming into the mortuary with a large wound on her forehead. That night, after the certificate was obtained, I found it torn up in the trash like the others and the cause of death was changed from blunt force trauma to Arteriosclerosis leading to a Myocardial Infarction. In other words, a violent death by blunt force trauma was adjusted to being a simple heart attack and looked like death by natural causes. This bore heavily on my mind. This person could have been murdered but now it was changed to natural causes. What if that happened to me one day?

So, a friend of a friend put me in touch with a Los Angeles Times reporter named Terry McGarry. He came to my house and looked over the recovered documents. He couldn't understand why the mortuary was doing this.

I explained that this was a way to streamline the death to an acceptable cause of death so that the deceased would not be routed to the Coroner's office. I didn't believe there was malice in my superior's actions but that it was more a way to get people buried without inconveniencing the families, and was a shortcut to 'turn and burn' each client. The faster a person was buried, the faster the mortuary would get paid.

One day I arrived at work and it was if a thunderstorm had hit inside that building. Apparently, my "We-Tip" phone tip had finally paid off with the mortuary being raided by officials from the State Registrar's Office, the County Sheriff's, the LAPD, the FBI and every other official agency that I can no longer remember. Files were raided and evidence was taken. It was extremely uncomfortable coming in and working knowing that I was responsible for the raid. After all the officials left with their evidence, each employee was taken into the office of the mortuary owner and interrogated at length. When my turn came, I lied saying I had no knowledge of what had happened. At the end of the interrogation, I remember my boss looking me straight in the eye and saying that when they found the person who had done this, that person would wish they had never done it and they could expect the repercussions to be greater than any person could imagine.

I took that to mean that death was an option. Apparently, my early demise was on the table.

Later that night, once the owners had left, I called Terry, the reporter from the L.A. Times. In no uncertain terms, he agreed that the owners would do anything to protect their business and that I should be concerned about my safety.

Terry decided quickly that he wanted to move on this story after having verified my story in conjunction with the events of that day. He and a photographer came down to the mortuary at three in the morning and did a quick photo shoot of me in the mortuary. I really didn't want to do the pictures but Terry said that this would ultimately save my life. Considering the alternative, I let him do the pictures.

The next night, Terry called and said the story was breaking on the front page of the L.A. Times that next Sunday morning and it was best advised that I leave prior to the story breaking.

I learned quickly that there is no glory in being a whistle blower. It is only pain and hiding. I walked away from my job that night and let the chips fall.

The chips fell like a wrecking ball in my life. I saw myself on the front page of the Los Angeles Metro section along with a long detailed story. It was a Sunday edition as well. It was not long afterward that I started receiving death threats on my phone. My girlfriend was scared and thought I was a complete moron for risking my life and hers. She promptly left me and told me she was never coming back. I remember hiding from television reporters who were stalking my home trying to get an interview.

One day, not long after that, my car mysteriously blew up. The Los Angeles Fire Department was able to assess that an "incendiary device" had been used to turn my car into a fireball. Although they were never able to pinpoint who did it, I didn't need a name written on a chalkboard to tell me that my former bosses were involved.

At the end of the day, when the dust had settled and all was forgotten, it was a great book to write.

It was after recalling my memory of this incident that I realized this event actually may have helped me on the jury questionnaire. I believed it showed me as a person who tried to do what was right no matter the cost.

At the same time, the other skeleton involving my parents and the failed court attempt may have shown me as favorable to the defense in that it showed I had experience with abuse and violence and that may impact any potential decisions I might make on the jury favoring the defendant.

I didn't know. I was starting to realize that I knew nothing about being on a jury.

I arrived for phase three of final jury selection dressed in a Ralph Lauren shirt with a different Jerry Garcia tie than I had worn the week previous. I had enough Garcia ties to last the length of a trial and looked forward to wearing a different one every day if I got selected.

I got to the thirteenth floor of Superior Court expecting a group of fifteen or twenty people only to be surprised at the fifty or sixty potential jurors waiting outside the courtroom for final jury selection. My confidence quickly ebbed into apprehension as we filed into the courtroom.

We each carried our numbers and I learned from someone in line that this pool came from three or four groups roughly the same size as our original group. We were called into the courtroom chronologically and I ended up in the far back corner of the courtroom with all the other potential jurors and sat uncomfortably on what can only be likened to as the church pews remembered as a child. The wood was hard and unforgiving. I remember thinking that I may as well let myself down now as my odds had become low on being on this jury. I sat in the far back corner not by choice but as the queue dictated.

The Judge noted that both sides had agreed on the sixteen jurors to be sat. The Bailiff began calling the selected jurors saying that their assigned numbers would be re-assigned as actual juror numbers.

"Juror number one is called and will be juror number one...Juror number four will become Juror number two, Juror number nine will now be Juror number three and so on" Each Juror began moving up to the actual juror section. My number was number one hundred and ninety eight and it clearly looked like I would not make the jury.

"Juror number one hundred forty-seven will be juror number twelve," she called as the juror moved from the wooden pews to the juror box.

I was stunned when the next number was called and I had become juror number thirteen. I wanted to jump up and fist pump but instead I remember thanking God for the opportunity as I made my way to the jury box.

Three more numbers were called and the jury was seated. I had never considered that sixteen jurors would be called instead of twelve. It was as if I had just made it under the wire.

The Judge thanked the roomful of potential jurors who had not been called and they were summarily dismissed not having to meet further potential jury summons obligation for another year.

I sat in the jury box in almost muted amazement. All my worries had been for naught. I also noticed that no one gave us congratulations and none of the seated jurors congratulated each other as one might expect. I had expected excitement and instead felt a weight of responsibility. It was a time of seriousness and not a time of exultation.

Cherie was sitting next to me and I almost smiled when I saw her name tag, which she had so presumptuously prepared in expectation of this day. I wanted to tell her congratulations but opted for silence and a comforting smile sent her direction.

The Judge asked us to stand as a unit and we took our oath. Just as quick as that, the jury was dismissed. We were expected to be there the next morning at 10:30 AM.

Sydney walked us in unison to the back hallway of the courtroom and she showed us the jury room.

She referred to the jury room as, "your home away from work". She showed us the simple room and I remember thinking that within the whole process I had said no more or no less than two words.

The words "I can" resonated in my head throughout the rest of the day.

If the circumstances had been laid out correctly and were paved by the rules of law, I couldn't help but wonder if push came to shove, would I be sentencing someone to death?

I truly hoped that God would guide me the right way.

I was really grateful that I could put my past to rest. The Voir Dire questionnaire had opened old wounds that could now be closed.

Dave Ramsey speaks of being "Gazelle Intense" when getting your financial affairs in order. I knew I would also have to be 'Gazelle Intense' to attack this book.

The door was open and I was ready. The best way to approach this trial and this book was one day at a time, a slogan I had long ago become familiar with. I was ready to walk through a door without knowing the end. I knew going into this project that the end could be anything.

The trial could be a mistrial. We might find the defendant guilty. We might not find the defendant guilty. A worst-case scenario would be the hung jury.

I thought of the victim, whom I knew nothing about, and resolved to remember him throughout the upcoming journey.

I said a prayer, grateful for this new journey of which I was about to embark. I also made a promise to Him that if I wrote this book that it would be honest, that something good would come out of it and that it would not forget the victim.

The victim's name was Dale Harrell and he was the reason we were here.

I would take it one day a time.

DAY 4

I, THE JURY

The first day of the trial was to begin the next morning at 10:30 AM. Although the trial had actually begun with the jury selection process, this would be the first day of testimony. I arrived at the Superior Court at 10:00, which would allow a half-hour for any potential delays. We had specific jury parking and a bus to take us downtown about eight blocks away. Our bus driver's name was Phillip and was nothing less than polite to every one of us. He looked more like an attorney than a bus driver with his tie, pressed shirt and pants. He was both affable and friendly.

I went to the thirteenth floor and made my way to the jury room our "home away from work." Most of the other sixteen jurors were already there. Our Bailiff, Sydney, was there and dispersed a handful of paperwork and folders that we were to use daily. Inside the three-ring binder, there were blank juror question sheets, the Rules of Law written by the Judge, pens and legal pads.

Certainly, we were concerned when they gave us blank evidence list sheets that had hundreds of lines for evidence documentation. There was also a calendar that was dated from the beginning of the trial in February through the month of April. The trial length was predicted by the attorneys to be approximately four to six months long with certain days off for holidays, spring break and so on. They also included a multi-page form that was titled "Arizona Lengthy Trial Fund Rules for Eligibility".

It was explained that this trial was scheduled to be a long-term trial and jurors could receive up to three hundred and fifty dollars a day for each juror whose work pay would be impacted by trial participation. If one provided the correct documents for employment and/or self-employment, jurors would be eligible to draw from the fund. Thankfully, the normal pay of twelve dollars a day would not apply to us and we would be able to survive the financial impact of the trial. Furthermore, we were to be compensated forty-four cents a mile for mileage based upon our address zip code.

The folder included blank question forms for the jurors. Arizona is unique from most other states in that jurors are allowed to ask questions after testimony and upon direction of the judge. If we had a question after a witness testified; after evidence was presented; and the prosecution and defense had completed their questioning, the jurors were allowed to write their question on this specified sheet without using their name or jury number. We would fill out the question and hand the question to the bailiff for presentation to the attorneys. If the attorneys and judge agreed that this was an appropriate question, the question would be asked without identifying the juror who submitted it. Personally, I thought that, although unique, this would be a valuable tool for us.

The jury room was nothing like I had pictured it might be from the movies or anything else I had seen in the past. The room was approximately twenty-five by twenty-five feet and packed the sixteen of us in there rather snuggly. The center of the room had a long wooden conference table in the center with padded armchairs juxtaposed next to the table and additional chairs lined the walls. There was a small refrigerator for our convenience along with a coffee pot and fresh water. There was a microwave included along with a jury call button behind the machine for our use should we need the bailiff for any reason. There was a side table loaded with snacks and Girl Scout cookies that the Judge was kind enough to purchase for the jurors, as he wanted to make us as comfortable as possible.

A laminated poster was on the wall that explained jury rules. The most important rule was that we were not to use any electronic devices in our search for information. All questions were to be routed through the bailiff. We were not to talk to attorneys or the Judge without following the rules of the process. We were to be seen and not heard until we were spoken to.

There was a restroom for both men and women located adjacent to the jury room so that we would have no contact with the public, attorneys or anyone involved in the case.

The bailiff officially gave us the "rules of engagement" fifteen minutes before we were to step into the jury box for the first time. Essentially, the rules entailed our not being able to leave the jury room without permission from the bailiff. We were not to discuss the trial amongst ourselves, nor with any outside parties including the media, our family or anyone involved in the case. Periodic breaks would be afforded to us at the Judge's discretion. The lunch break of one and a half hours was the only time we were allowed to leave the jury room. In addition, we had to be escorted by the bailiff to minimize any contact with any attorneys. If we happened to see attorneys involved in the case, we were allowed to offer a friendly "hello" and contact would be limited to just that.

I thought it ironic that after having met many of the jurors, that most of us had never been on a jury before and that we were being asked to make a decision with absolutely no experience or prior knowledge of the case. It would seem that we were all rookies and that's the way the court wanted it.

Finally, the time came when we were escorted to the courtroom from a hallway behind the courtroom. Everyone was standing as the jury was seated. None of us had assigned places to sit so we just filled the sixteen seats.

Judge Steinle, III introduced himself and members of the prosecution as well as the members of the defense. He also explained the great honor in being a jury member and mentioned it is the one thing he always wanted to do, but would never have this opportunity being a judge. We should be honored to be in such a critical role in our judicial system. I felt the honor as well as the weight of the responsibility.

The Judge also mentioned that when the trial moved onward to the next phase, a lottery would be held to remove four jurors when it came to the first deliberation stage. I always thought that the alternate jurors knew they were alternates in the beginning and was surprised to find out that was not the case. In a sense, we were all alternate jurors until deliberation time.

The morning was a matter of organizing and giving the jury an idea of what to expect. The Judge explained that the trial would take place in three phases with the first phase being the actual trial of Marissa DeVault for the first-degree murder charges that had been levied against her. We were to assume her innocence until the conclusion of the trial. Once we had reached a decision of first-degree murder, if that were the case, the trial would move to the aggravation or mitigation phase where we decided the aggravating factors that were entailed in the first-degree murder charge. I likened it to the difference between stabbing someone and stabbing someone and then twisting the knife inside. Was the murder particularly heinous and how would that affect our decision in the third phase?

The third phase was the decision by the jurors between life in prison and the death penalty. This had been the phase that the Jodi Arias trial had failed to reach a decision. At the time, it certainly seemed a long way off.

The Judge spent about thirty minutes explaining the law for us, and how we would eventually apply those rules of law to this case. I found him to be friendly and affable but at the same time we knew he was in charge of the room. He looked us each in the eye as he gave us a quick lesson on what we had become involved in.

The Judge was a short man with salt and pepper curly hair. He wore a black robe and peered over the courtroom from his seat, which was equal in height to the second row in the jury box.

Our jury duties were defined as to the court's expectations. We were to decide the facts on the case based on only evidence presented. We were not to speculate about witnesses, the defendant or facts of the case. We were not to be influenced by prejudice or empathy. The jury, and the jury alone, was the judge of the facts presented.

The Judge spent some time talking about direct evidence and how it was based on a physical exhibition of fact or the direct testimony of witnesses who actually saw the event. He then explained circumstantial evidence as that which proved a fact as interpreted from another fact of which that fact could be inferred. We were then to determine the weight of all evidence without regard to whether it is direct or circumstantial.

The Judge explained that we must keep an open mind and should always remember that the defendant is innocent until proven guilty. The State bears the burden of proof that a defendant is guilty beyond a reasonable doubt. Proof beyond a reasonable doubt is proof that leaves you firmly convinced of the defendant's guilt. He noted that in criminal cases, the law does not require proof that overcomes every doubt. I was sure this would be cause for hair-splitting when it came to jury deliberation.

When the Judge spoke of first-degree murder charges, he emphasized the importance of the prosecution proving this beyond a reasonable doubt. For a crime to be first-degree murder by premeditation, the State must prove that the defendant caused the death of another person and the defendant intended or knew that their actions would cause the death of another person and that the defendant acted with premeditation.

At some point, the Judge said (or had written in his Rules of Law) that if there had been past acts of domestic violence against the defendant by the victim, the state of mind of a reasonable person shall be determined from the perspective of a reasonable person who has been a victim of acts of domestic violence. The state has the burden of proving beyond a reasonable doubt that the defendant did not act with such justification. If the prosecution failed to carry this burden then the jury must find the defendant not guilty of the charge.

It was during this time, I realized that my personal experience with domestic violence might have an impact on how I thought of the charges and the case. It was the first time that I could assign value to my experiences with my family.

I did not have to look at the other jurors to know that they, like me, were taking notes furiously. It was not surprising given that we were all rookies in a capital murder trial.

We knew the trial had officially begun when Miss Arino, whom I believe was the Assistant Prosecutor, stepped up to the podium with her attention focused on the jury. She spoke calmly and carefully and if one were a casual observer, one wouldn't think she was speaking of first-degree murder. She would read her notes and then speak to us in phrases of paragraphs, pausing between each thought to check her notes.

"The first thing you will learn is that this defendant likes money and this is what precipitated the murder of her husband Dale Harrell."

"In 2007, Marissa DeVault met Allen Flores who was a very successful businessman. Marissa is the mother of three children and within thirty days of her meeting Allen Flores, she began borrowing money from him. The first time she borrowed money, it was under the assumption that it was to get her brakes fixed. In a very short time, she owed Allen Flores over $62, 000. After multiple requests for money, Allen Flores drew up a promissory note for the return of that money."

"Marissa DeVault claimed she was to receive an inheritance soon and this would be paid before the end of the year in 2008. She claimed that this was in litigation with her attorney."

"At some point, after getting tired of hearing false promises, Mr. Flores called her attorney only to find that there was no such case in litigation. At this point, Marissa owed him in excess of a quarter of a million dollars."

"It is clear that Marissa DeVault had no means to pay this back."

I listened intently and noticed at the same time that Michelle Arino was nervous. She had uncomfortable pauses and a number of sentences she had to restart. I had a feeling that this was her first murder case of this level.

"Marissa DeVault, the defendant that you see seated behind me on my right, planned to kill her husband on his birthday in December of 2008 after going to a local casino. She hired a hit man to take care of her husband when he went outside to the parking lot of the casino. However, the plan did not work out."

"In that, the evidence will show that Marissa DeVault came up with a second plan to kill him while her husband was sleeping. She then called Flores to say the hit had not happened. "

"At this time, given that the loans had accrued a $294,000, Allen Flores had another promissory note drawn up and the monies loaned would be due by the end of January of 2009."

"Allen Flores received a phone call from Marissa DeVault with her saying that her husband had been killed in some sort of confrontation. Her roommate at the time, Stanley Cook, confirmed that Dale Harrell had been killed with a tire iron and that he had seen it. Allen Flores immediately offered to come to the house to console Marissa DeVault but the defendant adamantly refused his offer telling him to stay away."

"The day before Dale Harrell's hammer attack, Allen Flores showed up at the defendant's house unannounced only to find out that the defendant was not at home and was instead out somewhere with her husband. This greatly concerned Mr. Flores because he thought the husband was dead."

"It was within twenty-four hours that the defendant, Marissa DeVault, called 911 to report the death of her husband at 2:45 in the morning. These phone calls are very revealing."

"The police arrive to find that Dale Harrell had been brutally attacked with a hammer. The Gilbert Police Department officers found Marissa DeVault in the driveway covered in blood. Over time, she explained to the police that she had asked for a divorce and that her husband had become enraged and raped her. Her roommate, Stanley Cook, ran into the bedroom brandishing a gun and had saved her life. She said that Stanley Cook had hit her husband with a hammer and that is how she got blood on her person."

"Dale Harrell was transported to the hospital and died twenty-seven days later from his injuries."

"The police department took pictures of the scene prior to the transport of Dale and the next twenty-four hours was spent on scene investigation."

"The police felt immediately that there were inconsistencies in Marissa's story. The blood spatter was not consistent with her rendition of what happened. It became the opinion of the Gilbert Police Department that Dale Harrell was laying down, probably sleeping, when he was brutally attacked."

"The blood that was seen on the clothes of Marissa DeVault was consistent with the swinging of a hammer and the blood on her roommate was not consistent with being the attacker."

"Further, the State will show that Marissa had an insurance policy taken out on her husband for one million dollars that was effective on the first of the year in 2009."

"It is no coincidence that Dale Harrell was attacked on the fourteenth of January."

"The defendant stuck to her story saying that her husband regularly abused her and that Stanley Cook had been her savior in the final attack when Dale had attacked her."

"You will see, at some point in the investigation, the police confronted Marissa on her story, stating that the evidence did not coincide with her account of the events of that early morning."

Michelle Arino stopped and picked up a bottle of water and sipped from it. She slowly screwed the cap back on as she glanced at her notes. She continued speaking, her nervousness less obvious, with focus.

"At this point, Marissa DeVault changed her story and said that because Dale was abusive and had raped her, that she was the one who actually killed Dale in self-defense."

"It was on February 7th, 2009 that the defendant changed the beneficiary on the million dollar policy from herself to the man that she owed almost $300,000, Allen Flores. Two days later, Dale Harrell died as a result of his injuries. Dale Harrell had lain in bed for twenty-seven days before he finally passed away from the brutal injuries he had received."

"It was shortly thereafter, that Stan Cook drafted a confession letter claiming that he had killed Dale Harrell. The evidence will show that this letter was written with the help of Marissa DeVault and with the guidance of her co-conspirator, Allen Flores."

"Ladies and Gentleman, the evidence will show that Stanley Cook could not have been the killer and the evidence will clearly show that Marissa DeVault is guilty of first-degree murder and planned to kill her husband prior to the attack of January 14, 2009."

The Judge dismissed the jury for the first of our many breaks. The hardest thing about this, and something we would have to learn to get used to, was the fact that we could not discuss what we had just heard amongst ourselves. We made ourselves content by using the restroom and getting some refreshments.

Many of us busied ourselves with checking for phone messages or burying our face in our Tablets. A nicely dressed juror made a phone call while we pretended not to listen.

"I'm calling back about the chicken fingers," she said on her cell phone. "Yes, Ma'am, I need to make sure that two-hundred fingers are ready for my kid's soccer team. I'll pick them up at 5:30."

She was dressed in a black and gold colored dress and looked like a lady who might be seen driving a Lexus or Mercedes. Her voice was calm and she aired a mother's authority. She struck me as classy.

"How much?" she asked.

I guessed that she should not pay more than one hundred dollars.

"That's great," she said. "I'll have the ninety dollars when I get there at 5:15."

I decided that I would remember her as "Wings" even though I didn't know her name, yet.

That first break was filled with gaps of silence as we busied ourselves talking trivialities such as how nice the weather had been with it staying stubbornly in the seventies even though it was early February. We were returned to the jury box fifteen minutes later to hear the defense opening arguments.

Alan Tavasoli of the defense presented their side of the case. The attorney was calm and warm as he explained that this was not a first-degree murder. He emphasized that as jury we must look at three things to find the defendant innocent. We must first acknowledge that Marissa DeVault called 911 immediately upon recognizing that Dale Harrell was hurt. Why would she call 911 if she were a murderer?

I noticed, again, that he pronounced her name as "DeVwah" in opposition of how Eric Basta and Michelle Arino pronounced her name.

The attorney explained the defendant had been a victim of both sexual and physical abuse giving her Post Traumatic Syndrome and her roommate owned multiple guns so why would someone use a hammer in a premeditated murder?

The defense also stated that Marissa DeVault owned a trust fund so she did not need money as a motive to kill her husband.

Alan Tavasoli directed our attention to Allen Flores and the fact that he had been given complete immunity as long as he testified. Allen Flores was a master manipulator and he alone controlled the situation. The attorney emphasized that we should focus on his immunity and that he could say anything to protect himself.

He noted that Allen Flores had manipulated Stan Cook's confession so that he would receive the benefits of a life insurance policy and this had nothing to do with Dale.

The attorney emphasized the fact that this case was about a history of domestic violence and was not about money at all. People hide domestic violence and this is what the jury needed to focus on despite the tragic end to Dale Harrell's life.

This case and the evidence presented would prove sexual assault, domestic violence and a misinterpretation of facts.

This defendant was justified in the death of Dale Harrell because she was merely protecting herself and her three children.

We broke for lunch with the weight of the case bared upon us. It seemed confusing and opposing in facts but I knew we were to remain non-judgmental until the end of the case when all facts had been presented.

Clearly, the hardest part after we were led back to the jury room was the fact that we could not speak to each other about the case. We each had to own the obligation and it was difficult not to say anything to those who had just witnessed opening statements. In fact, we couldn't talk to anyone and carried these secrets quietly within each of us.

The moment we returned to the jury box, Mr. Basta asked the court for permission to enter the first three pieces of evidence. He was granted permission and then he followed with a request to pass the items to the jury.

The first item to be passed into my hands was a clear plastic-wrapped box. Inside the box, a small black pistol had been mounted. I could see that it was a used gun with deposits of dirt along the inside of the trigger. I didn't remember a gun being used in opening arguments so I was a little confused as to the gun's importance.

The next item that we were passed was a gun clip and its unused bullets. The third exhibit was a bullet in a plastic bag and it was said to have been in the chamber of the gun.

The rest of the afternoon was spent with the prosecution presenting the three police officers that were first-responders on the scene: Clint Cobbett, Chris Dorenbush and Ryan Churchman.

The prosecution put its first pictures on the screen at the front of the courtroom for all to see. Officer Dorenbush had presence of mind to retrieve a digital camera from the trunk of his vehicle prior to emergency technicians arriving. He had only taken a couple of pictures during those first horrific moments but they were critical.

The first picture was haunting and, thankfully, slightly blurry. It was a picture of Dale Harrell, the victim, lying on the floor next to his bed with his head pressed against a nightstand. He was nude but still conscious and alive, with pictures being taken by the police who were first on the scene. Blood was everywhere including on the walls, in a blood soaked pillow, smeared on the sheets and on the upper torso of the victim.

One of the officers, Clint Cobbett, had pressed a towel against the open wound of Dale's head noting his skull was missing pieces and he was just trying to stop the profuse bleeding and was not successful. He thought it was a gunshot wound from a suicide attempt. He comforted and held Dale's head until the Gilbert Fire Department and Rescue came to move him to Mercy General Hospital.

On a small desk near the door, Officer Dorenbush, who took the picture, although blurry, captured a bloody hammer just lying on the table.

It was clearly the murder weapon although it had not been proven, yet. I could not see how the gun fit into the fabric of this story.

I knew the moment that I saw the picture of Dale lying on the floor, defenseless, that I would never forget it.

We, the jury, had our work cut out for us...

DAY 5

REALITY BITES

We had three days to think about things before returning to court on Monday. We all had the project of dealing with our work life and the reaction of our bosses. I can comfortably say that my boss was not happy about losing me to this trial for a period of four to six months. The Judge had warned us that our work would suddenly consider us "the best employee" they ever had and that they could not live without us for that period of time. He was absolutely right.

Furthermore, for us to get paid out of the Arizona Lengthy Trial Fund, we had to provide an enormous amount of documentation to prove what we would be losing while on jury duty. We were expected to provide copies of tax returns, three months of paycheck stubs as well as documentation of other monies normally received throughout the weeks that we would be on jury duty.

In my case, I worked and sold items regularly on eBay. This required my completion of an IRS W-9 along with supporting documents of what I normally received from eBay sales. Hopefully, my paperwork would effectively validate how long-term jury duty would impact the loss of sales, and subsequent income.

I certainly appreciated the availability of such a fund but it was not without detailed documentation. I likened it to an IRS Tax Audit in its complexity. To that end, I spent the weekend fighting with my workplace and coming up with a detailed financial review.

One of my goals that I set throughout the week was to learn the first names of each juror since we would be spending significant time together. I figured that if I learned the names of one or two jurors a day, I would know all the jurors in about two to three weeks given our court schedule.

The first juror that I reached out to was Cherie. One could tell she was a manager sort and dressed the part. She was African-American and dressed in sharp business apparel. She looked like a younger version of Whitney Houston. I met her on the first day of jury selection and throughout the process to this day, we had struck up a comfortable relationship. I genuinely liked her and respected her as a professional.

The one thing we had in common was our mutual ownership of dogs. She had seen my Chihuahua picture on my phone and thought he was gorgeous but a looked a little fat. I mentioned how happy my dog was every time I came home and how he liked to chase his tail and run around in circles to greet me. She pulled a book out of her business bag called, "The Secret Life of Dogs."

Evidently, she thought I might be interested in knowing why my dog chased his tail. I read the piece in the book and learned my dog had to see a doctor. I joked that my Rocky Balboa needed to see a psychiatrist.

The morning of our first week of jury duty, I brought in my book, "The Complete Dog Book" an official publication of the American Kennel Club. This book details every dog known to man and I wanted to learn about her dogs. She owned a variation of a Skye terrier and was happy to show me her multiple pictures on her tablet. Like me, she loved dogs. In that, I liked her. Dog people like dog people.

The first day of our first full week showed us immediately that we would be in for a lot of work. The thrill of being of juror was quickly over-ridden by the prospect of the amount of work we were going to face. The Judge had made two things clear. The first was that opening statements were not evidence. The second thing was that at the end, transcripts of the trial would not be allowed in the jury room. He warned us that we needed to take notes and it was from these notes that we would draw information when we reached the deliberation stage. In other words, we were advised to take good notes.

We were led into the courtroom at our designated time. The one thing that always felt honorable was that everyone had to remain standing until the jury was seated. It felt like an elevated position, as well as, an honorable defining of our importance as a juror.

I am a tall man and learned quickly that it was best if I was seated on the end cap of a row. In that way, I wouldn't block the view of other jurors. I learned that I preferred to be on an end and usually tried to choose the last seat in the first row. I also liked the fact that I could see the full profile of a witness as they testified. If one were looking at me from the gallery, I would be the furthest seat away at the end of the bottom row.

We were seated and I looked around the courtroom. I was a little surprised to see so few people in the public seats of the courtroom, which is also known as the gallery. The other thing one could not help noticing was the presence of live cameras. There were cameras located above the witness stand facing the courtroom as well as a long telescopic looking camera with a photographer standing behind it in the back courtroom.

The Judge had previously explained that the jurors would never be filmed in court, which protected us and made us comfortable.

Our Bailiff, Sydney, stood about five foot, six inches as she guided us to the direction of our jury seats and led us out every time the jury was dismissed. After she escorted us to our seats, she would then move to a seat on a lower level to the left of the Judge. There was also another awareness that stood out.

On the first day of the first week, Sydney gave us an indication of how much work we were facing because when she sat down, we could only see the tufts of her hair sticking out above boxes and boxes of bagged evidence and files. Numbers were on the front of each of these boxes and one could see that they were generally numbered one through four hundred and fifty. It was really quite intimidating, as you knew this was prosecutorial evidence. All I have to say about the first day can be explained in two words: hand cramps.

I should explain, before moving forward, my general process. We took notes throughout the day and then I would go home and create this journal of events. There was an incredible amount of information to be processed. We were not allowed to take notes home nor were we allowed to Google, watch TV or look up anything on the Internet. I had recused myself from CNN, HLN and any other form of news as directed by the Judge. In that regard, I quickly learned that there was no way that I could go home and remember all the evidence presented. Although, taking dubious notes and suffering through bouts of hand cramps did help to commit some of this information to memory.

I can comfortably say that probably only twenty percent of what we saw actually ended up in this journal of sorts. Furthermore, given that we could not discuss this case with anyone, I found that writing this journal helped to vent thoughts and feelings I would have told someone, had I been in a position where I was *allowed* to tell someone. The writing of this seemed to alleviate some of the pressure of the knowledge that we had to carry around in secrecy. At the very least, it kept me vested in the proceedings.

The first forty-eight hours of the crime scene had been treated as an aggravated assault since Dale Harrell had not yet passed away. The first two days at the scene consisted of evidence collection and documentation of the scene. It began with the second officer on the scene who was able to take those blurry photos of Dale Harrell, in the room on the floor before he was taken to the hospital.

It was interesting to watch policeman testify from my vantage point. Each one had to take a few moments to fit themselves into the witness stand chair. Their torso was wrapped in Kevlar with an enormous amount of gear hanging from their belts. One could see a Taser gun on their left side with a regular holstered gun on the right side. Their belt was adorned with tools, flashlights and hooks where presumably, handcuffs would be attached.

They sat as is if they were backing a car into a close fitting garage. We have come a long way from the 1970's when policeman's uniform consisted of a shirt, badge and gun.

It always took the officers some time to maneuver into their chairs. I also saw a microphone on each of the policeman's lapels. This must have been the device that recorded one of her encounters with the police upon their arrival.

One of the first pieces of evidence was a cell phone that had been discarded on the driveway by the defendant after she had called 911. The police officer that observed the defendant throwing the cell phone to the ground thought the behavior was very strange. Even more thought-provoking, was noticing that the 911 call had been disconnected by the defendant numerous times before the police first arrived on scene.

It was eight o'clock in the morning when a witness, Victoria McIlveen was dispatched to the scene. She was a Crime Scene Technician with over sixteen years of experience whose duty was to document and collect evidence of the scene. She took swabs, fingerprints, pictures and videos of the scene.

Her investigation yielded twenty or thirty pieces of evidence that were given Property ID numbers along with evidence numbers. The process of documentation by the jurors had begun with notes taken from the testimony of witnesses. We worked on completing an extensive log on evidence enumeration sheets.

Photographs were introduced of the bedroom including details of blood smears on walls, fingerprints on sheets, as well as bathroom pictures and everything else one could think of. It was surprising how quickly one got used to seeing the heavily bloodstained bed, sheets and pillow. Blood spatter covered the walls around the bed, above the bed and was seen across the room and even found in the remotest areas of the room. The process of our documenting this evidence forced us to write quickly and took the attention away from the drama of the scene.

My fellow jurors could be seen periodically stretching their hands, and flexing their fingers during their furious note taking.

We documented each piece of Stan Cook's clothing that was entered into evidence including his gray t-shirt, pants, socks, shoes, small gun and jacket.

There was a point when a police officer was asked if he had ever been able to talk with the victim, Dale Harrell. The only thing the officer heard was the groaning of Dale while he was lying on the floor in the bedroom and, while being accompanied by a police officer in the back of an ambulance, Dale's insistence that his right leg was uncomfortable. It was an odd thing to say but in consideration of the brain damage he had suffered, there was no surprise that wires would have been crossed in his head giving him false messages.

The gruesomeness of the scene was accentuated by, Andrew Bowers, the ambulance technician. He vividly recounted Dale's blood spilling out the back doors of the ambulance during transport to the hospital.

Police officers took the stand one by one as the documentation of the scene was revealed. A search warrant had been executed for the scene and details were enumerated as each piece of the scene was documented.

A significant sequence of evidence showed multiple pictures of the roommate, Stan Cook. Pictures were taken of him in the clothes he was wearing at the time police arrived. We saw pictures of his face, neck, chest, abdomen, crotch, legs, socks and shoes. The same sequence of pictures was done on his back in the same order as his front. Each picture had a property ID number along with an evidence number.

His gray t-shirt looked remarkably out of place with Grumpy from the Seven Dwarfs saying, "I'm right, you're wrong! Any questions?"

Pictures of a SKS rifle owned by Stan Cook were introduced with the rifle being found in a padded case in his closet. Evidence was presented of multiple computers that were seized including towers and the reverse side of these towers with manufacturer ID numbers on each of them.

The jury wrote furiously in longhand as these pieces of evidence were presented and discussed. By the end of the day, I can comfortably say that my writing hand hurt and my head hurt. It was absolute information overload.

The jury departed for the day and we were largely silent, each other focused on getting home and delving into rush hour traffic. At this point, we didn't know what to think except that a lot of evidence had come forward.

I remember thinking that we had only touched the surface of the mountain of evidence that Sydney had peeped out from behind in the courtroom. It was becoming apparent why this was expected to be a long trial.

If one were to look at a trial like the climbing of a mountain where the verdict is the peak of the mountain, then I think we were still in the pasture at the base of the mountain...

It was only the beginning of a long climb ahead of us...

DAY 6

ASSAULT OR MURDER

The first witness of the day was a former detective of the Gilbert Police Department, Detective Janssen Redcay. He was originally called to the scene of the assault of January 14, 2009 late in the morning and was to assist in the collection of evidence. He was also investigating the home of Allen Flores.

At some point in the morning, it was learned that Stan Cook went to the Gilbert Police Department with a confession letter. Shortly after Cooks' confession, police learned that Allen Flores was picking him up at the police station. The detectives, without his knowledge, followed Allen Flores to his residence.

A search warrant was executed and Allen Flores' house had been searched and documented for computers, various papers and the like that could be involved in what was now a murder. Dale Harrell had just passed away in the hospital's hospice unit with his father at his side.

Evidence was presented and it was learned that the birth certificate and Social Security card of Dale Harrell was found inside Allen Flores' residence.

That certainly sounded curious and it was obvious that this was a connection to Dale Harrell.

Detective Mike Bishop stepped to the witness stand and was questioned by the prosecution. This detective was one of the detectives who had followed Allen Flores to his residence. Detective Mike Bishop was also normally seated at the prosecution table as he represented the State of Arizona.

It was presented that in the evidence collection process, life insurance policies were confiscated and the name on those insurance policies was Marissa DeVault, the defendant. The effective date of those policies on Dale Harrell, were listed as January 1, 2009.

The horrific assault on Dale Harrell that eventually claimed his life occurred on January 14th, a mere two weeks after the execution of the policies. Was it just a coincidence?

The detective, upon further questioning revealed that a door-to-door search of neighbors was put in process, hoping for information. Neighbors all the way down the block on both sides of the street were interviewed. None of the neighbors had heard a dispute during the night of the attack. Furthermore, no witnesses could be found that had ever witnessed domestic violence at the residence.

We took notes furiously as the prosecution marched up countless witnesses to the stand. Most of them were from the

Gilbert Fire Department and were involved in the paramedic aspect of the scene. Marissa DeVault was reported as being nervous and sometimes hysterical. When paramedics took her vitals and looked her over, she complained about a pain in her neck from being strangled. The paramedics agreed that it was dark outside, but also stated that upon examining the area with a flashlight, they really didn't see any redness on her neck.

The court was given a fifteen-minute recess and we returned to the introduction of Captain Danny Grant, a twenty-year veteran of the Gilbert Arizona Fire Department. It was a lengthy direct examination by the prosecution and particularly vivid and gruesome details were revealed about the night of the assault and the condition of Dale.

He remembered seeing the victim as a person in his mid-thirties, lying on the floor bleeding profusely from his head. He took over for the policeman who was holding pressure on Dale's head to slow the bleeding. The Captain put a "C" Clamp on Dale's neck to prevent his head from moving. He did not know the extent of the injuries and noted that it looked like a shotgun wound had given the damage. He had seen depressions of the skull, cuts on the victims face and a profuse amount of bleeding.

He put Dale on a flat board to minimize movement during his transportation by ambulance. Dale was conscious and moaning. The Captain rode with the victim to the hospital remembering that while the victim was moaning; he was complaining of the brightness of the ambulance lights and that his leg was uncomfortable.

The captain explained that during the transport, the victim was given medication to dull the pain and they gave him Succinylcholine, a paralytic drug that allowed them to insert a breathing tube. It was explained that sometimes the drug was called "Succs" and this was done because without it, the natural reaction of the body would be to reject the breathing tube. Typically, the gag reflex prevents the insertion of the tube.

The testimony was quite revealing and uncomfortable at the same time.

Before the questioning ended, it was revealed that Dale had been able to recall his name and his age of thirty-four, but no other information was received from him.

We were relieved for the arrival of lunch recess and were sent downstairs. When one walked into the courtyard, you could choose an area to eat outside called "Change of Venue". Just inside, there was a cafeteria, vending machines and even a Starbucks. I happened to be following another juror and he chose to walk to an area across the street that featured a plethora of lunch restaurants surrounding a green courtyard.

I followed him to Chipotle Grille and we both ordered a burrito. He wasn't very talkative but I learned he was an insurance salesman for a national company. He was tall and big boned. Some might think he was a little goofy looking but he was an intelligent man.

We took our lunch back into the courthouse. He wanted to find the other jurors. After fifteen minutes of wandering down hallways, he gave up and sat down at a table by an escalator. He opened his lunch and then opened his Spiderman Logo wrapped tablet and put in his earbud headphones.

We didn't say much throughout lunch.

We returned to the jury box after lunch and Andrew Bowers was introduced, the paramedic engineer. He had accompanied the victim and prior witness to the hospital in the ambulance. He spoke in depth about Dale Harrell's extensive injuries and was amazed at the amount of blood. The victim was suffering through extreme trauma and had severe swelling in his eye.

He originally thought this victim was an attempted suicide by shotgun. He saw copious amounts of blood and the blood-soaked pillow above where Dale had been lying prior to transport. He recalled that in the transport of a victim and the urgency involved, it would be expected that paramedics would toss gloves and medical packaging aside at the scene given the priority of the victim's transport. He further recalled seeing a bloodied hammer lying on a nightstand by the door.

The afternoon witness was a female by the name of Brenda Tomory who was a detective for the Gilbert Police Department with a focus on sexual assault examinations.

Pictures were presented of Marissa DeVault taken during the sexual assault examination. Pictures were presented of her face, neck, abdomen and legs. Photographs were taken of both her front side and back side. A particular photo stood out of what looked like fingermarks on the inside of her thighs. When Marissa was questioned about those marks, she claimed it was from making love to Dale.

There was also a picture of some redness on the right side of her face and Marissa explained this mark. She said that it was from her roommate, Stan Cook, whom she had asked to slap her in the face to 'wake her up from a dream' or to 'prove she wasn't dreaming'.

It was noted that there was dried blood present on Marissa's red acrylic nail cuticles and on her right knee.

There was a point when the defense approached the witness and it was learned that Marissa had consented to a sexual assault examination voluntarily. This examination was meticulous and it took almost six hours to complete. There was a point where it was asked if the defendant had been "Mirandized". It was explained that this was not necessary because the defendant was not under arrest and was being treated as a victim. The case was being treated as an assault and since no one had died, murder was not a consideration.

The day ended with the prosecution's direct examination of Detective Mike Bishop. It was learned that Dale Harrell had never been able to tell what happened due to his injuries and the amount of medication in his system.

The detective walked us through a timeline and noted the investigation had changed course when Dale died of his injuries. It further changed direction again, when it was discovered that Stan Cook's confession was not consistent with the facts of the scene. Prior to those two events, there was no feeling that a search warrant had been needed.

It was a long day of testimony and my hand cramps were in full swing.

At this point, I knew not to speculate anything. I knew that this was only the beginning of the case and there was a lot more to come.

I could only imagine the pain that Dale must have gone through in his final two weeks of life.

DAY 7

MIXING MORTAR

I liked Doc. She was warm, friendly and had a deep from the heart laugh. She didn't take disrespect from anyone. I imagined her as a young girl and imagined that in the schoolyard, the bullies were afraid of her. I could see why she was on the jury. She was levelheaded and intelligent.

Doc was a smoker like me. I met her in the smoking area of the public courtyard. Even though it is a large space that leads to the Superior Courthouse, it is a small area afforded for smokers. We stood in the shadow of the thirteen-story courthouse as pedestrians, lawyers, defendants, police officers and good-looking secretary types converged toward the security doors that lead into the building.

Doc and I smoked and looked across the open area toward "Change of Venue", the outdoor seating for the restaurants on the other side.

We were amazed as we observed how people dressed for their upcoming court appearances. One saw as many hoodies as one did suits on lawyers. It was hard to believe how many people arrived in pajama bottoms and fuzzy bedroom slippers. Who goes to a courthouse in sleepwear? It reeks of disrespect for the court and makes a silent statement about them.

Doc told me that the other jurors had dubbed me the 'Professor' because of the shirt and tie I wore every day. I took that as a compliment.

No matter when I saw her, she always gave the feeling of being a genuinely happy person. She had a Doctorate in Pharmacology, worked as a pharmacist and paid dearly for that education in student loans. Student loans seemed to be her only worry in the world. She did not seem to think that two hundred thousand dollars would be that difficult to pay back. I was jealous of her confidence.

She had the unique position of loving both her job and the fact that her parents loved her. She recognized that, and I think too few people recognize what blessings they have. It was special to see that aura. So, when it came time for a lunch break, we were always sure to hang out on the way to lunch and would meet up first thing in the morning before court began.

When the time came, a half-hour before court was to begin for the day, we made our way in.

By this time, I had become somewhat of an expert on entering the building. You knew you were going to pass through a metal detector daily. The first few days weren't all that smooth for me.

Initially, I had spent time retrieving a tiny Swiss Army knife that was on my keychain the first day. Security confiscates the item, tags the item, you are then given a copy of the receipt and may retrieve it later.

The Sheriff's Office runs the security protocol for entering the building. I learned to respect them for the thousands of people they must screen daily yet always remain patient and focused on their task at hand.

The second day I went through security, my leather keychain was confiscated because when it was taken apart, there was a sharp edge to it. I didn't know it was there until it was pointed out. The retrieval process is fairly easy but after being in court all day, it's an inconvenient trip to go retrieve confiscated items. It's the last thing that you want to bother your mind with.

A person is also required to take off their belt and put it through the metal detector and X-ray machine. Hence, that required me to buy a new belt that had a nice slippery underside to it as opposed to a brushed leather underside. It made taking your belt on and off a lot easier.

It also made me conscious of the waistband of my pants. Normally, you can get away with a waist size being a size too big with a belt on. Once you took your belt off and went through security, you felt self-conscious as you steadfastly held your own pants up by a loop.

The other thing I learned to eliminate was carrying a pocketful of change. It was just another useless step since I never saw any vending machines in the building heading toward our courtroom.

I learned not to follow Doc through security. She usually carried a large green purse and her lunch in another bag. It took them awhile to scan and take apart the purse. She usually had a roll of quarters that drew attention and loose keys in the base of her purse. I remember them being pulled out one by one and she didn't know what the keys were for. It was amusing.

We walked into the jury room a short time later and we all started sitting in regular seats. Some jurors liked sitting at the wooden long table while others sat in their same spots along the walls. I liked the far corner because I could see everything in front of me. I like to be conscious of my surroundings and it makes me comfortable not having to look behind me.

The way we sat in the jury room also seemed to designate where we would sit in the jury box. For instance, the doorway to the courtroom from the jury room is at the front of our room. In that, we would file out from the wall first, then those from the long jury table would follow and those along the opposing wall would file out last. This is how we ended up the same jury seats every day and almost every time. If you happened to be out of sequence leaving the jury room, then you ended up in a foreign seat in the jury box.

There was no assigned seating and everyone instinctively just knew that you didn't claim the seats where you sat the previous day. You were seated as the queue dictated.

I can sum up the day's proceedings as likened to someone taking a 500 pc jigsaw puzzle box, opening it and throwing the pieces in front of a big blow fan in front of the jury. Imagine each piece having to be documented with a Property Identification Number as well as an Evidence Identification number and then adding a description to each piece.

We had little time to do anything but write continuously. It was not like television where a piece of evidence is presented and then the attorneys discuss it.

There were witnesses brought forward to discuss pieces, but I think the prosecution wanted to get all the pieces introduced so that they could be later discussed piece by piece. It would be like getting the bricks together to build a house but you don't have mortar to connect the pieces.

We labored through the logging of the different pieces of evidence regarding the serology results obtained from Marissa DeVault during her sexual assault examination. These included pictures, smears and swabs. There were breast swabs, mouth swab evidence, fingernail bed swabs, anal swabs and numerous others forgotten since I left court. Conclusions were not established as I think the focus was getting as many pieces in as possible.

We saw and logged more exhibits of Stan Cook's shirt, pants and every other piece of apparel he was wearing. I couldn't wait to meet this witness.

At some point, we got to see the plastic-wrapped box that contained the gun he was carrying and the clip and the rounds in the gun. The gun was found in his pocket and would fit right in the palm of your hand. It was never fired.

A particularly interesting piece was in regards to the testing of the bloodied claw hammer found at the scene. The hammer was wrapped in white plastic and secured in a cellophane wrapped box. One tried not visualizing its use in the murder. There were no statements yet on whose blood was on it.

Another segment of the trial included the entering of evidence such as the test results of every item that had blood on it. If one were to look at the jury at that time, I bet we looked somewhat like the 1920's type reporters documenting a World Series game with their eyes peeping up momentarily to glance at a play on the field. We were doing the same thing; recording a piece of evidence and then glancing up to see the presenter or witness, while we would quickly return to documenting them on our own evidence logs.

It was really quite daunting how much evidence would be walked through. I am also surprised that by the time I arrive home to record my day in my journal, how little I can remember by the time I get there.

It is funny how being a juror begins changing how you think. Not only does your mind start becoming attuned to being analytical, you also become aware of how much the law is in our lives daily.

I remember driving home with my head swimming in details and I suddenly became conscious of how I was driving. It was expected that I be a good driver and obey the laws. I am certainly not saying I have wonton disregard of the law, I am just noticing that I am looking at my speedometer more often, I'm making sure that I wear my seatbelt and exercise that little extra ounce of caution that the law of driving dictates.

It was curious how this trial was beginning to impact how I had previously looked at things. It was as if I was paying more attention and thus making me more aware of things.

I was beginning to feel like a responsible citizen.

BITS AND PIECES

Today was the most interesting day of the trial thus far. The first things that were presented were DNA studies of evidence in the room where the assault occurred. Clothes had been analyzed along with bed sheets, walls, pillows and the smears on doors, tables and tissues in the trash.

The prosecutor made a point of saying that a tissue had been found in the bathroom trashcan. He pointed out that the trashcan had no liner. I was not sure of the significance of it.

I don't remember the exact order of how these things were presented but some facts did rise to the surface. In essence, there were only three people and their various DNA samples were brought to light. It was said that accuracy of this DNA was one in three hundred and seventy quadrillion which represented a one with fifteen zero's following it. It sounded accurate and trustworthy to me.

There were three people determined to be in the room at the time of this assault. They included the victim, Dale Harrell; the defendant, Marissa DeVault; and Stan Cook, the roommate. DNA tests showed that Marissa and Dale's DNA were found in the bed. Dale's semen was found in the bed sheets as well.

The clothes that Marissa was wearing at the time of her questioning showed Dale's DNA. The shirt that Stan Cook was wearing also carried Dale's DNA on it. Dale's DNA was under Marissa's fingernails and a swab test taken in the bathroom showed a mixture of Dale and Stan's DNA.

The hammer was tested and the results were inconclusive although it was clear that it did have a lot of blood on it. It was explained that blood tests are not always perfect as it depends upon the environment of which the samples were taken. The factors that can inhibit sampling results can depend upon heat, age, temperature and drying so results may not be surmised all of the time. However, sperm is very hearty.

Detective Sy Ray was introduced as a witness who had been with the Gilbert Police Department for over fifteen years. He was with the violent crimes unit and specialized in blood spatter interpretation.

Although it was imperceptible except to me, it looked that some of the ladies on the jury seemed to have a more piqued interest with this witness than over others we had seen. I surmised that it was because he was an amazingly good-looking man. I didn't see a wedding ring on his finger and wouldn't be surprised if that had solicited additional interest. He resembled the chiseled physique of Superman in both facial features and physique.

Detective Sy Ray was able to look at the blood spatter on the walls and found it easy to draw a conclusion before an in-depth analysis was done.

It was explained that one could determine the point of convergence of the blood spatter by seeing the profusion of blood beginning on the blood soaked pillow. Arising from the pillow toward the walls and ceiling was the blood spatter evidence. Further, after looking at the clothes Marissa was wearing and the clothes that Stan had been wearing, it was certain that Marissa was closest to receive the impact blood that had hit her prior to the same blood spatter hitting Stan Cook.

This detective then saw the video of Marissa's interrogation and determined that her original story of events did not match the signs at the scene. Her version of events was clearly not consistent with the story that the scene told. The detective delegated a blood spatter expert, Steve McGibbon, to do an analysis of the scene.

We were excused for a break. I heard Doc say that she loved blood spatter analysis. It was certainly interesting once one looked past the horror of the scene. I knew we wanted to talk about it but we were restrained by our position.

The trial resumed with the next witness introduced as Dr. Laura Fulginiti. She was quite animated and reminded one of a favorite teacher in college. Whereas the police as witnesses were stoic and clinical, I found her to be enjoyable and educational. One could tell that she was passionate about her work and loved to teach people how she did her work.

The doctor was a forensic Anthropologist and specialized in looking at skeletal remains. She specialized in trauma to the skeleton and was given the project of analyzing Dale Harrell's skull. Pictures were placed on the screen of the remains of the right side of Dale's skull. There were thirteen pieces photographed with the first picture being what looked to be a random pile of skull pieces. Further pictures were presented as she reassembled the right side of the skull and put it together like a jigsaw puzzle.

The doctor was able to explain in layman's terms the points of convergence where she could place the impacts of the hammer and the damage done to the skull. She spoke of scalloping as to how these pieces fragment. She was able to explain that these pieces did not act like glass because the skull is generally held together by muscle and skin so reconstruction would not have been as difficult as one might expect with shattered glass.

She was able to see at least two areas of convergence and believed the injuries to be consistent with being impacted by a claw hammer that was found on the scene. She was even able to determine the part of the skull that was impacted first.

At one point, she was questioned about the term, 'maceration'. We learned that prior to the analysis; she had put the pieces of skull in an enzyme solution so that the enzymes would eat away the remaining bits of flesh and only left bone pieces remaining. Once the maceration process was complete, she was able to reconstruct the skull and determined that there were at least three blows, probably more, to the right side of the head and the weapon was consistent with being the hammer.

A juror submitted a question after her testimony and it was asked if there were any other impact areas on the skull. She responded that she was only given the right side of Dale's skull to complete analysis.

The next witness was equally as fascinating as the prosecution brought forward Steve McGibbon who had been delegated to do the blood spatter analysis of the crime scene. He was a forensic consultant who specialized in bloodstain analysis. This witness also had fifteen or more years in the field.

I remember the first day of trial when the picture of Dale Harrell was put up on the screen. He was lying on the floor with his head tucked up against the nightstand next to the bed. I remember the visual of lots of blood everywhere and it had looked meaningless and grotesque in its horror. I can comfortably say that I knew nothing about bloodstain analysis until Steve McGibbon took stand.

This was a fascinating window into this very specific study. The doctor explained that he focused on the shape, size and distribution of blood spatter and was able to make determinations based on the evidence found at the scene. He further elaborated that his goal in bloodstain analysis was to study the where, when and how of blood spatter and that determinations were based on viscosity, surface tension, temperature and pressure.

This is where I learned that blood is thicker than water and will sink in water. Blood has its own surface tension and reacts in verifiable ways when contact happens. The surface where blood hits is very important, as materials made from cloth will react much differently than those of walls. Blood behaves differently depending upon the surface it strikes.

Typically, blood spatter is broken into three categories: Drip, impact and mist. Misting is typically seen in gunshot wounds while drip refers to a bleeding or dripping wound, and impact spatter is how blood reacts when going through the air. Blood in flight has angle and direction and one can make scientific determinations from that by taking the width of a blood spatter mark and dividing it by its' length which then determines its direction of impact.

The doctor then explained the difference between impact, cast-off and transfer spatter. These droplets have different characteristics when they are left on an object such as a wall. An impact spatter mark begins showing after an object is hit twice. The first impact does not create spatter but the following impacts do create spatter, as blood vessels have been broken. Cast-off spatter is seen when blood clings to a swinging instrument while transfer spatter is that blood that has been transferred from one object to another.

I feel as if I can look at a blood droplet and tell its properties and what it means. It is passive if it is round and tells you the person was stationary when it fell. I can see that if it is elliptical, it is a form of medium velocity blood spatter. I can tell where it came from by the smaller end it exhibits, for instance, on a wall. It would be called directional blood spatter. The amount of knowledge we received in a short amount of time was interesting, educational and simply fascinating.

Doc positively glowed during testimony.

We then were shown a multiplicity of pictures of the scene, which showed the various types of spatter involved. One particular sequence was abundantly interesting. The doctor showed a picture of the wall and ceiling behind and over the bed. There were pencil drawn lines that were broken into four different categories noted as A, B, C and D. Within each of these groupings, one could see pencil drawn lines that seemed to run upwards from the pillow toward the ceiling and each grouping had significant different directions. Then, there were the numbers one through twelve within the existing groupings under each letter.

The jury was able to submit a question as to how those numbers were determined. It was explained that twelve drops were picked out of each grouping based on clear characteristics that other spots of blood did not show. At the base of these groupings, all the spatter centered on a point of convergence, the center point where the spatter had originated.

Furthermore, it detailed spots that were absent of blood called void patterns. These patterns are created by an object or item that shadows an area where blood would normally hit. For example, if one were to throw an orange at a wall and a bookshelf is nearby, the bookshelf will receive the orange juice spatter but the wall behind it will not because the bookshelf would be in the way. It would create a void pattern.

The morning was spent detailing direction and impact of blood by various pictures throughout the room. It was incredibly detailed and scientific in its approach and had me believing every word that was said.

It was concluded, based on the blood spatter evidence that, in all probability, Dale was lying down, facing away from his attacker, when the impact of the hammer occurred.

We learned that the shirt Stan Cook was wearing put him a significant distance away from the spatter but it did show spatter. The shirt that Marissa was wearing was in all likelihood within close contact of the spatter and was significantly different than that of the spatter on Stan Cook's shirt. Marissa's shirt showed directional cast-off blood at such an angle that it determined her to be holding the object that caused the impact spatter.

The forensic evidence was able to show that the bedroom door was partially open. It was able to determine that Dale had sheets and a blanket partially covering him when the impacts occurred. It further showed what was believed to be a bloodied handprint on the bed facing toward the edge of the bed.

The blood spatter evidence also told us that Stan was not wearing his shoes when the attack happened and that he had transfer blood on the bottom of his socks telling us that he had walked in wet blood.

The forensics overall concluded that: Marissa's shirt was the one being worn when impact spatter had hit; Stan was in the room when the impacts hit, Dale was lying down and partially covered when the impacts occurred.

Cast-off blood showed the swinging of an object and that object was more than likely a hammer. The shirt that Marissa was wearing at the time the blood spatter left the victim was denoted by the angle of spatter on her shirt and was consistent with a right-handed swing.

It was determined that the impact was made from the ball of the hammer and not likely to have been from the claw side.

It was a fascinating day of testimony. I still found it interesting how the original visual of blood and gruesomeness turned clinical and how quickly we got engaged in its secrets...

THE PINK ELEPHANT

"Nine-one-one, what's your emergency?" the male voice asked.

"Uh, uh, something's wrong..."

"What's your emergency, ma'am?" the operator repeats calmly.

"Something's happened! I don't know..."

Click. The phone disconnects.

"Nine-one-one, what's your emergency?" the same male voice questions.

"I need help! He was hurting me..." the female voice responds. It was jerky and hysterical sounding. The voice can be heard faintly and then disappears.

"We have help on the way, ma'am," the operator states.

"Can you tell me what happened? Who attacked you?"

"He was raping me. I was fighting. I grabbed a hammer and hit him and then I put it down and Stan hit him with a hammer. Oh, my God," she says and starts crying in a haltering way.

"Where is he now?" the operator asked. "Ma'am?"

All of us are listening intently in the jury box. We were listening to CD's of the 911 calls. The first call was made at 2:45 AM. This was a change of pace for us and gave us time to assimilate some of the evidence we had seen and tie it to a voice. It was certainly the voice of the defendant.

My mind was picturing Marissa on the phone and then trying to place her location. At this point, we knew the assault happened in the master bedroom at the south side of the house. There are three other bedrooms that are down the same hallway as the single story house. The bedroom closest to the master bedroom would belong to the oldest daughter, Rhiannon, who is thirteen years old.

The next room down the hallway would be for the other two daughters, Khiernan and Diahnon who were ten and eight respectively.

The final door is that of the roommate, Stan Cook. At this point, we know Stan was in the room with Marissa. Next, we were wondering where the girls were during all of this. Did they hear anything? Why isn't there noise in the background of the 911 calls? How long did it take to call 911 after the attack?

"Hello?" The operator asks again.

There is only a muted silence. One can't tell if someone is on the phone or not. There is no dial tone but the phone appears to be still connected. It struck me as weird.

"Hello?" the operator asks again.

There is no response.

A dial tone can be heard as the call is disconnected.

"Nine-one-one, what's your emergency?" the same male voice questions.

"I don't know what happened," a hysterical female voice answers. "He was attacking me. He was trying to strangle me. There was a hammer. Are they coming?"

"Yes, ma'am. Can you tell me what happened? Who attacked you?"

We listened intently and I wondered if she was faking it.

Heavy breathing can be heard on the other end. There are muffled sounds in the background.

Click. The phone goes dead again.

The prosecutor walked up to a CD player and changed the disc. The court was silent after the eeriness of the 911 phone calls. The new disc begins playing and it appears to have been recorded from the officer's microphone, probably the same type of microphone that I had seen officers wear when they took the witness stand.

The recording is remarkably clear. Marissa is either standing in front of or very near the officer.

"I'm sorry. I'm sorry. I'm sorry," she says distraughtly. "He had a hammer. I don't know what happened. He was choking me and he got hit with a hammer. I couldn't stop screaming. I couldn't stop! Where are my kids? How are my kids?"

This recording took place over the next two hours with her being near the officer who was recording it. I believe that it was Officer Cobbett, one of the first to arrive on the scene. This is a general idea of the events that took place after the murder and when the police and paramedics arrived.

Marissa is standing in front of the house when the first police car arrives. She has her cell phone in her hands and this was the same phone she used when calling 911.

When the first police car pulls up, Marissa takes her flip cell-phone and throws it on the driveway while the officer tries to calm her down. She is wearing a torn t-shirt and she is covered in blood. There is a line across her forehead that the officer thinks is a cut. She is barefoot and hysterically speaking in fragmented phrases.

Meanwhile, another officer sees a black man stepping out of the house and orders him to raise his hands. This man appears calm as raises his hands as ordered. The officer carefully approaches him and does a pat down for weapons. He then tells the officer there is a gun in his left pocket. The officer can feel the gun and carefully removes it from his pocket and steps back telling the man to keep his arms raised and not to move. The officer completes a felony prone search.

At the same time, another officer, whom I believe was Officer Ryan Churchman, enters the dwelling with his gun drawn. The house is dark except for a room down the hallway. The officer comes to a closed door and opens it. He sees two children sleeping. He slowly closes the door. He continues down the hallway and comes to another closed door which he carefully opens. He sees a thirteen-year-old girl and she questions him about what is going on. He tells the girl to stay in her room and he closes the door.

The officer continues down the hall toward a lighted room where the door is open. He comes through the door and sees a naked thirty-year-old man lying on the floor next to the bed. He sees blood sprayed everywhere with a significant amount of blood on the bed and notes a blood soaked pillow.

The victim is propped with his body on the floor while his head is vertical to the front of the nightstand drawers and he is bleeding profusely. The victim's position looks awkward with his face and body facing the bed and his face is cornered between the dresser and mattress. His first impression was this was a shotgun blast to the head and looked like an attempted suicide.

The officer runs to the man and kneels down and begins the search to identify where the blood is coming from. He sees a large depression in the man's head and his eye socket is swollen. He grabs a cloth and tries to cover the wound on the side of the man's head where the blood is coming from. He is trying to apply pressure but the wound is soft and fragmented. Blood runs freely. He does the best he can and radios for emergency services.

Another officer, Chris Dorenbush, comes into the room and sees his partner trying to apply aid to the victim. He immediately leaves and hurries out to his car. He goes into the trunk and pulls out a digital camera. He returns to the bedroom where the victim is and begins to snap what pictures he can before medical help arrives. He wants to capture the scene as fresh as he can before items begin to be disturbed in the transport process. He gets pictures of the victim and a picture of a bloodied hammer lying on a table next to the entrance to the room. It is a gut wrenching scene and the officer neglects to check the focus before he shoots the pictures.

The deep diesel rumble of fire rescue can be heard pulling up. There are sounds of equipment being pulled out and the clicking of a gurney being transported.

An officer can be heard asking questions of the female that he has led toward his car.

"Can you tell me your name?"

"Marissa," she says in between heaves of crying. "M-A-R-I-S-S-A", she spells.

"Who is the black man?" the officer asks.

"That's Stan," she answers. "He's a roommate. He's my savior. He saved my life."

"How did he do that?" the officer asks.

"I don't know. I was being choked and he saved me."

"Who was choking you?"

"My husband, Dale", she answers. She starts crying and getting hysterical again.

"There are children in the house," the officer says. "Are they yours?"

She nods and cries. "We have three kids."

The officer asks their names and she spells out their names. It takes some time because she is still crying.

"How is he?" she asks the officer.

"I don't know, ma'am," the officer responds. "It looks like he's been hurt pretty badly. We could hear him trying to speak so he is alive. Don't worry, we're getting him help. Let me put you in the car and I'm going to close the door. It's pretty cold out here."

One can hear the car door close. The sounds of Marissa become muted and unintelligible.

A short time later, the officer comes back and opens the door of the police car where Marissa is waiting. "Can you tell me what happened?" he asks.

"I don't know," Marissa says. "I woke up and he was choking me. I think I passed out. I remember a lot of blood and Stan was there. I don't know what happened..." she says as she starts crying again.

"Who was choking you?"

"My husband was choking me. I think he was raping me. My neck hurts."

"Let me see your neck," the officer says. "It looks like I see some redness there. Is that where he was choking you?" he asks.

"Yes," she answers.

"Your face looks red on one side. Was he hitting you?"

"No," she responds. "Stan did that because I told him to. I wanted him to wake me up so I told him to slap me."

That statement got my attention because it made no sense whatsoever.

"How long have you known Stan?" the officer asks.

She is still crying and making hiccupping sounds. She manages to speak brokenly. "He's like family. He's lived with us eight years or so. He has brain damage. It's weird. He has a bizarre memory problem. He was riding a motorcycle and got into a car accident. He went all the way through the front and back window of a pick-up truck. He's never been the same after that so we take care of each other. He's like family."

"Very good," the officer responds.

One can hear a new person enter the scene. It is a paramedic who is checking her vitals. "Where are you injured?" he asks.

She says her neck hurts and her legs hurt.

"This looks like a cut on your forehead. Did you get cut?" the paramedic asks.

"I don't think so," she says. "My neck hurts and it's hard to swallow. I don't know what happened. It was all at once. He was choking me and then I passed out. There was blood everywhere. I think I pushed him off me. Is he going to be okay?" she asks.

"Don't worry about him," the paramedic, Andrew Bowers, answers. "We are transporting him right now."

"I got this phone from your daughter," an officer says. "Do you want to call anyone?"

Marissa answers in the affirmative.

One can hear her as she fumbles with the phone. She is still breathing deeply.   "Mom? Mom?" She questions into the phone. "Can you come down right away? Something's happened and I need you to watch the kids."

She starts crying uncontrollably only saying a word or two into the phone. "Please, Mom, I know…"

I remember that the courtroom was silent as the CD played. I stole a glance toward the defendant and her head was down with her hair masking her face. This was the first time we had heard her voice and it was uncomfortable and even eerie. One could imagine her husband dying in the bedroom with his head damaged the way it was. I'm not sure why I would even look at the defendant. It was not as if she could provide any answers as to what had happened and I was sure we wouldn't see her testify.

But...there was still that innate curiosity.

The Judge adjourned court for the day, and bailiff escorted the jury from the courtroom, as everyone remained standing. We were following each other from the jury box and through the hallway that leads to the jury room. Suddenly, I heard someone whisper in my ear.

"I wish he would pop it."

I turned around to see that it was Jeebs. He and I walked to Crazy Jim's for lunch and ordered some pepperoni pizza slices to go. We ate lunch on a park bench in the courtyard across from the police museum. The pizza was wonderful with a river of clear grease floating on top of the double cheese.

I asked Jeebs where he got his name from and he said he used to be called J.B. and then someone decided that he looked like a porky little butler when he was a kid. The name had stuck with him and now he was used to it.

"Pop what?" I said under my breath as we followed each other down the single file hallway.

"What is that thing on the prosecutor's forehead? You think it's a spider bite?" he asked as we filed in the jury room.

I looked at him and smiled. I proceeded to get my things ready and Jeebs saw that I had a Crazy Jim's carry out menu.

"Can I have that?" he asked.

"Sure," I said as I handed it to him.

"I can't have my wife thinking I was eating double cheese pepperoni pizza. " He opened the paper menu and looked at. "I think I had the Goat Cheese Chicken Salad with spring mix. Sounds good, doesn't it?"

"Pizza was better," I responded with a smile.

Jeebs was fun.

The drive home had me wondering if the other jurors were thinking as I was. There were weird things about the recordings. For one thing, there were parts that didn't sound genuine. This is hard to pinpoint but there was a hollowness and eeriness to the recordings. Some things just didn't ring to be true. Maybe it was the creepiness of the situation that was clouding my judgment.

However, the other side of this was that you were trying to put yourself in the defendant's shoes. You did not know how you would react if you were in the same position. Maybe her reaction was typical in a scene like that. I would suspect all people act differently when enveloped in a crisis of that nature.

The one thing that no one tells you about in jury duty is that the wheel does not stop turning just because the court day ended. The thoughts of the trial just keep going around and around. I would remember remnants in my dreams.

The deeper we dove into this trial, the murkier the waters got.

If there was a gun in the room, why did she use a hammer to attack him? Wasn't he lying down and facing away from her?

I suspected that the list of questions was going to grow substantially.

The next day, we lost our first juror.

THE CONFESSIONS

It was the final day of our first full week as a jury. We were falling into the rhythm of the system.

I would usually wave to Phillip, the jury coach driver, and then choose to walk the seven or eight blocks to the courthouse. I think it was the thought of confinement in the courthouse making me want the last few breaths of freedom before hearing evidence.

I walked up the steps to the courthouse and saw that a few of the other jurors had gathered in the smoking area. We were becoming regulars. Doc greeted me with a smile.

"Hi, I'm Annie," a middle aged lady said with her hand outstretched. "We call you the Professor."

I laughed and shook her hand. "My intent was to look like Richard Gere in American Gigolo. I didn't expect to look like a professor but I'm complimented."

The other girl there introduced her name as Althea. She said her parents had been big Grateful Dead fans and that's where her name came from. I knew we would get along immediately with this in common. I had even followed The Dead for a short period twenty years prior. She said she was too young to have followed them but surely would have enjoyed it. I liked her tie-dyed peace earrings. She blushed when I told her.

She was named after the song, "Althea" and it made her charming.

We finished our cigarettes and disappeared into the bowels of security. I made my way to the elevators and caught Cherie.

"Good Morning," I said cheerfully.

"Good Morning to you," she returned with a pleasant smile. We followed each other into the elevator headed to the thirteenth floor. She set her briefcase down and began digging through it.

"I've got something for you." She dug for a minute and then pulled out an object.

She had to squat down as she was wearing a black business suit skirt. She had lilies on her black and white silk ruffled shirt. She always dressed tastefully and I'm sure many would have thought her another attorney walking the halls of the courthouse had they seen her at first glance.

I couldn't believe it. It was a clear plastic holder for our juror badge. It was the same case I had thought presumptuous back in the jury selection phase.

"It bothers me that you wear these expensive shirts and you put holes in them from the badges they give us. Now you can just clip it on your collar. "

"Thank you," I said. "That was extremely thoughtful."

Cherie was special.

We walked into the jury room after being buzzed in by Donna, who was the Judge's office manager.

One could always expect to see Butthead sitting at the front side of the table. He would have a two-liter plastic bottle of Diet Mountain Dew standing in watch of his open laptop with a gallon-sized drink cup. He would have a microphone in his ear and one could hear him doing codes for a large computer firm. It looked like he was another IT Specialist.

I had learned that Cherie was a manager of IT personnel.

Butthead had introduced himself to me as Butthead. That was immediately disturbing to me. How in the heck could I call someone "Butthead" with a straight face? The other thing that was curious about him was that he arrived at 8:00 AM when the jury room opened for us and would not leave until we were dismissed for the day. I couldn't understand how someone could have that much information overload in such a confined space without going stir crazy. While we always left for lunch together, he would stay in the jury room throughout.

He always sat behind me in the jury box. I knew he was there by the sound of his drinking when he drank from his gallon beverage. Some people are just loud.

We got settled in the jury room and watched as Wings came in just after 10:00 and set up the coffee pot. The jurors would stream in afterwards and people greeted each other friendly tones. The funny thing is that we were starting to feel guilty that we didn't know each other's names.

The easiest way for a juror to draw unwanted attention was to arrive any time after 10:15. We could always expect a visit from Sydney, our bailiff, who performed a quick headcount. Parker inevitably arrived at 10:16. This usually got a small eyebrow raise from Sydney.

In every jury, there is always one juror that tries the patience of the bailiff. Our jury was no different and the one juror that drove Sydney to the point of drinking, speaking figuratively, was Ted. Ted was the youngest of all the jurors, and he was between twenty-three and twenty-five years of age. He would walk into the juror room at 10:29 AM with court being scheduled at 10:30 AM. The jurors didn't sweat it but one could see Sydney get a little more frantic as the minutes passed.

We were waiting for Ted when Sydney peeked in, asking if we had any questions for the Judge. We were not allowed to communicate to the Judge unless we used an official jury question form. It was expected that we avoid submitting dumb questions. Although it was never said, common sense dictated that you did not want to annoy the court. In other words, think about the question before you ask it and exercise that right judiciously.

Surprisingly, two people submitted a communication to the Judge. The first was Althea, my fellow smoker and the second was James, whom I knew nothing about.

James kept to himself and usually didn't engage in anyone's conversation. It did not mean he was suspicious, but rather he was probably more shy than most of us in the room. We had a good group of people who got along. He usually sat next to the small refrigerator by himself and watched everyone. Sometimes he could be seen looking at his phone but he was really quiet overall.

Ted came in at 10:27 AM and some jurors commented that he was early. He had black hair and wore sunglasses and a zippered gray hoodie when he came in. It was February so it was still cool in the mornings. We thought he looked like the Unabomber. He was quite the opposite. He was a dancer at a local casino, and said "Disney owned his ass". He also waited tables at a national chain restaurant.

He could usually be seen taking off his hoodie and sunglasses and throwing them on the back of his chair. He would have an open oxford shirt worn over a t-shirt. This t-shirt featured Pink Floyd and his oxford shirt looked like it had sat in the dryer overnight after being washed. At least, it was clean, I suppose.

Somehow, we made it into the jury box complete as sixteen and on time. I could only imagine Sydney's relief.

Judge Steinle III ran a quick paced courtroom. He did not bother with the courtroom greetings and he didn't let the attorneys get off track. This morning was no different except that he opened with a statement before we were to hear from the attorneys.

"I received a jury question. Juror Number Six?"

James stood up who was seated a few seats down from me.

"The court has received your note and the court dismisses Juror Number Six. This is why we have alternates," he said moving some papers in front of him.

James sat down and the Judge looked up over the rims of his glasses. "You are dismissed," he said.

"Do you want me to leave now?"

"Yes. The court appreciates your service and Sydney will lead you out."

James walked in front of me and exited the jury box toward the jury room. The court was silent and we never saw him again and never knew what was in that note. It reminded us that we were dispensable and that there were still three random alternates who would never make it to the deliberation room.

Eric Basta introduced a lengthy interrogation tape as evidence to the court and it was accepted by the defense. This interrogation was done in a room at the Gilbert Police Department, and was conducted in the afternoon hours following the hammer assault on Dale Harrell. I believe it began at three in the afternoon. This must have been done after her hospital examination that we had already heard testimony about.

We learned that we would see this tape-recorded interrogation that had been transferred onto a CD, and that it may take a couple of days to present.

We would finally get to see Marissa DeVault the day of the assault. I was looking forward to this segment of evidence.

DAY 10: PART II

TENUOUS AT BEST

There is a video camera located in an interrogation room. The room is plain with white walls. There is a table with two chairs. One chair faces the direction of the camera lens while another chair is at a forty-five degree angle to the camera. On the table there is a white plastic bag with items in it. There is also a legal pad of paper as well as a pen lying on the table. One can see the back of a female detective's head, and her hair coloring is brown and black.

The other chair has Marissa DeVault in it. She is wearing a light blue sweatpants outfit with a zippered hoodie top hanging off her back. She is not wearing a bra and her hair is tied back. It is curly on the ends.

"Let's go back to last night," the interrogator says. "I know we've covered this but I want to make sure I'm clear on everything." Both the pen and notepad lie on the table in front of them; but neither is being used.

"He didn't start choking me right away. We had a session, I think."

"What do you mean, "A session?""

"I should say sex but I was asleep."

"So, you had intercourse?"

"We must have," she says furrowing her eyebrows. "I was wet down there. I had to wipe myself in the bathroom. I don't remember. I was asleep and his hands were around my neck."

"Wait a moment," Detective Brenda Tomory says. Her back is to the camera and one can see this large annoying curl going down the back of her head. Sometimes, she blocks the camera forcing us to listen to the audio without benefit of seeing Marissa's facial reactions. "I need to see who is in the house. Who is in the house when this is happening?"

Marissa thinks a moment and then says, "Stan was in his room. I remember his light was on. The kids were asleep."

"Where are the kids? Are they in the same room?"

"My oldest is in the room closest to the master bedroom. She has her own room."

"Is this Rhiannon?"

"Yes, the thirteen year-old. Diahnon and Khiernan are in the bedroom next to hers. They're all sleeping."

"These are your biological daughters?"

"Yes," Marissa says. Then, she thinks about it. "Well, I had Rhiannon when I was seventeen. Her father left me. I had Khiernan and Diahnon with Dale. I had a twin son with Rhiannon but he was stillborn."

"I'm so sorry," Detective Tomory responds. "So, you don't know where the father is?"

"I have no idea. I'm used to it. My father died when I was young."

"It must have been hard."

"It's okay," she says offhandedly. "Maybe it was for the best."

"I have a clearer picture now. So, he is choking you and you are asleep?"

"Yes."

"Is that common? Has he done that before? Is that normally how you had sex?"

"When we fight, he forces me to have sex whether I want it or not."

"Are you saying that you don't have a say in the matter?"

Marissa looks down at her fingernails. She looks up and appears to be close to crying. "I do what the wife is expected to do. I don't have a choice."

"Does he normally put his hands around your neck?

"He does it a lot. He likes to do it, well, when I'm no fun," Marissa says. She partially covers her mouth. She then takes her legs and tucks them under her on the chair.

"Do you have sex often?"

"We have sex every day."

"It sounds like he was rough."

Marissa laughs. "Well, he's rough when I don't want to have sex."

"How often is that?"

"I'd say about four times a week I don't want to have sex but he has it anyway."

"Are you saying he rapes you?"

"Sometimes," Marissa answers. "He likes to put his hands around my neck. I think it excites him."

"So, getting back to last night, you said he had his hands around your neck. How did he have his hands around your neck?"

Marissa gets out of her chair and walks over to the interrogator with her hands raises and demonstrates how he put his hands around her neck. "Like this," she says. "He pushes me downward."

"I see."

Marissa returns to her seat and tucks her legs under her. "I don't know if he had sex with me because I passed out. I remember waking up and he was on top of me. He said something like, 'This pussy is mine' and something else. I think I passed out and when I woke I could feel drops falling on me and I wanted him off of me and I pushed him. I couldn't breathe, I couldn't swallow."

"Were there any lights on?"

"I don't remember. I think the bathroom light was on and I think the TV was on. I remember screaming really loudly. I was shaking. I jumped up and called 911. I can't remember what I said. I think I said my husband was dead. I threw down the phone and ran back in the room."

Marissa laughs nervously and then continues. "Stan was there. He had a hammer in his hands."

"Where did the hammer come from?" the interrogator asks.

"I don't know. I don't know. Oh wait," Marissa says pausing. "I was in the bedroom earlier and had to hang a picture. I couldn't get Dale to do it. He never has time to do the things I want him to do. I finally got fed up and hung the picture myself. I think I must have left the hammer on the table or whatever it is by the door. Dale would get pissed if he knew I didn't put his tools away. He doesn't like when I use his tools."

"So, then what?" Detective Tomory asks.

"I was looking at Stan with the hammer in his hands. I was shaking. I couldn't stop shaking and then Stan asked if I was okay?"

"What did you say?"

"I was confused. I kept looking at Stan. He asked me if I was okay. He said Dale was hurting me. I think I called 911 again and I couldn't get the words out."

"Then what happened?"

"I told Stan to slap me. It was like I couldn't wake up. I wanted him to slap me to wake me up."

"Were you mad at Stan?"

"Oh, no, it was nothing like that. Dale was on the floor and he had just attacked me. I should have been used to it but I guess since I had lost consciousness, it made me confused."

"That's understandable," the detective said. "What happened next?"

"It's frustrating because nothing makes sense. Everything was in pieces. The next thing I remember is there was a cop at the door. I was still shaking and I wasn't even making sense to myself. Stan did the right thing, I know he did."

"Did your husband threaten you in any way earlier? Maybe he threatened you with the hammer?"

"Well, I'll be honest. We fought a lot. We fought every other day and I shouldn't have been surprised with how it happened," Marissa said looking toward the floor.

"Was he abusive to the children?

"Oh no, he was only abusive to me."

"Did Stan ever see that?"

"I think Stan saw it a lot and that's why he tried to protect me. He knew I was trying to get a divorce."

"When did you file for divorce?"

"I didn't actually file for divorce." She laughs a little and then continues. "I saw a lawyer about a month ago. I just had the papers drawn up."

"Stan had a gun in his pocket. Why didn't he use that?"

Marissa shakes her head and looks toward the ceiling and then toward the floor and then looks again at the interrogator. She clicks her manicured nails on the table. "I don't know. Maybe the hammer was at the door and he heard me screaming and panicked. Maybe it was the first thing he saw."

"Was that Stan's gun?"

"Uh, no. My boss gave it to me for protection. He knew I was having problems."

"If that was your gun, why did Stan have it?"

"I don't like guns. I really don't like guns. We have kids in the house and I'm scared of guns."

"Why did you take the gun from your boss if you don't like guns?" the interrogator asked.

"He was very insistent and I didn't want to hurt his feelings. I guessed that it would best if Stan held on to it just in case. He already had other guns and I knew he understood how to use it. Guns really scare me..." she said as her voice drifted off.

"Getting back to Dale," the interrogator continued, "was he always abusive toward you?"

"No. Before we were married he was my Dale. We got along great. We lived in Lake Havasu and things were good between us. We got married in '99 and things changed almost right away. It was as if he owned me. He got very abusive," Marissa said.

"Can you give me any examples? Did anyone know about it?"

"I think a lot of people knew about it. Maybe they didn't know he was raping me because I figured that was part of my duty as a wife. Aside from that, though, things happened all the time. One time he threw me on the bed and broke my collarbone. There was another time that he hit me and scratched my eye. I went to the hospital. He was always very sorry," Marissa said with a sarcastic laugh.

"How did he hit you? Did he normally slap you?"

"With a fist," Marissa said.

"So, he used a fist. He didn't slap you?" the interrogator asked.

"He liked to use his fist. I think it made him excited."

"Did you ever call the police on these incidents?"

"No, I didn't. We both got marriage counselors. I don't like counselors and he didn't either. He had anger management issues over bills, stress and his job. I think I got a pamphlet on domestic abuse but never really did anything with it. Wait a minute," Marissa said. "I think I did call the cops a couple years ago when we lived in Glendale. He threw me into the wall and put a hole in it. I don't think the police did anything because by the time they got there, Dale had calmed down. We covered the wall so the police couldn't see it."

"What do you think started these fights? Were you sleeping with Stan?"

Marissa starts laughing and then leans over to the interrogator as if she was telling a secret.

"I wasn't sleeping with Stan," she said and leans closer as if she's telling a great secret. "I think he's gay. We could be driving down the street and I would point out this hot girl walking by and he would be like no big deal. One time I was in his room and saw he had cartoons. But, they weren't like Bugs Bunny. They were weird. Anime, I think they call it. It's like cartoons having sex with each other. It's really weird but I was like, whatever."

"So, you never had sex."

Marissa laughs again. "He's not my type. I really like him as a friend and I think I felt protected from Dale when Stan was around. He knew what was going on, though. I had confided in him many times and Stan had said he would never let Dale hurt me. He was really sweet."

"Have you ever seen Stan get mad or show violent tendencies?"

"Stan wasn't violent. He was just sweet, although he had seen Dale slap me, little bitch slaps, you could say. He saw me get hit in the eye with a coffee mug and Stan told Dale to knock it off. I thought they were going to have a confrontation but it never happened. I knew that Stan was concerned but I didn't want to involve him."

"...so he never protected you physically?"

"I think he wanted to. On Christmas Eve last year, Dale got pissed at me for something stupid and threw me on the driveway and began kicking me. I could tell Stan wanted to do something but he was laid off. I went to the emergency room."

"How was New Year's Eve? Were there any incidents?"

"No, not really," Marissa said, stopping to contemplate for a moment. "I had a lot going on by then. I was trying to get in the police academy so I was pretty busy with that. I was running, working out and had taken my written and physical tests."

"Really," the interrogator said obviously intrigued.

"I think that pissed Dale off. It was like I was showing my independence and he didn't like that one bit. I was bold and said it was for me. It gave me the courage to ask him for a divorce."

"When did you ask him that?"

"Last weekend I told him that I loved him but the "us" part wasn't working out anymore."

"How did he react to that news?"

"I thought he would be really pissed but I think he saw that we weren't very happy. He didn't get confrontational and I don't like confrontations. I think he said that we should go back to counseling," Marissa said pensively.

"Did you think that's why he attacked you?"

Marissa looked at the floor, brushed some dust off her sweatshirt and started picked at her manicured nails. "I couldn't tell you," she said. "It just happened so fast."

"Tell me what you did that evening before the incident. Did you fight at all?"

"We always had little fights but he was nice that night. It was nice being with the Dale I had fallen in love with ten years ago. We had put the kids to bed. We went out and got some hot chocolate for Rhiannon that night, because she got in trouble at school for someone putting a dirty picture in her notebook. She was very upset and we wanted to calm her down so we went down the street. When we came back, we made love and it was really nice."

"Okay?" the officer prodded, "Then, what?"

"I couldn't sleep so I went to the garage to smoke a cigarette. Stan must have heard something and then he came out and we chatted awhile. I remember Dale coming out in his red plaid shorts. I hated those shorts. They were really ugly," she says laughing.

"...and then what?"

"We all went back in and I was still restless. Dale had lain down and gone to sleep but I still couldn't sleep. Something was bothering me and I don't know what it was. I smoked lots and lots of cigarettes. Eventually I went back in the house and went to bed." Marissa picks at her fingernails and inspects them.

"The next thing I remember is that he was choking me and trying to have sex with me," Marissa explains.

"Something had to have set him off. Did he think you and Stan were doing something? Was he mad that you kept going outside? Maybe you were waking him up."

Marissa appears to think. "No, no, there wasn't really anything. Well, I did tell him about Allen when we were in the garage."

"What did you tell him?"

"I just said that we were friends and I had a right to have friends. He didn't like most of my friends," Marissa responded.

The female interrogator looked Marissa in the eyes. "It doesn't make sense to me, Marissa. You say he gets mad at you all the time in your marriage, but he doesn't get mad at you that night? What triggered him? There's something that had to have set him off at that moment."

"I'm being honest, I don't know," Marissa says sincerely. "That's the way our marriage was. He would get violent over the simplest things and he would just blow up..."

There was a tap at the door to the interrogation room. It is outside the view of the camera but one can see that another person has joined the interview. He sounds soft-spoken and empathetic toward Marissa.

Marissa removes her legs from under her and puts her feet on the floor giving the investigator her attention. She acts as if she recognizes the officer.

"Haven't we met at the academy?" she asks him.

The detective is Sy Ray, the same one that made some of the girls act giggly. He extends his hand to Marissa and nods at her as if he might recognize her.

Marissa suddenly seems comfortable and looks at the officer with interest, as if she is very concerned.

The officer begins speaking. "Look, Marissa, I'm here because we understand your situation. It sounds like you've suffered a lot of physical and emotional abuse in your marriage and we can really understand that."

Marissa nods her head in agreement.

"I've been at the scene all day and have spoken with a lot of investigators at the scene. First, I want to let you know that Dale is in the hospital being worked on and your kids are with your mom in a hotel. I wanted to let you know that they're safe," he says.

Marissa says softly, "Thank you".

"But I've got to let you know that you have an opportunity to tell us what's going on. This is why we have an officer with you," he says in reference to Detective Tomory. I understand abuse and what you have been through but there are things at the scene that just can't be accounted for according to what you have told us thus far."

Marissa queries, "What do you mean? I mean I've been telling you what I remember but there are parts I can't remember what happened. It's in little pieces."

"I understand that. But, you need to understand that for us to get to the bottom of this and find some answers, you have to be truthful with us. This is your opportunity to come clean on everything and I promise things will go better in the long run..."

Marissa looks toward the floor and the officer gets up outside of the view of the camera. One can hear the door click shut as he leaves.

Marissa is silent.

The prosecutor shuts off the CD.

The court is silent.

The judge resumes court business. "Before we close for the day, I need to mention that we have received a question from one of the jurors. I will paraphrase it to say that this juror has been notified from their place of employment that due to the hours of the trial that their status has been changed from full-time to part-time and due to that, this juror has lost their benefits," he said.

"I would like to make something clear. This court will not tolerate jurors being penalized for their service. I will be personally dealing with this employer and will do so to protect all jurors. We need to understand that employers cannot walk on the wrong side of the law. If there are any others jurors who feel they have been penalized for being a juror in this court, I need to know about it. Please submit a message through the bailiff. We will sit down with the attorneys of both sides and we will get this cleared up."

The Judge recessed court for the day.

I realized that it must have been Althea's question from the morning and thought her treatment was unfair. I respected the Judge for standing up to her issue.

I had a funny feeling and decided to call my work where I was employed as a bartender.

Sherry answered the phone at my work. I had known Sherry for five years and she virtually ran the front desk taking carry out orders as well as seating Guests. Although she was near sixty, one could never tell as she had the energy of a twenty-year-old. I could picture her on the other end of the line with her long blonde hair tied back in her signature bun.

"Can you tell me my schedule this weekend?" I asked her.

"You're not on the schedule, honey," she said. She called everyone 'honey'. "You were fired, weren't you?"

"Fired? I wasn't fired," I said.

"Honey, your name isn't on the schedule."

"Can I speak to the General Manager?" I asked.

"He's on vacation, Sweetie. He's back in a week."

I thanked her and hung up the phone. I was incredulous and stunned. It did not take a rocket scientist to figure out that this was illegal.

I decided to write a note to the Judge at our next court appearance.

It was time he knew of my termination...

DAY 11

BRAIN TRAUMA

"Doctor, can you explain to the court your diagnosis and subsequent treatment of your patient, Dale Harrell?" Mr. Basta asked.

I liked his style. Some of the jurors thought he looked like Jim Carrey, and I thought there might have been a loose fit in resemblance. He had a very good energy and never showed anger toward the defendant. I wonder if he approached it that way to allow the evidence to speak for itself. He never threw a snide comment toward the defense. I thought that was peculiar but good. He was not theatrical although he did have a sense of humor. He made witnesses feel comfortable and I felt that he kept a good pace.

The one thing I liked about his questioning was that he used an outline that he relied upon at the podium. He would look at his notes, step forward and question the witness and then he would step back to the podium and check an item off of his outline. It was a brilliant move in making points succinct without being theatrical.

Mr. Basta stepped forward and allowed the witness to answer the question.

Dr. Joseph Zambransky, a board-certified specialist in Neurosurgery, spoke slowly and carefully. He spoke clinically and without emotion or empathy. He reminded me a bit of my father in the way he carried himself. He spoke in a way similar to the way a jury might think, as they must be devoid of sympathy or empathy.

He was detailed and self-assured. He felt trustworthy, and if I were in the same position as Dale, this is how I would want my doctor to be.

"I was called on this case a short time after Dale Harrell was brought to the emergency room. I arrived within fifteen minutes in response to a severe brain trauma case. I looked at the pictures of Mr. Harrell and knew that he needed emergency surgery. We performed CAT scans and determined there was severe facial and brain trauma. I got in touch with Doctors on staff and we were able to communicate through his images sent over the Internet. It was really quite amazing and probably saved his life," he said somewhat proudly.

I looked to my left in the courtroom and on the screen was a picture of Dale Harrell lying in a hospital bed. It is the most gruesome picture of anything I have ever seen. I had to look at the picture in small pieces and glimpses while taking notes. I was afraid that I would get queasy. I busied myself taking notes only looking at the picture when the doctor pointed something out.

The picture of Dale showed him lying on his back in a hospital bed. One could see the blue arm railing at his side. One could almost hear the hum of the machines around him as they worked and monitored him to keep him alive.

Tubes ran from his leg and over his body. An IV hung from one side while a large tube and wiring protruded from Dale's mouth. His head had been shaved recently but his dark hair was starting to grow back.

The damage that she had caused with the hammer had clearly destroyed the side of his eye. His right eye was purple, swollen and disfigured. A large area of swollen brain could be seen behind his ear. The ear was pulled from its base. An elongated "C" plastic piece ran along the side of the wound and half-inch black staples could be seen.

Dale had lived in that state for twenty-seven days due to the defendant's assault. Once seen, I knew it was an image scarred on my brain for the rest of my days.

The doctor began pointing to Dale's image on the wall.

"The patient had an avulsed ear, meaning it was not fully attached to his skull, and he had a facial maxillary fracture, the top part of the jaw was broken, right here," he said pointing to the picture on the wall. The skull had a depressed fracture behind the eye, which would have indicated at least one blow to the right side of the skull. Further, the patient had multiple hematomas, also known as blood clots, underneath the surface of the skull," he said in reference to the picture.

"We were extremely concerned about the multiple skull fragments as these edges are sharp and can cause further damage when moved. Finally, he had a contusion on the brain in this area here. The swelling of this part of the brain greatly concerned us and surgery needed to be done as soon as possible."

"Thank you," the prosecutor said. "Can you tell us what the surgery was and give us an overall picture of what you did?"

"The first thing we had to do was to stop the swelling. The brain can asphyxiate itself if this isn't controlled quickly. In that, we made a question mark type cut into the skull bone," he said pointing to the posted picture, "right through here. We removed the large pieces of skull and made attempts to stop the bleeding by sealing the vessels that the bleeding originates from. After this we removed a significantly large piece of bone because the edges would have caused more damage and we needed the brain to swell without this piece in there. Unfortunately, the patient expired before a new piece could be put in."

"Let me ask you," the prosecutor queried, "Do you think this patient would ever have fully recovered?"

The doctor thought for a moment and appeared to brush a piece of lint from his pants. "No, counselor, I do not. That isn't to say that he wasn't improving however. We were doing tests on him when he was conscious and he was able to move parts of the right side of his body such as his leg, fingers and so on. The right side of the brain controls the left side and vice versa. I don't know why that it is, it is just how we are built. We did not have movement on the left side of his body and I don't know that we ever would have. I believe he would have needed assistance the rest of his life."

I stole a quick glance toward the defendant, Marissa, while the testimony of the doctor continued. She had her head in her hands and one could see she was visibly shaking. It appeared she was crying but one couldn't quite tell as her long hair covered her face. I looked away just as quickly not wanting to speculate any further.

"You said he was improving," the prosecutor pointed out, "but then he passed away? Why is that?"

"Certainly the injury he suffered was the manner of death but the cause of death was a pulmonary embolism. This was the thing we were most worried about so we had filters put in his system to capture blood clots before they got to the heart, which is generally fatal. He also had a filter in his femoral artery over his abdomen," he said pointing to the right side of his stomach.

He pointed toward Dale's thigh. "This is where the clot ultimately came from. It took twenty minutes to resuscitate him but the damage had been done and his brain was asphyxiated. This is usually a natural result of the trauma he received."

"One more question," Mr. Basta asked, "were you able to see any bite marks or scratch marks on Dale Harrell's body, either before, during or after surgery?"

"This was not something I would normally look for," the doctor answered, "I did look at the surface of his body as we were going through surgery and the only trauma I saw was the damage to the right side of his skull. I think I saw a scrape mark on his calf but that could have happened during any of his periods of transport."

"Thank you," the prosecutor responded. He sat down.

"Does the defense have any questions of this witness?" the judge asked.

"No, Judge," Mr. Tavasoli answered as he sat back down.

"Very well, then," the Judge said and recessed the court for lunch.

Sydney, the bailiff, led us back to the jury room. I knew everyone wanted to say something or comment about the picture of Dale that we had just seen but all chose to busy ourselves getting ready for lunch. I think I speak for all when I say we just wanted to get out of the building to see some normalcy of regular life. The hustle and bustle of downtown and the process of getting lunch would erase those images like medicine to a sick man. Most of us went to Crazy Jim's led by Cherie. She was a good tour director knowing all the best places to eat downtown.

"They have the best salads ever," she said.

I joined the group and talked with Jeebs, who was always dressed sharply but conservatively. He was a genuinely nice guy who carpooled with a few of the other jurors every day. His drive was about ninety miles round trip and that didn't seem to bother him. I liked his warm sense of humor.

We were waiting to order when he asked me. "I heard you don't drink. How can you be a bartender?"

I laughed. "That's like asking a person who is on Weight Watchers why they work in a restaurant? Whether I drink or not, I sell the stuff. It doesn't mean I have to partake in the inventory."

We returned to the courtroom refreshed and the first thing we saw was the continuation of Marissa's video interrogation. She was still in the interrogation room with the female investigator, Detective Brenda Tomory, and I remembered that the officer, Sy Ray, the juror's dreamboat, had just left the interrogation room.

Marissa was sitting in her chair and looking down. She was quiet for about two minutes while Detective Tomory looked at her. Suddenly, one got the feeling that she was about to confess. The other feeling you got was that she was about to change her story. One could feel the tension of silence.

"Marissa," the investigator prompted, "we know that you've suffered eight or nine years of abuse. But like the other investigator said, things don't match what you're telling us."

Marissa kept looking down and did not answer the investigator. Suddenly, she reached over the table and pulled the legal notepad to herself and began writing. It looked like she was crying. She finishes writing and slides the notepad back toward the officer.

Officer Tomory read it aloud. "Husbands can't rape their wives."

"I lied, I lied," she said breaking down.

Marissa leans forward and then leans back in her chair and puts her hands in her face. She was crying. "I know what happened and I don't know. I woke up and Dale was on top of me, he was inside me. I bit and scratched at him. Stan wasn't in the room then, I'm sure of it. Somehow I pushed him off me and I don't know how I got the hammer. I had it in both my hands and I hit him. I don't remember the hammer going in," she said pausing to catch her breath.

"I said you don't own me and I hit him again. Then, Stan was in the room. He grabbed me and stopped me. He grabbed the hammer..."she said with her voice trailing off. "I didn't mean to do it," she cried. She slumped over in her chair with her head in her hands.

The investigator leaned over and started rubbing her back in small circles. One could hear the roughness of her hands over the faux velour of her sweatshirt. She continued to rub her back, and Marissa cried.

"How did your shirt get ripped?" the investigator asked after a couple minutes.

Marissa appeared to get it under control. She took a deep breath. "I think Dale ripped it when he was grabbing at me. Look I don't want to go to jail. My kids will grow up with no mother..."

The investigator rubbed her back one more time and stepped out of the room leaving Marissa alone. Marissa paces around the room, then walks to a corner on the left side of the screen. She slides down the wall in the corner and cries as she tucks her body into a ball.

A short time later, the investigator comes in and tells her that she'll be arrested for attempted homicide and that she'll be going to the Fourth Avenue Jail. She lets her know that she will be seeing a judge and he'll probably set bail.

Marissa looks defeated and deflated. "Can we have one more cigarette before I get arrested?" Marissa asks.

The female investigator thinks about it decides it is okay and the two of them leave the room.

The video continues recording the empty room, and then Marissa steps back into the room alone. She takes her pack of cigarettes, the box looks like imported cigarettes, and puts them in the plastic bag on the table. She feels around in the bag and finds her cell phone. We watch as she makes a call.

She speaks softly. "Yes, Mom", she says looking toward the floor. "I'm being arrested. They say that the forensics results are making them arrest me. I guess I moved to the wrong side of the room or something." She slowly disconnects the phone.

She begins pacing and looking at her phone. She scrolls until she finds a number and presses a key, which meant the number was on speed dial. It is someone familiar to her.

"Listen, you and I need to talk in private."

She pauses and listens to the person on the other end. "We have to have," she says, thinking, "We have to have boundaries. I'm being arrested for attempted homicide, something about forensics that doesn't fit. I'll need help with bail. I'll know in the morning. Tell Stan I'm sorry," she says. "I love you."

The video ends before Marissa is handcuffed and processed but we knew it happened.

My biggest problem was the lie. What else did she lie about?

The judge recessed court for the day. We filed back to the jury room and Sydney tapped me on the shoulder.

"Was that you who submitted the note about being terminated?"

"Yes, that was me," I answered.

"Okay, wait here a minute and the Judge will call you soon," she said.

The rest of the jury left for the day and I waited in the jury room by myself. It was really nerve racking. I don't know why I was nervous but I was. I knew I hadn't done anything wrong and the last thing I wanted was the spotlight pointed on me. At the same time, I knew there had to be resolution for a couple of reasons. The first reason was obvious, as money was crucial for paying bills.

The second reason was that if I had been terminated, I wouldn't be able to meet the requirements for collecting unemployment during the duration of the trial. The state requires, generally, that you are to be actively looking for work five days a week. The trial would have inhibited that requirement.

It seemed like forever but was only twenty minutes before Sydney came in the jury room and led me to the Judge's chambers. I was flanked on either side by the defense attorney, Andrew

Clemency, on one side and by Mr. Basta, the prosecutor, on the other side. I was directed to a chair in the middle of the room and each attorney was about ten feet from me seated on either side.

I noticed the court reporter came in with her equipment and began typing the moment the Judge began speaking to me.

I must say that the Judge's chambers were extremely nice compared to the sterile environment of the courtroom. Wood paneling lined the walls. Light was furnished by the incandescence of warm lamps. The Judge appeared to be seated above me in front of me but maybe I thought that because I was used to that seat in the courtroom.

"I need you to tell me in a short, concise manner what the issue is with your work and what I can do about it," he said looking me in the eye.

I quickly gave him a rundown of what had happened including my being removed the work schedule. I mentioned some of the torment I had been put through and finished with, "I feel like I'm being punished by my employer for my commitment to this trial." I know my voice showed nervousness and it may have cracked like that of a teenage boy going through puberty. I couldn't believe how nervous I was.

The stenographer stopped typing while we waited for the Judge's response. He thought for a moment and began writing something down.

"I need you to go to your work and have your employer put into writing that you've been terminated. I'll need that by Monday. What they are doing is against the law. On the way, please give my assistant the name and contact information for your general manager. I will be writing them a letter. Is there anything else?" he asked.

"No, Sir," I responded. I took that as my cue to exit. I felt like I stood up and backed out of the room.

I never wanted to be in that seat again. It crossed my mind that the last time that I had been in a Judge's chambers was in 1976. The result of that did not go well.

However, in this instance, it felt completely different. I think it was because I felt that the court had my back as opposed to what had happened almost forty years ago. It was as if things had come full circle only this time I was on the right side of the deal.

I gave the Judge's assistant the information he had asked for and left the courthouse as soon as possible. I hoped I had done the right thing.

The next night I went into work for what normally would have been my shift, had I not been removed from the schedule and I was prepared. I knew I had to follow the judge's orders and prove I was terminated. Given that, I needed to do three things.

The first thing I had to have readied was the camera on my phone. I knew that when I swiped my magnetic strip card that the computer screen would say one of two things. (1) I had been terminated and no longer worked for the company. (2) The screen would read that I was not on the system. I understood this process after having been a manager, and knowing what happens with terminated employees.

The next thing I had to do was take a picture of the posted schedule in the employee break room to further prove I was not scheduled.

Finally, I had to get a signature from them saying I was terminated. I knew that if I had been terminated, there would be no willingness to help me out by verifying this in a letter. So, I prepared a couple of simple statements on a pre-prepared letter from me and directed it to, "to whom it may concern". I left a spot on the bottom for a manager to date and sign, acknowledging that I arrived for work on time and that I no longer worked for the company.

I went into work very prepared with my phone in hand set to camera mode. I attempted to clock in and the screen read, "You are not on the schedule." I then went to the employee break room and took a picture of the posted schedule showing that I was not on it. I put the phone in my pocket and went looking for a manager. It was just my luck that it was Roberto, the manager that had treated me like garbage the week before. In my hands, behind me, I had the paper that I needed him to sign.

"Hi, Roberto," I said in a friendly tone, "Where am I working tonight?"

He absolutely surprised me. The man who had thrown me under the bus the week before was suddenly the nicest guy in the world. "Oh, Papi! Good to see you. I can use you behind the bar. We're going to be very busy. I'm really glad you're here!" he said.

I followed him to a computer and he clocked me in and I went to work, crunching the pre-written note into my back pocket.

That night, I was treated like the best employee they ever hired. Roberto even bought me dinner for helping out. There was no vindictiveness, vengeance or even the slightest hint that there was any discontent. Of course, the rest of my co-workers seemed surprised with most commenting they thought I had been fired. I assured them I had not been and worked a solid shift.

I think they got a phone call from the Judge and I would have loved being a fly on that wall...

DAY 12

SEEKING ARRANGEMENTS.COM

The jury was led to the jury box while the court was standing. Seated in the witness chair was Allen Flores. We had heard this name many times in other testimony, but this was our first time seeing him. His name did not reflect what I expected him to look like. I expected a tall, self-confident businessman who would be sharply dressed and maybe somewhat older.

Allen Flores was not a tall man by any sense. He wore what looked like a black polyester suit that didn't fit him quite right. I expected an Armani suit and saw a Walmart suit instead. He looked like a cross between Mr. Magoo with his baldhead and Scrooge with his stringy hair below the crown of his head.

The best that I can characterize how he spoke was closest to the character on Office Space, the guy with the stapler and the office in the basement. He spoke half through his nose, and struck me as a meek man.

I didn't like him right off the bat. I knew he had immunity and he was critical to the prosecution's case. He seemed like a snitch. He felt like what a jailhouse snitch might look like. I bet he had a clammy handshake.

I watched as he sat in the witness chair and looked ahead of time at the seat as if there were a 'whoopee cushion' in it. He sat in the witness armchair and then leaned forward. He nervously moved the microphone toward him.

From my seat, I could see his profile and saw his rubber-soled shoes making me think he liked comfort over style. His butt was pushed back at the seat. His fingers were touching end to end over his knees. That seemed weird. He didn't seem to be shaking but he did look nervous. I suppose he did pretty well considering the position he was in.

He also began as a very eager witness offering more information than needed on questions.

For instance, when he was asked if he knew the defendant, Marissa DeVault, he quickly answered in the affirmative stating the names of her three daughters. "...Her daughters are Rhiannon, Khiernan and Diahnon. I used to..."

The judge admonished him to stick to the questions asked. One could feel that this was a very delicate witness. He was on the stand three times in two and a half days and we exited the courtroom on a good number of occasions.

The strangest thing about watching his testimony was trying to figure out why a decent looking girl would be with a creepy looking guy like this. I listened and tried to focus on his testimony. It was hard not to speculate.

Allen had met Marissa in 2007. He happened to be online cancelling his membership on an adult website called 'seeking arrangements.com'. This website features ladies who are looking for discreet relationships with some sort of financial arrangement. It just "so happened" that he saw Marissa's ad on this website and recognized her after seeing her at a local grocery store. I believe it was Basha's Supermarket.

"Coincidentally", he accidentally saw her again at a local pizza place where he had started a conversation with her.

Marissa told him she was a divorced mother of three.

They had sex on their first date.

Allen considered himself a wealthy man. He grew up in England, earned a Doctorate from Yale University and specialized in supply chain optimization for large corporations. This field apparently deals with inventory, cost effectiveness and supplies for inventory.

I had never heard of such a job.

He was proud to say that he was licensed in life insurance sales and considered himself an expert.

To me, he was proud of this in the same respect, as a man might be proud of a hobby. Who does insurance in their spare time? I can understand golf or camping but his obvious interest seemed off key.

Allen started seeing Marissa on a daily basis in the afternoons. He said they had sex almost daily. The first money he loaned her was to replace the brakes on her car. Within three months, she owed him over ten thousand dollars. This was not a lot of money to Allen at the time and he kept loaning her money. She promised that they would split the difference and she would pay half of it back.

The money trail was endless as verified by Allen. He talked with Marissa and she told him not to worry. She had a trust fund from her deceased father, Michael Wright. She was going to receive 1.8 million dollars as soon as it cleared litigation. He was happy to help out this struggling mother who seemed overwhelmed in bills.

He paid her phone bills, gas bills and water bills. He loaned her cash whenever she asked. He took her and her kids to his timeshare in Florida and charged her fifty percent on Disney tickets, food and so on. Whenever she asked, he willingly gave.

They continued to have sex.

Marissa also continued to tell him stories of her impending payout from her estate. Early on, Allen started keeping spreadsheets of loans he gave her. They mounted up so quickly that he wanted to get a handle on the situation. Every couple of days, Allen would log more monies paid on his spreadsheets on his computer.

Eventually, when returns were not coming back to him, he started charging two and a half percent per month in interest charges he felt he was owed. The prosecutor pointed out that this was thirty percent per year.

Allen started paying the mortgage on her house and was frustrated that she couldn't come up with the papers for the house. She said the house had ownership issues so there was no paperwork as it was tied up in court. Allen believed her and paid the three grand a month due every month.

At one point, Allen finally sat down with her because the amount she owed had surpassed a quarter of a million dollars and he felt like he was getting the runaround on the trust money she was due. She swore up and down that the payment would be at the end of January.

Six weeks before the killing, things started getting strange. Allen learned that Michael Wright was not dead. Marisa said she made a mistake and it was her grandmother's trust and not to worry. Michael Wright had recovered from being terminally ill.

Things would get paid as promised, she swore to him. They got a joint bank account together while Marissa was working at Macy's Department Store. Allen said the bank account was a good way to get her finances under control.

Marissa always seemed to show up with past due bills and this irritated Allen. He was fastidious about money and thought that if she put her paychecks in the bank account via direct deposits, things would surely balance out.

He told her a hundred times that she needed to use their account but she rarely did.

They continued to have sex regularly.

Allen asked why her direct deposits from work were not going into the account. Marissa claimed there was some foul up and because she had bad credit, her money wasn't being honored due to some bank misunderstanding.

She told him it would be straightened out. He had nothing to worry about. There would be plenty of money in January. Allen continued giving her money.

One day, while Allen was at the Annual Gilbert Rodeo, he called Marissa at home to see if she wanted to join him. Stan Cook answered the telephone and Stan said Marissa and Dale were out to dinner. This didn't make sense to Allen. He thought that Dale was her ex-husband and lived elsewhere. He couldn't get it off his mind and drove to her house.

Dale was putting up Christmas lights; hammer in hand...

The next day, he confronted Marissa. What was going on? Why was he there? Didn't he abuse her?

Marissa assured him that they were not together. Dale was just having some financial problems. She let him move back in temporarily because he had lost his apartment. The kids were not his anyway. They were from a previous marriage.

Allen thought that Marissa had a restraining order on Dale. He told her it wasn't a good idea to have him live there. Marissa agreed and said she would work on following through with the restraining order on him.

She then borrowed fifteen thousand dollars to help get him a new place.

Allen felt sorry for her and the position that she was in. It seemed awful to have to deal with this violent abuser that she couldn't get out of her life. Allen was concerned for the kids and Marissa insisted that a will be made in case something happened to her. She wanted the kids protected and wanted Allen to be the beneficiary.

After all, the kids weren't Dale's and she didn't want him to end up with custody. They would surely be abused and she trusted Allen. They each signed the will.

It was less than a month before Dale's demise that Marissa approached Allen. She wanted to borrow money so that she could take Dale out to a local casino for his birthday. He wanted to resist but she said this would be a great opportunity for her to ask Dale to move out.

Allen loaned her a few thousand.

Allen then learned that Marissa wanted to pay a friend of hers to take Dale out.

"What do you mean 'take him out'?" Allen asked her.

"I mean what it says. Take him out. Make him go away," she said offhandedly.

He didn't think she was serious the first time she brought it up.

Marissa told him she couldn't deal with the abuse anymore and she was afraid for her three girls. She was going to give the money to her friend, Travis Tatro.

She told Allen that she used to date him in the early 2000's when she worked at a club. She said Travis was a tough guy who had no issues taking someone out. She would get Dale drunk and then send him to the parking lot. While he was in the parking lot, Dale would be shot dead and she would just claim Dale tried to rape her. It was simple. Travis saved her life by shooting him.

It was about this time that Allen started to realize that he might be getting in over his head. He knew he was owed almost three hundred thousand dollars and if she would take out Dale that easily, what would she do to him?

The next day his fears abated when they got together and had sex.

The holidays passed and a week into 2009, Marissa approached him again. Dale had not moved out and had been abusive with her.

Marissa begged Allen for a gun.

"Please, honey," she said, "It's for the kids' safety. One of these days he will go too far and I need protection!"

Allen agreed and loaned her a small gun. He taught her how to use it and said it would be perfect for her, as it would fit in her purse. She readily accepted the pistol.

Allen was surprised to get a phone call from Marissa a few days later. She was distraught and beside herself. She was even hysterical. Marissa told him that Dale was dead.

"What happened?" Allen asked with surprise in his voice.

"Dale became violent and attacked me. Stan heard the whole thing. He came in with a tire iron and hit him over the head! I can't believe he's dead!" she said.

Allen was incredulous.

"He died on the way to the hospital," she said.

"What can I do to help?" Allen asked, genuinely concerned.

"Don't worry about me," Marissa said. "At least he's gone..."

"Let me come over," Allen offered.

"No, Allen, I'm fine. There's family here and there's too much going on. Please stay away until I get this figured out."

Allen agreed he wouldn't come over but he was gravely concerned for her. She had been through such a hard time and he wished he could do more to help. It was awful what she had gone through and he realized how much he cared for her. He even believed he loved her and felt the pain as she must have been feeling. He would do anything to help her.

But, Allen learned that Dale was still alive quite by accident. He had called her thinking it would be a good idea to get her out of the house. Once again, Stan answered and said that she and Dale were out of the house and would be back later in the evening.

Allen hung up the phone and stood there trying to take it in. He was starting to realize that everything she had been telling him were lies.

A few days later, Allen received a phone call from Marissa. She was in jail and needed bail money. He asked her what in the world for?

Marissa said she had been arrested for attempted homicide on Dale.

He wondered if she was lying again but she did sound upset and defeated. She said the police tricked her into saying that she killed Dale when it was really Stan. She said she had memory issues from being raped by Dale and didn't know exactly what happened but she was sure she didn't do it.

"How much do you need, Reese?" he asked her using her nickname.

"They want fifty thousand dollars."

Allen rubbed his head and sighed. "Yes, Reese, I'll take care of it..."

A week later, Marissa and Stan were at Allen's house. She had stayed there virtually every night since the incident. The sex was good.

"Take a look at this," Marissa said to Allen handing him a sheet of paper. Will you look it over and let me know if this will work for the police?"

"No, Marissa," Allen said. "I don't want anything to do with this."

Marissa started crying and begging him. "Please read it. You're my only friend in the world who understands me. I want to kill myself and want to leave something so that the girls will know what really happened. Please read it," she said with tear-filled eyes.

Allen hesitantly took the sheet of paper and read it. He expected it to be her will in her emotional state.

Instead, it was a type written letter. It was Stan's confession. He had attacked Dale and not Marissa. Allen said it was believable and made some editing suggestions.

He figured that while he was at it, she needed to sign his latest spreadsheet and promissory note. She owed him over three hundred and sixty thousand dollars.

Marissa signed it willingly.

"Do you still love her," Michelle Arino, the Assistant Prosecuting Attorney asked him.

"No," Allen responded almost inaudibly.

"No more questions, Judge," Michelle said as she went back to the prosecution table.

DAY 12: PART II

WILD, WILD WEST

.   The afternoon began with the appearance of DeVault attorney, Andrew Clemency. He had an interesting last name for the case and made for comments just as we had previously with a bump on someone's forehead.

Andrew Clemency had made a few appearances throughout the trial and he was interesting to watch. He would walk toward the witness and pause in front of the podium. He would push his coat tails back with his hands and put his hands on his hips. He'd look at the floor and then, ever so imperceptibly, you could see him rock as he looked toward the witness and then back at the jury. He would hold our gaze and then look back at the witness.

Each question was fired as if it were a dart headed toward a board.   One felt like each question could be of the utmost importance. Had there not been the seriousness to the trial, one might have thought it almost funny.

"You have been granted complete immunity from the state, haven't you Mr. Flores?" Andrew asked as his eyes drifted toward the jury box.

"Yes," Allen answered.

"Had you not been granted immunity, you would have been charged in this case, wouldn't you have?"

"Yes," Alan answered.

"Isn't it true that you would have been charged with being an accessory to murder?"

"Yes," Allen Flores answered.

"Is it also true that you would have been charged with hindering a police investigation?"

"Yes."

"Wasn't Stan's letter of confession found on your computer?" the attorney asked, looking toward the jury.

"Yes but it was on there because it was on a thumb drive and..."

Judge Steinle, III interrupted. "Just answer the question as you have been asked, Mr. Flores."

"Yes, Sir," Allen responded timidly. He put his face back up toward the microphone.

"For the record, was Stan Cook's confession found on your computer?"

"Yes, it was" Allen answered.

"Are you aware of the videos that we found on your computer," the attorney asked.

"Videos?" Allen questioned.

"Yes, videos. Wasn't it your practice to film videos of you having sex with various women?"

"I did," Allen answered. "That was a few years ago."

"Was it? Didn't you videotape yourself and the defendant, Marissa DeVault, having sex?"

Allen looked toward the floor of the witness stand. "Yes, I did."

"Did the defendant know that you were taping her while having sex?"

"I told her later."

"How long later?" the attorney asked.

"It was about six weeks afterwards."

"How did the defendant react when she found out?"

"She was fine with it," he answered.

Andrew Clemency rocked on his heels and looked toward the jury.

"Isn't it true that your sexual interests include sadism and masochism? Most people know it as S & M? Don't those interests include bondage and such?" Andrew asked him.

He had no longer looked at the jury when Mr. Basta shouted an objection.

"Your Honor! Mr. Flores sex life is not on trial."

"Move on, counselor. You're walking in dangerous territory," the Judge said.

"Yes, Sir," Andrew responded.

The attorney walked back to the podium and pulled out a sheet of paper. "You were also granted immunity from a charge that would have carried with it a life sentence. Are you aware of that?"

"Yes," Allen answered.

"The charge that carries a life sentence is the possession of child pornography found on your computer. Did you have child pornography on your computer?"

"Yes but that was a long time ago..."

"Your response requires a yes or a no. Is it not true that child pornography was found on your computer?"

"It is true," Allen answered.

The trial was not about this item on his computer but it surely didn't make him look good. At the same time, I kind of felt sorry for this guy.

He looked lonely and looked like he had a lot of secrets. I think he was trying to grasp at something with the defendant but was tricking himself into believing something was there when it wasn't. I think every time he gave her money, he thought this would bring the two of them closer or maybe it would cement their relationship by being responsible to him for this debt. It was his way of controlling her.

I don't think he wanted to admit he was just a 'Sugar Daddy' to Marissa.

One couldn't argue the fact that they were doomed to begin with. He was twenty years her senior with his being fifty-one and her being thirty-one when the incident happened.

She was an expensive date and for sure had only been 'seeking an   arrangement'.

BRAIN DAMAGE

The prosecution presented Dr. Chen, the forensic pathologist who conducted the autopsy on Dale Harrell. Her primary job was to determine the manner and cause of death of the decedent.

Dr. Chen was a female doctor who had a degree in both law and medicine. She was a slight woman dressed in black and was obviously well learned in her field.

When she spoke, she spoke with care and in phrases. She would use her hands to clarify points. There were sometimes long pauses when she spoke as if she was trying to be very careful with her words.

Dr. Chen spoke of the autopsy reports and pictures were included for the jury. Fortunately, since I had worked for a mortuary for some time, the pictures were not as uncomfortable as they might have been without the experience.

Ironically, I thought the photos of him in the hospital were almost more gruesome than the autopsy photos. I kept visualizing my memory of Dale lying in a hospital bed with a long tube coming from his mouth.

I could still see the large staples that went around the "C" of his skull on the right side of his head. I could see the brain swollen outside of where the skull was supposed to be. I remember a plastic piece sticking out of his head above the wound. I knew, without a doubt, those pictures would be permanently etched in my memory.

The prosecutor presented each picture, while the doctor explained to the jury what we were looking at. We first saw Dale, as he lay prostrate on a table before the autopsy began. One could see the severe swelling of his eye and the damage to his brain on his right side.

The doctor walked us through the process of the autopsy explaining that the process is very mechanical. Autopsies generally have the same procedure and process. The first part of the process included a physical examination of the body.

Dr. Chen carefully pointed out the obvious damage to Dale's head noting the swollen and bruised eye, the defect of the skull on the right side and the fact that his jaw had been wired shut. She explained that the healing process had begun with evidence of scarring and bruising. She pointed out that Dale had a broken rib and this was most probably due to cardiopulmonary resuscitation (CPR) shortly before his death and how it is not uncommon for a rib to crack during the process.

The doctor was careful to point out bruising on various parts of his body including the legs and on his abdomen. These bruises were due to medical intervention with the variety of tubes placed in him such a feeding tube, a tracheostomy and a tube that went from the femoral artery in his abdomen including the filter meant to cease blood clots.

She also footnoted that Dale could not use blood thinners as this would cause damage to the wounded part of his head. The veins and arteries in his head needed to have a clotting ability.

We were able to see the brain as it was autopsied and the damage on the right side was severe. The left side of the brain also showed damage via blood clotting and gathering, and this was due to a subsequent stroke suffered while he was in the healing process; but was an end result of the damage caused to the right side of the brain.

Dale also had pneumonia in the lungs, also a probable contributor to his death.

It was verified that Dale died from a pulmonary embolism, which is a blood clot causing asphyxiation to the brain.

The most important thing that came out of her testimony was that there were no signs of scratching or bite marks anywhere on his body. Additionally, Dr. Chen made no mention of shin burns.

I remember looking over to the defendant, Marissa. We had gotten out of our regular order when leaving the jury room to the jury box and I ended up on the top row, closest to the gallery. I was able to see the defense table as well as the profile of the defendant.

At first, I thought she was dutifully taking notes of the graphic images on the screen. After a couple of glances, I could see her writing with a short number two pencil. She began erasing

162

something in broad strokes. I watched as she brushed the eraser particles from her sheet of paper.

A short time later I realized that she wasn't engaged in taking notes but rather drawing pictures as if she were an artist in the park on a Sunday afternoon. It struck me as severely inappropriate. I thought I remembered Jodi Arias doing the same thing at her trial.

We broke for lunch and I found myself tagging along with Ted and Jarod. I didn't know Jarod very well although he seemed nice enough. He had a dark complexion and had a funny haircut with very short hair on the sides with long hair on top. It looked like an overgrown Mohawk.

We decided to have sushi for lunch even though I knew I couldn't afford it. Little fruit flies flew into Ted's soy sauce and dampened his appetite. It was amusing.

We returned to court and the prosecution called up one of the most desired witnesses to the stand.

"Your Honor, the State calls Stanley Cook to the stand."

An African-American man walked toward the witness stand and the court remained silent, all attention riveted to him. He was kind of a dumpy guy and dressed in pants that had not seen an iron in years. The creases were long gone.

I didn't need to look at the other jurors to know that their interest was piqued. This gentleman had been spoken of multiple times and the only time we had seen a picture of him was when earlier evidence showed him in his bloodstained clothes shortly after the incident.

I remember the olive green t-shirt that he was wearing the night of the assault, spattered in blood with the shirt having a caption from Snow White and the Seven Dwarfs. I believe the shirt had Grumpy on the front speaking in a balloon saying, "I'm right, you're wrong. Any questions?"

I remember the large droplets of spatter on the shirt and the forensics telling us he was in the room and probably behind Marissa. The spatter said he came in around the fourth or fifth blow.

Stanley Cook was important. We knew he could provide some important answers. We knew he could clear the murkiness of the water.

What we received was certainly not what we expected.

"What is your name?" Miss Arino asked.

"Stanley Cook, Jr."

"Is it true that you were in the armed forces?"

"Yes, Ma'am. I was in the Air Force."

"What did you do in the Air Force?"

"I was an Aircraft Armament Technician."

"Did you go to school after the Air Force?"

"Yes. I went to DeVry University."

"What was your degree?"

"I was a computer software technician."

"Did you get a job in that capacity?" she asked.

"Yes. I worked for a billing company in the computer department."

"Are you still working for the same company?" Miss Arino asked.

"No, ma'am."

"Why don't you work there?"

"I was fired."

"Why were you fired, Mr. Cook?"

"I was unsuitable for the position."

At first, everything seemed normal in the questioning of the witness. He answered clearly and succinctly but he did not look very comfortable on the stand. He was dressed in khaki pants, a black t-shirt, wore rubber-soled shoes, wore glasses and had a shaved head. He fidgeted with his fingers over his knees nervously and held his blue windbreaker uncomfortably on his lap.

He did, however, sit forward eager to answer questions but one could see that he had to struggle a little.

"Can you explain why you were terminated?" Miss Arino asked.

"I don't really remember."

"Can you tell us why not?"

"I had a motorcycle accident. I hit a truck at forty miles an hour and can't remember stuff sometimes."

"Do you know the defendant, Marissa DeVault?"

"Yes, Ma'am," he answered.

"Can you point her out for me?"

Stan's eyes looked over the courtroom and they eventually focused on the defendant. "She's right there," he said pointing toward the defense table.

"Can you describe her for the court?"

"She's wearing a black sweater with a white shirt and she has black hair and is wearing glasses," he said pointing in her direction.

"Where did you meet the defendant?"

"I met Reese at DeVry. I always called her Reese," he said.

"When did you meet the defendant?" she asked.

"I don't remember. I just know I met her at school and we became friends."

"That's okay," Miss Arino said. "Was there a point in time that you lived with the defendant?"

"Yes. I lived with her about four years."

"Were you close to the family?"

"Yes, Ma'am. They called me Uncle Stan. I was like an uncle to the three girls."

"So, you spent a lot of time with the family?"

"Yes, Ma'am."

"Did you take trips together?"

"Yes, Ma'am."

"Did you go to Disneyland or Disney World together?"

"Yes, Ma'am," he answered.

"Which one did you go to, Disney World or Disneyland," she offered.

He appeared to think for a minute, as if he was putting pieces together. "I think it was Disney World. That's in Florida, right?" he questioned.

"Yes, it is. Now let me ask you, where were you on January 14th, 2009?"

Stan looked down and fumbled with the zipper on his windbreaker on his lap. He appeared lost for a moment.

"Mr. Cook, where were you on January fourteenth, 2009?" she asked again.

"I don't remember," he said. "I can't remember last week much less five years ago. I think I was there."

I was avidly trying to take notes when I almost fell out of my chair. I had to think about what he just said. It also crossed my mind that Miss Arino had just assassinated her witness. How could anything he said be of any value?

"Did you have a gun?" she asked, apparently oblivious to his response.

"A gun?"

"Yes, a gun. Didn't you have a gun in your pocket the morning of January 14, 2009?"

Stan looked at his lap and appeared to struggle internally.

"I have a rifle in the closet. It's an SKS. It's in a case, though," he said eagerly.

For a moment, it looked like Miss Arino was getting irritated. His answers had disrupted the flow of questioning.

"I am talking about the. 22, Stan," she stated. "Didn't you have a .22 in your pocket?"

"I think so," Stan finally said.

"Where did you get the gun?"

"I don't remember," he said. "Probably from Reese."

"Did you have blood on you that morning?"

"Apparently," he answered.

For some reason, Michelle went after Stan. She asked questions and the answers were null and void and she asked anyway. I stopped taking notes because there was no longer a point.

"Did you hit Dale Harrell with a hammer?"

"I'm not sure," he said hesitantly. His answers seemed weak and without merit.

The prosecutor went over to the podium and pulled out a plastic bag containing a sheet of paper. She removed it from the plastic casing and handed it to Stan.

"Do you recognize this?" she asked.

She held a packet of papers. I was unclear as to what it was.

"Is that your signature?" she asked him.

Stan looked at the front of it and then the back. "That's my signature," he said.

"Do you remember it?"

"No," he answered.

"Did you write this or did someone help you?"

"Apparently," he answered.

"Is it true that Marissa helps you remember things?"

"Well, yes," he answered. "So does Wikipedia. I don't think a person can put memories in my brain."

"Do you remember discussing wedding rings with Marissa?"

"Yes," he said.

"You two were planning on getting married, weren't you?' Michelle Arino pointed out.

"I think so. We might have talked about it. I can't remember for sure." One could see his brow furrowed in confusion.

"Did you hit Marissa with a sledgehammer to make it look like Dale abused her?"

"I can't remember," Stan said, matter-of-factly.

The rest of the afternoon was spent with the prosecutor asking him questions and he generally had only three responses.

"I can't remember", "Evidently", and "Apparently" encompassed most of his answers.

It was uncomfortable sitting in the jury box as we watched Stan struggle with each of his responses.

"Do you love her?" the prosecutor asked.

"Yes," he answered.

The prosecutor sat down and the defense attorney got up and approached the witness.

"Do you remember me," he asked.

"No," Stan answered.

"We've had many meetings together. Are you sure you don't remember me?" Mr. Tavasoli asked. He approached Stan as one might approach a tiger in a cage. He walked delicately.

Stan looked at him and appeared to think about the question. "Maybe," he finally answered.

"Do you have an immunity agreement with the State," the defense attorney asked.

"Yes," Stan answered.

In my opinion, nobody could get him off the stand fast enough. I don't know that Stan proved anything except that he couldn't be relied on to remember anything. One could have told him he was a Martian from another planet and I expect he would have responded with, "Apparently." Personally, I thought he was faking his memory loss.

I am still not sure why the prosecution put him on the stand except to say that he wasn't in control. I think the idea may have been to show that he was a patsy, someone that could be used to take the blame.

For now, we will leave that to be discussed in the jury room when it came time.

The only live witness in the room aside from the defendant may as well have been blind.

I wondered if we would hear from the three other witnesses in the house.

DAY 14

DEAD OR ALIVE

Today featured a short appearance of Detective Sy Ray for the prosecution. We had seen Detective Ray on the stand early on in the trial. I didn't have to look at the lady jurors to know they gave this witness undivided attention with his perfect hair, well-defined face and the way he carried himself. He was confident but not overbearing. He was friendly and seemed the type of guy you would happily invite over for an afternoon barbeque.

Sy Ray was not on the stand very long except to provide some information regarding the video interrogation tape of Marissa prior to being arrested. He was the officer who had stepped in late on the video to tell Marissa that she might be more straightforward about the incident the night Dale was attacked. In essence, he had told her she was lying.

It was presented that he had used well-learned interrogation techniques when speaking with her. One of those techniques involved befriending the suspect to obtain information. These techniques were ploys.

The moment that Sy Ray had acknowledged that he may have remembered her from police academy training, it was a ruse as well. It seemed that the more confident and relatable that Marissa was, the more fertile the ground for lies.

The defense asked only one question of Detective Sy Ray, "Is it an acceptable technique to lie to a suspect in interrogation?"

"You're allowed to lie", the detective responded casually.

Detective Mike Bishop took the witness stand as the lead detective but not as the third man on the prosecution team representing the State of Arizona.

One could tell that Detective Mike Bishop was a seasoned street cop, and probably more comfortable at a police station investigating crimes as opposed to being in a courtroom all day. He was the lead case agent for the DeVault investigation since the beginning.

The prosecutor asked questions specifically about details mentioned in Marissa's interrogation tapes. He had detailed each piece of information she had spoken of in the tapes including names of neighbors she had mentioned, hospital names she had dropped and had checked police agencies that she had said she had made reports to of domestic violence. He researched areas she had lived including Glendale, Gilbert, Tempe and Lake Havasu by contacting police departments and hospitals in each locale.

Essentially, Detective Mike Bishop had found no corroboration of virtually anything she had said in the interrogation. Neighbors and friends had been interviewed and no one seemed to have been a witness to any domestic violence.

He had contacted all police agencies in the area and found no evidence that she had called anyone to report incidences with her husband, Dale. Further, he called all local hospitals and there was no record of her having a cracked skull or anything else to corroborate her story of ever having been abused by Dale.

Just to top everything off, there was no evidence supporting her statement that she had ever given birth to a twin when Rhiannon was born.

There was also no evidence of any divorce papers being filed for her marriage to Dale.

The defense team asked if he had interviewed the children living in the house, for information regarding any domestic violence. He responded in the negative.

The prosecution redirected their questioning of Detective Bishop. It was determined that another detective had handled those interviews along with a child specialist.

It was starting to look like Marissa DeVault had a problem with not only telling the truth but with telling stories that, in some cases, seemed unnecessary. It was beyond speculation to assume that anything she said could be trusted. I knew that these lies would complicate issues once we got to the deliberation room one day.

There was one more thing that had come out in the questioning of Detective Bishop.

Marissa DeVault's stepfather was alive and well living in Chandler, Arizona.

I thought he was dead...

DAY 15

REESY CUP

"Please call your next witness." Judge Steinle asked.

"Yes, Your Honor. The State would like to present Travis Tatro."

The back doors of the courtroom opened and we watched the next witness being led in by the prosecutor.

The court was quietly taking in his six foot, five inch presence. This was the hit man we had heard about earlier in the trial. As he walked toward the front, it was as if he owned the entire courtroom.

He walked past the podium and to the right of the Judge in the center of the courtroom.

"Do you swear to tell the whole truth and nothing but the truth? So help you God."

Travis had his right hand raised and said, "I do."

I was in rapt amazement of this gentleman. He was a large man and one would say was big-boned but not fat. He easily stood six-foot-three. He wore a black suit that hung loosely on his frame, and a red shirt that boldly made him stand out.

His face was incredibly interesting and uncommon. He had a large round head with a small nose ring tucked under his nose and close to his face. The whole of his head was shaved clean except for a spot in the back of his head that looked like it was crowned by a yarmulke but was actually his hair cut into a perfect four inch circle. A two-foot long loose braid of hair protruded and hung down his back, out of the center of the yarmulke cut.

His face aired confidence and the nose ring was not particularly noticeable due the two-foot long braided beard that prominently hung from his chin. The sides of his head had a squared off sideburn that ran across the length of his chin to his small beard.

He sat in the witness chair and made himself comfortable, as if he was sitting in the easy chair of his living room. He held the arms of the chair as if he could stand up at any second and heave the chair across the room.

He leaned forward and moved the microphone stand closer to him. On his left hand, in the area between the thumb and forefinger on the back of his hand, there was a tattooed spider web. In the same spot on the right hand, there was a tattooed 8-legged spider.

"Do you know the defendant, Marissa DeVault?" the prosecutor asked.

"Oh yeah," Travis said in a booming voice.

"When did you first meet her?"

"I met her seven or eight years ago. Probably '02 or '03?"

"So, it was a long time ago. Did the defendant look like she does today?"

"It was long time ago, man," he said. "We were all different. Did you ever see Brad Pitt in "I Am Legend?"

"Yes," Mr. Basta answered.

"I looked like Brad Pitt." I heard somebody chuckle in the gallery. " If I remember, Reese had red hair back then."

"Where did you meet the defendant?"

"I was a bouncer for a club downtown called Knockers. She worked there."

"Did you know her beyond a work relationship?"

"Oh sure," Travis said smiling. "I used to date her. I dated her for about eight or nine months. I think it was less than a year."

"Very good," the prosecutor responded. "Was she married when you were dating?"

"Oh, yeah. "

"Did that bother you, Mr. Tatro?" Mr. Basta asked.

"I didn't care. At that time, she was talking about breaking up with her husband. She said he was hitting her pretty good and pretty regular."

"Hitting her?"

"Yeah, she was getting slapped around so it didn't bother me that I was going out with her," he said. He paused. "I don't like woman-beater pieces of shit."

I saw the Judge look toward Travis but he did not say anything. I suspected this was the type of witness who did not change for anyone. It did not matter if he was in court or not.

"Eventually you broke up?"

"Yeah, we did. Look she was a sweet girl and pretty hot but she had a bad habit of lying and I didn't need to deal with that."

"When would you say you broke up?"

He thought for a minute. "I'd say in 2004."

"Was there a time when she contacted you again?"

"Yeah. It was five years later in January of 2009 she called me at work."

"Were you surprised to hear from her?"

"I was surprised. It had been a long time."

"What did she want?"

"She wanted to get together. She said Dale was hitting her again."

"Did that strike you as strange?"

He laughed. "It struck me as fucking weird."

Judge Steinle gave him a dirty look.

"Why is that?"

"She told me her husband had died of stomach cancer a long time ago."

"Stomach cancer?"

"Yes."

"Did you get together at some point?"

"I did," he said. "Let's put it this way. She can be pretty persuasive when she wants to be. I thought I'd hear her out."

"What happened when you got together?"

"She wanted me to take care of him."

"She wanted you to take care of whom?" Mr. Basta asked.

"Her husband, Dale."

"What do you mean when you say 'take care of him'?"

"I figured she wanted me to slap him around a bit."

"Didn't she ask you to kill him?"

"No. She never quite said that. I did go out to her house when we talked about it and Dale was there. He tried to shake my hand but I wouldn't."

"Why not?" the prosecutor asked.

"Like I said before, I don't shake hands with woman-beating pieces of shit."

"Did he strike you as that type of person?"

"Not really. He struck me as a decent guy."

"What happened then?"

"Shit," he said. "I wanted out. I realized that this dude was back from the dead and I wanted nothing to do with it."

"Did she say anything else?"

"She said she would take care of it in her way."

"What did you take that to mean?"

"I figured she wanted him whacked or some shit. I don't know. She lies at the drop of a hat and I wanted out and I got out."

"No more questions," the prosecutor said.

The defense asked a few questions and then the jury was prompted for questions. A couple of us wrote our question and the Bailiff picked them up and brought them to the circle of prosecutors, defense attorneys and the Judge.

They discussed them briefly and then the Judge brought the questions back up to the bench. He read each question and waited for the answer from Travis Tatro.

"While you were dating, was there any evidence that she had ever been hurt by her husband?"

"Nah," he answered nonchalantly.

The Judge read the next question. "You said she worked at a club. Was she a bartender, cocktail waitress or entertainer?"

Travis laughed. "The place was called Knockers. It was a strip club. She was a stripper. Her name was Reesy Cup."

I looked toward the defense table and Mr. Tavasoli and Andrew Clemency showed no emotion on their faces. It still could not have been a good moment.

Travis was dismissed and I thought he was the strongest, yet the most ironic of witnesses. It worked against him that he worked for a strip club as there is a visual that this is somehow part of an underworld of nastiness. But, he was the strongest of witnesses because he had nothing to hide. We knew at this point that nothing Marissa ever said could be trusted. The prosecution was successful in proving she was a liar on more than one occasion. The interrogation tapes had been ripped apart from the testimony of Michael Bishop.

Allen Flores had a lot to hide and I didn't find him trustworthy. He was into sadism and masochism, and he liked to film his conquests without their knowledge. To top it off, his offenses were to be protected by immunity. In that, his testimony seemed weak at best.

When one looked at Stan Cook, the other witness in the room when Dale died, it was not that he had something to hide but rather his memory was so poor that one could not say he was a reliable witness by any stretch of the imagination. I wondered how much of his testimony was performed and rehearsed.

Travis Tatro had nothing to hide and I believe all the other jurors felt the same way that I did. He was genuine, although a caricature to be sure, he seemed honest. He was the most honest and enduring because he had nothing to gain.

The prosecution then brought in a computer forensics expert, Detective Scott Zuberbeuhler, who was able to establish, amidst a lot of computer jargon, that Marissa had a document created on her computer on Feb. 4, 2009. That particular document ended up on Allen Flores' computer. On that same day, Stan Cook brought his confession letter to both the Tempe and Gilbert Police Departments. The document on Flores' computer turned out to be the confession letter of Stan Cook.

The final evidence the prosecution brought forward were tapes from the Buckeye Jail of Marissa calling Stan Cook via collect phone calls.

This segment was an absolute debacle. We would have to re-listen to these pieces of evidence because the CD's that played from the computer through the small computer speakers were muffled and distorted. All I could get from these is that Marissa was questioning why the police didn't accept Stan's confession and something about her losing out on an insurance policy in April of 2009. This had presentation issues.

The prosecution rested.

Judge Steinle informed us that we were to reserve judgment until we heard the defense part of the case. We still had a long way to go.

There was one thing on my mind and I would have to wait to see if the rest of the jury wondered the same thing.

There were a total of six people in the house, including Dale when he was attacked. We had heard from Dale through his gruesome photos taken while still alive and then dead. We had heard from Marissa and Stan Cook who were in the room the night Dale was attacked.

However, the other three witnesses in the house had not been brought forward which were the three daughters. I believe that two of the girls were eight and ten years old. The third daughter was thirteen at the time of the attack. I remembered the testimony from the first police officer to enter the home, saying that she was awake while the other two were sleeping.

I wondered about the thirteen year-old and if she would ever be on the witness stand...

There was a question that still nagged me. Where is all the money?

ADMONISHMENT

Today it was uncomfortable to be a juror. The last time I had felt this uncomfortable in a jury box was the second day of jury selection, the shooting gallery. I am sure every one of us felt the same way.

"I received a question from one of the jurors today in regards to the tapes that were played the last time we were in session," Judge Steinle said in the direction of the jury.

This was the first thing in the morning.

He paused and looked down. Then he raised his head, looked over the rims of his glasses and looked at us again.

"I did not appreciate the tone used in this question. The evidence is what it is and we provide means for you to listen to the evidence when it goes back to the jury room. I have been a Judge for thirty-five years and let me tell you something," he emphasized," If this were 1979, the jury would not get the opportunity to use the notepads that we provide. The jury would not receive a detailed list of exhibits. The jury would sit there and listen. You would go back to the jury room with far less than you have today. You would hash it out.

He paused. "Again, the tone used in this was unnecessary," he said firmly. He shuffled a piece of paper and said, "Has the prosecution rested?"

"Yes, your Honor," the prosecution answered.

"Defense, present your first witness," he said, closing the jury matter.

This is my first and probably only jury I will ever be on but I have learned a few things.

The first thing I learned, after my employment experience with the Judge, was that one is to be seen and not heard. I realize that we have a jury question system where we can contact the Judge with any issues that arise. Furthermore, I also understand the importance of maintaining the integrity between the jury, judge and the attorneys of both sides. One wants to eliminate the risk of bias on any party giving the defendant a completely fair trial. This is a critically important aspect.

At the same time, just because the option is available, it isn't there to interrupt the court process. In other words, I would think that one would use this only at critical times and use it sparingly. Most importantly, always treat the court with respect. It sounds as if this question was either sarcastic or demeaning to the court.

I had a feeling I knew who submitted the question.

Coincidentally, I submitted a question prior to court beginning today. I don't regret it but the timing wasn't the best given the judge's mood after that question but it is what it is. I was polite about it, though.

I had gone to the Jury Commissioner's Office to pick up my check. They asked me what juror number I was and I told them number thirteen. I'm proud of that number as it's always been my lucky number as I was born on the thirteenth. The kind lady who distributes the checks looked on the list and said I was listed as juror fifteen.

I thought about it all weekend. There's always been the alternate juror factor in the back of my mind. We considered this an island and there were three of us who would be kicked off the island when the lottery was held at the conclusion of both sides of the case. I did not want to be kicked off the island and I don't think anyone else did either. The thought was: imagine vesting all this time in the matter and then not being able to deliberate when we counted.

Then, I thought, I wished I had not submitted it. It seemed trivial in the face of the trial.

The other weird thing about today was that the court reporter kept turning around in her chair and looking at me.

The court reporter reigns over her little kingdom in the courtroom. She steadfastly works a typist code and monitors testimony on a computer. Nobody is to talk to her except for the Judge, and this is a rare occurrence unless testimony needs to be reread. I can comfortably say that Judge Steinle was afraid of her.

She wore glasses and looked over her rims directly at me, and she did it at least four times. I thought that maybe she was redoing our juror numbers. The juror behind me, Butthead, informed me that the court reporter was hearing some sort of sound and thought I was making the sound. I have no idea what anyone was talking about as I was engrossed in the testimony.

The funny thing is, I went to great lengths to be quiet. I didn't want to be the jury member with a cold who was coughing and generally interrupting everything. Even though I didn't have a cold, it was always inevitable that I would get a tickle in my throat. I started bringing cough drops. The best thing about cough drops by Halls was that they are wrapped in paper instead of cellophane and make very little noise when opening them.

I still wonder why she kept looking my direction.

It was just a really uncomfortable day to be a juror because we all felt admonished by the judge. Especially disconcerting, for we all knew one should never write a note without the utmost courtesy to the court.

The various unwritten etiquette rules about being a juror include being seen and not heard, being early for court times, dressing appropriately, acting professional at all times, not talking to each other in the jury box and, did I mention, to be seen and not be heard?

That was the thing about Butthead. He has a great big heart. But, he was starting to stick out a little.

Butthead was about forty or forty-five, a little heavy set and was a computer tech guy. He was the juror who was the first one in the jury room every day. He always brought in his laptop and could be seen tapping away at something or another. He was the only one to stay in the jury room throughout the duration of our hour and a half lunch.

Butthead has been married for thirty-five years, and was really a good guy. That piece of information told me that his wife had a lot of patience.

Butthead was one of those guys who knew exactly who to contact in any given situation. He was the MacGyver of anything computers. He could fix anything.

One morning, after we arrived in the jury room, a couple of us laughed at how long it took the elevators to get to the thirteenth floor. The elevators would also seem to randomly stop for no apparent reason. These stops would generally be a pause and nothing to be alarmed about. Well, Butthead decided to contact the City of Phoenix Facilities department and lodge a claim and work order to get them out to inspect the elevators.

"Really?" I thought. The most powerful men in the city ride these elevators daily, and I believe that if there were an issue, they would handle it. We laughed it off but it was still odd of him to get involved in it.

Butthead was also in the minority in another sense. I believe he and Cherie were the only jurors to have been seated on a jury before. I asked him how the experience was.

He casually said he had been dismissed from that trial, because he helped the prosecution team fix their computer. I suppose I can understand how that would happen. It might show jury favoritism toward the prosecution team by befriending them in the process of fixing the computer. A situation, which could later be interpreted as unfair bias to the other side. I remember thinking it was a little odd that he ended up on the jury.

Butthead may have been odd but he had a great big heart.

A couple of days ago, I almost fell out of my jury chair while in the box. There came a point where the Judge called the attorneys up to his bench for a sidebar, when all the parties communicate with each other outside the ears of the court. They usually speak in low and hushed tones.

"Excuse me, your Honor," a booming voice said behind me. I half turned to see Butthead in his usual spot at the end of the second row behind me.

"I can hear what you are saying," Butthead said loudly.

I think I speak for the other jurors when I say, that the rest of us wanted to sink in our chairs.

The Judge said he appreciated the comment but they were just working on some scheduling issues.

The whole of us looked back at the Judge and pretended we didn't know who Butthead was.

The defense began laying their groundwork with two witnesses. The first witness was Dr. Jon Conte, a specialist in child abuse who teaches at the University of Washington. He was detailed and clearly knowledgeable in the field.

He did not directly speak how his testimony was related to the defendant, Marissa DeVault. I did take exceptional interest, however, because of my experience being an abused child.

He explained that historically, the serious study of child abuse really began in about 1979 with the rape crisis and the field's focus on child abuse. He explained that it wasn't until the 1980's that serious studies began in child abuse and the effects of that abuse on children.

He also explained the general difference between discipline and abuse, something I have always struggled with in my mind. For instance, I knew my upbringing favored a disciplinarian approach; but at what point does it become abuse? He explained that discipline may be a smack on the rear end but once one starts leaving marks, it can be categorized as abuse.

My father was a doctor and I can remember him writing notes to the gym teacher telling him that a medical condition existed, that would keep me out of his class for three or four months. This would happen when a spanking turned into a vent of rage that would leave me out of class for months at a time. My parents would check my legs periodically and eventually release me back to gym class when the bruising healed.

He spoke of how parents are critical in child development and how abusive behaviors during the growth process virtually determined the future onset of such things as alcoholism, gambling problems, sexual addictions, violent behavior and a host of other issues.

Dr. Conte talked about Post Traumatic Stress Syndrome as a result of trauma in childhood. He reminded me of the powerlessness and betrayal I felt as a child; when my parents would leave awful bruises or wield punishment to the point that I would ask myself, "Weren't they here to protect me?" Why were my parents the only ones that I was most afraid of in the world? I also remember the isolation I felt as a child because I couldn't tell anyone the awful secrets that were happening behind closed doors.

It was no wonder that my brother had tried to kill himself over five years ago. He felt worthless inside because we had been told on more than one occasion that my parents wished we had never been born. It was no wonder that he became violent or that I never settled down with anyone. I wasn't afraid of commitment. I was afraid of becoming the man my father was.

The doctor spoke of sexual abuse and how it gives one in their adult life an altered sense of reality and its effect of phobias, isolation, fear and anxieties.

Fortunately, I think the only real damage to me was my escape into alcohol to minimize the memories. It only took hitting rock bottom and a realization that my life had hit a fork in the road where I had to choose life or death. I chose life and started over.

The doctor admitted, that there is no way to predict the damage abuse can cause. Different people react in different ways in order to protect themselves, as they grow older.

The lesson in abuse was interesting and I was curious to see how it would apply to the defendant.

The defense presented a second doctor who was trained in sociology as opposed to psychology. He was experienced in training police departments and social agencies on violence and where it occurs.

I believe this was Dr. King.

This doctor primarily focused on 'intimate partner homicide', those homicides happening between couples. He was a fact person quoting studies and documents and knew his statistics. One statistic that stood out was that eighty-three percent of violence between couples usually involved women as being the victim.

He said that sixty-percent of women who were murdered in a relationship were either in the process of divorce or dissolving their relationship. He also said that women are often victims because they isolate themselves, because they don't believe the system can help them and oftentimes never call the police or counselor.

He talked in detail about the few times that the woman kills, and that it will happen at a time when their partner is defenseless.

Usually their partner is physically bigger than they are, so it is better when the victim is in a position where they can't fight back.

An example might be when the partner is sleeping or incapacitated.

He noted that when a woman kills, it is usually through blunt force trauma and guns are rarely used.

I found it all interesting but wondered how this applied to Marissa.

The prosecution had only one question at the conclusion of testimony.

"Has there ever been an established correlation between abuse and homicide?" Mr. Basta asked pointedly.

"No, but..."

"No further questions," the prosecutor said, cutting off the witness.

There were a few things that I had noticed about Marissa as the prosecution laid out their case.

For one thing, I thought it was odd that she was married but never took her husband's last name. She had spoken of this in the interrogation tapes and brushed it off as something she never got around to.

Another thing that I thought odd was that she appeared distant from her family. For instance, testimony had shown she was a stripper less than three years after she was married. I'll try not to recognize the fact that she had her affair with Allen Flores for almost two years.

There was also the fact that I didn't seem to know anything or had heard very little about her mother and father. Was she a stepchild from another marriage? What was the relationship with her and her stepfather? Would it have bearing, considering how many times she had said he was dead when, in fact, he was alive? Where was her father and did the above doctor's testimony refer to him?

I will let the defense present their case and stay away from speculating but they are worthy thoughts to be sure.

Let's hope there are no more admonishments to the jury...

MALINGERING

The defense presented three witnesses today with two in the morning and one in the afternoon.

The first witness was a friend of Marissa's who knew her from her kids' school. Her name was Ayesha Hale who worked for Wells Fargo Bank as an underwriter. She felt she was very close with Marissa, but when asked could not remember any of the kids' names.

She was asked about her relationship with Dale. She said she was uncomfortable around Dale and he wasn't involved in the children's lives. She felt a tension between Dale and Marissa and had even seen the black eye that Marissa covered with sunglasses.

Ayesha would visit Marissa from time to time and felt that as time passed, Marissa seemed to have lost weight. Further, she witnessed the farm animals at Marissa's house not being fed. It seemed to her that Marissa and Dale were having problems; however she had never witnessed Dale abusing Marissa.

The prosecution took her apart fairly quickly. It was answered again that she had not witnessed any abuse from Dale toward Marissa. She was asked if Marissa had told her that Dale had lost his job.

"No," she answered. Before the prosecution could pursue that answer, she quickly changed it to the affirmative.

"Did Marissa ever talk to you about the night that Dale Harrell was assaulted?"

"Yes," she answered.

"Who did she say hit Dale with a hammer that night?"

"Stanley Cook," she answered softly. "She had a lot of stories about that night," she recalled.

"Nothing further," the prosecutor stated as he was sitting down.

The second witness was Lisa Kohl, a close friend of Marissa. She wore a pink blouse and tennis shoes while answering questions on the stand. She was bubbly and friendly seeming somewhat eager to answer questions. She knew the family mostly from sleepovers that the kids would have at each other's house.

Lisa was able to say that Marissa was warm and friendly and a good mother to the kids. She had not witnessed any abuse from Dale but had witnessed Marissa having a black eye. She also said that she always felt a tension between Dale and Marissa. She felt that Marissa would never be allowed to talk to anyone unless he was there. She said the tension was palpable.

She mentioned a story that one night she had woken up at three in the morning to hear screaming. She looked across toward Dale and Marissa's house and didn't see anything.

"Look," she said, "I'm a Jack Catholic. I don't really go to church anymore and I don't believe in weird stuff and this was weird. I don't know what woke me up but I was sure I heard screaming. When I looked toward Marissa's house, all the windows were dark. The next day though, I did see Marissa with a black eye."

"Was she able to tell you where that black eye came from?" the defense asked.

"She said she was clumsy."

"Did she eventually tell you where that came from?" the defense pursued.

"Yes," Lisa answered. "About a week later she said that Dale was abusing her."

"Thank you," the defense answered. "No more questions."

Mr. Basta, the prosecutor, stood and asked: "Did you ever witness Dale hitting Marissa DeVault?"

"No," she answered.

"Do you know who was screaming the night you said you heard it?"

"No," she answered.

The afternoon was spent with Dr. Cheryl Karp on the witness stand.

I remember Dr. Conte saying that he was married to Dr. Karp.

Dr. Karp was the author of four books on psychology and had spent a significant amount of time training lawyers on the importance of having a psychologist involved in investigations. Although she was short, her size was made up for in her extensive knowledge in the field.

She had given Marissa a cacophony of psychological tests between 2010 and 2013. These tests included a Trauma Symptom Inventory Test both older and a more current variation of the same test. There was a MacArthur Competence Assessment Tool – Fitness to Plead (Mac CAT-FP) Test along with the more commonly known Detailed Assessment of Posttraumatic Stress Test also known as the DAPS. She also mentioned the Multi-Phasic Personality Test and the Personality Assessment Inventory Test.

This doctor had spent sixty hours studying the defendant and the conclusion of all of her tests said that Marissa suffered a psychotic episode in her past although it was not defined what the episode was. She concluded that Marissa showed signs of severe depression and definite signs of PTSD (Post-traumatic Stress Disorder) with dis-associative features complicated by depression and anxiety. She also mentioned that there were signs of a bi-polar disorder.

In the middle of this testimony, I remember glancing toward the gallery where the open public can sit and was surprised to see Juan Martinez sitting in the back row. Juan Martinez was the lead prosecutor for the Jodi Arias case of a year earlier.

Coincidentally, the prosecution asked the witness of her involvement in the Jodi Arias trial and of her testimony for the defense of that trial.

The Doctor adamantly explained that she had only filled out a report for that trial and had never been a witness on the stand in that trial.

I wondered why Juan Martinez was there and speculated he wanted to see this witness and how she performed on the witness stand. This was only conjecture on my part but I did find it interesting that he was there. I never saw him leave.

The prosecution was able to get into the testimony of Dr. Karp and tear it apart. Mr. Basta pulled out volumes of psychological reports on Marissa and presented them to the witness. Item by item was pointed out and the witness did her best to stand her ground on the assessment of Marissa.

"Did you find that the defendant was competent, that she had a rational state of mind?" he asked.

"Yes," the doctor answered.

"Did the defendant, Marissa DeVault, understand the gravity of the charges against her?"

"Yes, but she still has mental issues that have to be considered," she answered.

"A 'Yes' or 'No' will suffice." Mr. Basta responded.

Mr. Basta pulled another large three ring binder from his desk. One could see Post-Its marking pages to be looked at. He brought one of the binders forward to the witness and placed it in front of her and asked her to read it to herself.

"Yes?" she questioned after reading the page in question.

"Do you not say in that passage that you just read that Marissa suffers from a Borderline Personality Disorder?"

"Yes," the doctor answered.

"Will you explain the characteristics of having a Borderline Personality Disorder?"

"Certainly," she answered. "Typically, a person with that disorder will show signs of having a conduct disorder. This person will typically not show signs of remorse. They will show a pervasive action of not respecting the rights of others. They tend to be deceitful and characteristically lie when confronted. They also show a history of conning others."

"But you did not include this in your final diagnosis..." the prosecutor said, prodding for an answer.

"I didn't feel that it was important in the final diagnosis."

"You were hired by the defense team, weren't you?"

"Yes."

"What are you being paid for your testimony?"

"I am paid two hundred and fifty dollars and hour," she answered. "Normally, I charge three hundred an hour but I lowered it for this case."

"How many hours have you billed for this case?" he asked.

The doctor fumbled through her volumes of paperwork and appeared to have found the sheet she was looking for. "I have billed sixty hours in this case including my interview times."

"Do you know what malingering is?" the prosecutor asked.

"Yes," she answered.

"Will you explain the term 'malingering' for the court?"

"This would be what we call 'faking good' or 'faking bad' when a patient answers questions on their various tests."

"In other words, you could say a person would be lying on their tests. Is that a fair assessment of the term?"

"Yes," she answered.

"How do you know when a patient is malingering on these exams?"

"This information is put into a computer. The computer then checks for consistencies and inconsistencies on these various tests."

"Are these tests compared to each other when looking for malingering?"

"Not necessarily. Each test is different from each other so malingering is checked for test to test."

"So you do not compare results from test to test? Is that correct?"

"The system is not set up to perform in that manner."

"Did you compare the results of the 2010 tests to those of the 2013 results?"

"Yes," she answered.

"So you are able to show that her individual responses from 2010 match the responses of the tests taken in 2013?"

"Well, no. It doesn't work that way. We only check that results of these exams match the results of any secondary tests. We do not compare line by line."

"Are you saying that the defendant could not have faked her answers for a desired result?"

"No, I'm not saying that. All I am saying is that the results of all tests are similar and I am confident that these answers were not faked."

"In your experience, have patients shown signs of malingering in the taking of these psychological tests?"

"It happens but I have found that it is rare," she answered. "The computer is very good at showing inconsistencies from test to test. I believe with a reasonable amount of probability that there are no signs of malingering."

The prosecution sat down after finishing with the witness.

The Judge asked the jury if there were any questions and I submitted my folded paper forward to the Bailiff.

I watched as the judge and the lawyers discussed the questions we submitted. My question to the psychologist was "You said the defendant suffers from PTSD. Can you define the root cause of trauma that the PTSD is from as coming from: A) the trauma of the night of the assault, B) the trauma of being arrested or C) the trauma of incarceration?"

The Judge declined to have that question submitted to the witness.

My thought was the question was either too broad or it was too prejudicial toward the defendant. I thought it was a good point, though.

I don't know exactly how I feel about the psychologist's testimony except to say that from what I have seen of Marissa and her past behaviors, I think her telling the truth in any given situation is rare. In that, I am starting to think that her test results would be impacted by her regular action of lying. Why would she suddenly start telling the truth?

The odds of malingering were high given that the psychologist did not first see her until a year after the assault. Marissa would have had plenty of time to think and to manipulate.

I hate to say it in fear of not being open-minded but I was starting to dislike the defendant. She could not be trusted. She manipulates people and I feel like she would manipulate her answers in this multiplicity of subjective examinations.

I think the prosecution was successful in damaging the testimony of this well learned psychologist.

Judge Steinle dismissed the court for spring break. He told us that testimony would resume with the final witness of the defense next Tuesday. Once he told us who the next witness was going to be, I knew that everything resided on that witness...

Absolutely everything!

SPECULATIVELY

We were headed into two weeks of spring break for the trial. It gave me time to catch up on my personal life as well as enjoy a well-deserved break from the trial. Thoughts of the trial had been rolling in my head like a gerbil going crazy on a wheel. Things would tumble over and over again and was especially accelerated by the fact that there was only one witness left for the defense.

Here's where I stood right now based on the evidence presented. I have not made up my mind by any stretch of the imagination and I knew final results would really depend upon what the other jurors perceived. The picture, however, was coming clearer as the days passed.

The night of the assault was marked by Marissa's phone call to 9-1-1 at 2:45 AM. I remember that phone call as sounding disingenuous, hollow and creepy. The evidence shows that prior to that phone call Marissa and Stan were in the bedroom when Dale was attacked. Even further, the blood evidence clearly shows that Marissa was the first recipient of the blood spatter and that Stan was behind her. It is not clear whether Stan was in the room when Dale was first attacked, but it tends to look like Stan came in after the first blows that created the blood spatter.

The opening statements by the defense pointed out that Stan had a gun and that Marissa called emergency services. The question was raised that we should pay attention to the fact that the gun was not used. A theory was coming clear in my head based in part on the five and a half hour interrogation tapes with Marissa.

When one looks at those tapes, tapes that I think we will need to look at again the jury room, one must use a filter to detract truths and lies. We have already learned that much of what Marissa has said were falsehoods.

However, there are little clues that remain. One of them is that Marissa was adamant that she was afraid of guns. If one were to assume that her explanation behind getting the gun were false, saying that she needed it to protect herself from Dale, then a problem is created in why the gun was there in the first place?

It looks like Marissa was planning on Stan firing the gun at some point. I don't find it beyond belief that she was using Stan to be the killer. I think that Stan was reasonable enough not to put himself in a situation where he would use the gun. Besides, the other fact is that there was already a gun in the house owned by Stan. I think Marissa wanted it in his hands to facilitate the idea that he would shoot in self-defense.

The other reason I think she was using Stan to her benefit is because she thought he was too dumb to know any better. I think she was wrong to think that.

Just because Stan had memory problems, it didn't mean he had a loss in his moral compass. I also look at how she behaved after her arrest. I remember the computer expert getting up and speaking of his confession being created on February 4 and then Stan was sucked into confessing on February 9. I don't see Stan as being complicit in the assault but rather see him as a convenient dupe to take the fall.

I also remember the jailhouse tape when Marissa acted surprised that the police wouldn't believe his story about his confession. One would think that she would have known that the confession wouldn't carry. I think she thought people were pretty dumb, and that her plan would work.

One cannot go forward without considering Allen Flore's involvement. I don't find that he was a trustworthy witness and one must filter out truths in his involvement.

The moment I didn't trust him was when he said he was ending a subscription to an adult website and happened to run into Marissa's picture. He had a relationship with her to be sure but the basis of that relationship is tenuous at best.

Consider that her being on this website was akin to prostitution. Why would a normal housewife be putting herself on websites of this nature? It looked to me like he wanted to be a Sugar Daddy because he couldn't get attention elsewhere. Certainly, a major part of their relationship was financial given all the money he had given her. Did he actually think she would pay him back?

Allen Flores had originally lied to police when he said their relationship was not sexual when, in fact, it was. In that, and given the child pornography on his computer, he is very untrustworthy.

There was something beyond this that bothered me.

He had a significant age difference and he was not good looking by any stretch of the imagination. So, why would Marissa be with him to begin with? The obvious answer would be the money but why did she make so many promises to pay it back when she probably didn't even need to? I think he would have given her anything in trade for her company.

The scary part is that Allen had proudly admitted he was certified to sell life insurance. Is it possible that she had a target on him in the very beginning? Did she attack Dale to pay Allen back? Or did she attack Dale for the bigger picture, the life insurance policies?

I think she could have run a tab of a million dollars with Allen and he would have waited forever to get it and bought every story she sold.

He liked the sex with her. It was a drug to him. She liked the money from him. Sex was her way to get it.

I don't feel her debt to Allen was the impetus for the attack. It is starting to look like she may have set this plan in motion for at least a year prior, if not more.

Marissa is an interesting character to say the least. She was married in 1999 and by 2002 she was a stripper? How does that transition happen?

We also know that in 2007 when she met Allen, she was featured on an adult Swingers type website with financial compensation. Where does that come from? Another thing that sticks out is that she said she is deadly afraid of guns but in 2008, she tries to join the police academy. That would be the last career anyone would want if afraid of guns.

Is it possible that she knew that Dale was going to mysteriously die and this would go toward her being the less likely suspect?

She had a thing about lying. Clearly, she lied to everyone and at times for the most unimportant reasons. Was she trying to make herself feel more important? She doesn't lie to protect herself. She lies to get something in return.

A defense psychologist had said that abused people lie to protect themselves. I can understand that to a degree but it doesn't explain why she kept lying about various trusts and inheritances that didn't exist.

One of the biggest questions that has not been answered is where in the world did two hundred and fifty thousand dollars go in less than two years?

We have the ledgers of Allen Flores that say she received the monies but I didn't see any signs where this money went. Wasn't Dale working and employed? Why weren't the bills getting paid? I remember Allen Flores saying that she would show up with past due bills and he would pay them. How was Dale letting bills go long past due?

I'm not saying it is the man of the household's responsibility to pay bills but I would certainly expect him to be involved after ten years of marriage.

The hammer is an issue also. How did it end up in the room? Marissa said she had put up a picture earlier in the day before Dale was attacked and the hammer happened to be in the room.

This didn't quite ring true to me. I remember the crime scene photos of the bedroom where Dale was attacked and it was askew and messy with clothes tossed everywhere.

In my experience, if I hang a picture and judge it's being level, I would naturally want to straighten up the room because you want to see the picture in relation to its surroundings. I may be reaching but it is odd that the hammer happened to be within reach.

We heard very little about Dale in the trial except how he spoke to us in the face of death.

How was he paying the bills? Did he know about the depth of the relationship between her and Allen? Did he know she was a stripper in 2002? Did he know about the website she was on? Did he know she lied as frequently as she did? I would expect he knew of some of her behaviors.

Most importantly to the defense team of Marissa: I don't see the abuse that they speak of. We heard of a black eye and learned that her numerous stories of visits to local hospitals were hogwash. The neighbors and friends who testified could not definitively say they had ever seen Dale hurt Marissa. The best they could come up with was a black eye, of unknown origin and they felt tension between Marissa and Dale.

This does not show a pattern of abuse and doesn't support her story that Dale attacked her the night she said he raped her. There was semen on the bed but that does nothing more than to show a natural expectation between a husband and wife. Is it possible that she had sex with him that night with the intent to show that as a basis for rape?

The interrogation tapes had her telling us that she kept going out to the garage all night to smoke cigarettes, because something was bothering her and she felt all this restlessness. Is it possible that her restlessness was due to her building up courage to lay the killing blows to his skull?

She said at some point in the tapes that when he attacked her, he had said 'this pussy's mine'. That bothers me because I don't feel that a husband of ten years would say that to his wife. It sounds like something from a pornography tape or something from a crummy movie. It doesn't sound natural.

Up to this point, the biggest factor that was going against Marissa was Travis Tatro, the bouncer whom she had dated when she was a stripper. Like I said earlier, I don't see a reason for him to lie and his story was consistent with everything else we had heard about Marissa.

The close of court had signaled that the final defense witness was coming forward. I don't know that this witness would realize how much was on her back. It was said that the final witness would be Rhiannon, the oldest daughter who would have been thirteen at the time of the incident. She was one of three other people in the house aside from Dale, Marissa and Stan.

The other girls had been said to be sleeping when the police arrived that morning so I can understand why they might not have value as a witness. However, the police had said the thirteen-year-old girl was awake behind a closed bedroom door when they arrived.

Did she hear the incident? Was she aware of the abuse that Marissa said she had suffered? What did she think when they were going on trips to Orlando with Allen Flores? Had she seen Marissa abused in the past?

These were only a few of the many questions on my mind at the recess for Spring Break. She had the power to validate or invalidate much of the testimony we heard. In that, I don't want to speculate further until we meet her face to face. She literally had her mother's life in her hands.

One could not argue the forensics. The picture was clear on who had swung the hammer. The real question at the end of the day was why?

Would Rhiannon have the information needed to clear her mother? Was she biased? What did she hear? What did she witness?

It looked like Dale was sleeping on his left side. It is unclear whether a light was on except possibly the dimness of the television splayed long shadows across the room. The time was early in the morning.

A hammer contacted his head from the right side. It struck at least four times spraying the walls and ceiling with blood.

Dale didn't know it was coming.

Did Rhiannon hear the crushing blows?

DAY 19

THE ISLAND

The day before we were released for spring break, I was unwittingly trapped in the jury room restroom. I was drying my hands off when I heard Cherie speaking with Butthead. Apparently, the rest of the jury had left for the week.

"Butthead, are you the one who wrote the letter to the Judge?"

My hand was on the door handle.

"That was me," he answered.

"What are you doing? Do you know you made us all look bad?"

"We couldn't hear the recordings. What was I supposed to do?"

"Butthead, leave it alone. You know we'll get to hear this stuff when we get back here. What's up with the attitude you displayed?"

"I didn't know the Judge would get mad," he answered.

"Don't tell me that," Cherie said. "You knew he would get mad and if you didn't know, then you need to pay better attention."

"I'm sorry."

"While we're at it," Cherie continued, "let's keep our noses out of the Court's business. If the elevators are slow, then they are slow. There's no need to be pestering the city with this nonsense. Your job is to be a juror," she said firmly.

"I'm sorry about that," he said. "I thought people would want my help."

"I understand that. The best help you can give us is what you are hired for. You are here to deliberate and you are not here to change the system. These things have been going on for over two hundred years and we don't need you trying to fix everything."

"Sorry about that," he said.

"While I'm at it, will you please quiet down in the jury box? I'm tired of getting dirty looks from the Court Reporter."

"I'm not that loud," he defended.

"You are loud, Butthead. I sit eight people away from you and I can hear you drink your water, unwrap your mints and the noises you make when you are playing with your three-ring binder. We don't need to hear everything you do," Cherie said. "I've been hard enough on you. Just think about what I said and have a terrific weekend. I appreciate your work and I appreciate your hearing me out."

I waited at the door until I heard someone leave. I came out of the restroom and saw Cherie picking up her bag. I pretended I hadn't heard anything.

Cherie looked at me with surprise when I came out. I grabbed my leftover pizza from lunch and picked up my bag.

"Shall we go?" I asked her.

"Sure," she said.

We walked down the hallway and pressed the button, waiting for the elevator. A few minutes later, the door opened. We stepped inside and were surprised to see that Judge Steinle had followed us in. I was holding my leftover pizza horizontally in a box.

The Judge hit the button for the lobby.

"Nice tie," the Judge said to me.

"Oh, thank you," I said.

"I don't have a neck," he said. "I can't wear ties."

I smiled.

"I like leftover pizza," he said.

"It's from a new place called 'Pizza Unlimited'," I said.

"I have a stone brick oven at home," he offered. "It keeps the crust from getting soggy."

"That's a good idea," I said.

Cherie and I looked at each other. It was an honor to be in the same elevator as the Judge.

The doors opened signifying our stop at the lobby. We stepped out and went on our way.

Being in the jury room was akin to the people one might know at an Alcoholics Anonymous meeting. Everyone knew each other by their first names only. We drank coffee and enjoyed snacks brought in by other juror members. A meeting room carries secrets that must remain untold. A recovering alcoholic cannot tell stories of drunken conquests while a jury cannot talk about incidents they've witnessed in a courtroom.

There was a tension that always existed that no one wanted to talk about. We were deep into the trial and we knew the time was steadily drawing near when the final selection of twelve would happen. We had lost one juror very early in the trial. There were still three on the chopping block.

Many of us joked that we should be able to kick people off the island but the system only allows a random lottery, which is held prior to the case being handed to the jury.

There was part of me that wanted to come in early every day to begin organizing the four hundred and thirty-six pieces of evidence put before us. Even though we had built evidence logs, much of the evidence was not presented in numerical order; which then created a potential organization issue. I didn't want to jinx things and I felt if I got carried away putting in extra time, it would certainly jinx me off the jury. I likened it to a twist on Murphy's Law. It would figure that you did a bunch of extra work only to find it was for naught.

I enjoyed coming into the jury room every day. We had a good energy between us.

The first person you would see is Butthead, sitting at one end of the center table, his laptop open in front of him. He usually had a Bluetooth device in his ear and would be talking computer tech things seemingly into the air.

Butthead works for a nationally known computer company. I'm guessing he was a tech guy. He's been married thirty-five years and I would suspect his wife is a very patient and understanding woman.

Seated next to Butthead was Sunny. She was retired and her kids were happy to have her out of the house. She laughed when they said that jury duty was her job. She always brought in her lunch, and I usually joined her at the *Change of Venue*, located in front of the courthouse. She said that she loved lying in the sun by the pool and working on her tan, that went well with her blond hair. She always had a smile and she was a pleasure to be around.

Parker sat on the left side of the table. He carried a tablet with a Spider-Man portfolio case with him daily along with some ear buds. He was a salesman for a nationally known life insurance company but he looked more like a computer guy. He always had a gadget or game to play on his tablet and was happy to introduce others to those games. Free was always the best price.

Parker had an interesting hobby. I liked to collect 'Hot Wheels' and he liked to collect tennis shoes. He owned all the best Air Jordan sport shoes and limited editions that people would wait in line all day to be the first to receive them. Many of these shoes were worth hundreds of dollars a pair. One of us asked him the value of his collection and casually responded that it was worth upwards of seventy thousand dollars He owned ninety-five pairs of shoes...never worn.

Parker's computer rival sat across from him and was certainly my pick as the potential jury foreman. Cherie was always in early and ready to go, all the while juggling her management job. She had all the qualities of being a good leader. She was focused, organized, prepared and got along with everyone. Her vote for foreperson was etched in stone after my hearing her talk with Butthead.

Wings, was a sharp-looking lady that one might equate to being a soccer mom of sorts. She was extremely involved in her kids' affairs and showed she was always there to support them.

Wings, was also a flight attendant for a major airline. She worked a schedule of "Three up, four down" which meant she flew three days a week and her four days were spent on the jury. I couldn't tell you how many times that she would be leaving court and by the evening she would be in a faraway land such as Tokyo or some other far corner of the world.

Wings and Lucy always sat next to each other and were like peas in a pod. They had become friends instantly. One could always hear them whispering back and forth.

It looked like they had been best friends forever. Lucy was a tall dark-haired girl that belonged on the cover of Vogue Magazine. I could picture her driving a Lexus SUV and living in the well-to-do Scottsdale area. I was jealous when she said she was going to Cabo San Lucas, Mexico for spring break. She was smart and had a great and infectious laugh.

Seated across from her was Annie, who was one of my smoker friends. She had a large family and they were always over visiting. I liked the sound of her cousins coming over for the week in their RV. She almost enjoyed court as a means of escaping from home for a little peace of mind.

Jeebs was seated next to her. He was a quiet but jocular guy with a great disposition. I loved his sense of humor. One could watch him as he listened to other people discussing something at the table and you could swear he was up to something with a little smile on face. It was as if he knew of something humorous that nobody else was aware of yet. He was a great person to talk with.

Bruce always sat to the right of me. He had an extremely pleasant disposition and was glad as hell that he was retired. He used to manage a nationally known computer-shipping department. He was always dressed in a pressed shirt with matching pressed Khaki pants. Every time I came in the jury room to sit down, he always had a warm handshake. He loved tooling around on his laptop checking his latest stock values.

Seated to the left of me was Victoria. She always showed up wearing a professional looking blouse and neat skirt. She was friendly and had a great giggle. She could be seen reading a book or chewing on some animal crackers that she had bagged from home. She was into the "Divergence" series as we moved through the trial. She had a "Live to read and read to live" personality and would often be seen discussing the latest books on the market with Althea and Doc.

Doc sat next to Victoria and always wore something bright. She was the pharmacist who had the family that loved her to death and she always had great beagle stories since she owned two of the little troublemakers.

She was another one of my smoking buddies. She was easily considered the loudest of jurors with her hearty laugh. I referred to her as one of my "Homies" whom I would congregate with in the smoking area every day after lunch outside in the Change of Venue. Wings would joke that I was going to see one of my "Peeps".

Althea sat next to Doc and was great to talk with. She was married to a man she loved. There was something about her that was very endearing and I can't put my finger on what it was but I can say she was a special person. She was in charge of knowing how to get our paychecks from the Jury Commissioners Office.

Jarod was a fun guy. I'm not sure of his ethnicity but he was dark-skinned and may have been Puerto Rican or Jamaican. I can hear him laughing as he reads this, and will probably ask why I thought that. He always dressed extremely casual and his head was shaved on the sides but he left the top long and wavy, almost like an Elvis wave coming across the top. I joked that he missed a spot right after a haircut he had gotten. He was single and worked for a nationally known company's warehouse distribution center.

Then, there was Ted. He worked for a restaurant but had a dream of being a professional dancer. He dressed casual like Jarod but brought it to new levels. One day he work a Pink Floyd T-shirt with a collared Ralph Lauren long sleeve shirt hanging unbuttoned and untucked in his pants. He didn't like ironing his clothes for added effect.

We nicknamed him Ted because he oftentimes wore a hoodie with sunglasses. It was getting warmer out so he didn't wear his signature attire as often as he did at the beginning of the trial. He had an extremely easygoing personality and we got along especially given our similar jobs in the restaurant business. He was twenty-five with a child and girlfriend at home.

I can comfortably say that he was Sydney's thorn in her side with his punctuality issues.

I never wanted to be the juror who arrived late for risk of facing the judge's wrath. I told him to set his clocks ahead all over his house to fifteen minutes ahead and he'd never worry about being late again.

A story got into the jury room from the news. Someone had heard about a court reporter who had been busted for writing, "I hate my job" over and over again for the duration of thirty trials. I couldn't imagine the cost of all the mistrials she caused.

It reminded me of Stephen King's, "The Shining" when Jack Nicholson had written, "All work and no play makes Jack a dull boy," for the duration of a book.

I couldn't help thinking that our court reporter was probably writing, "I hate the jury, I hate the jury, I hate the jury," for the duration of our trial.

Three of us were going to be pulled off the island and I hoped I was not one of them.

"DALE, BUDDY, STAY WITH ME..."

The day began with Rhiannon Harrell taking the stand. She was stunningly beautiful at age eighteen. She wore a red formal coat with a white dress and matching red shoes. Her hair was blonde and was remarkably different looking than her mother, Marissa.

Rhiannon was eighteen and one got the feeling that she was well protected. She was thirteen at the time of the assault. She was going to college in Prescott, Arizona, about two hours north of Phoenix.

Her voice was soft, delicate and spoke in a way that a teenager would speak. She held an innocence that enveloped her. She seemed balanced and comfortable in her own skin but she was nervous.

I noticed there were no cameras in the courtroom.

Mr. Tavasoli of the defense asked her questions, as we knew she was the final defense witness, our curiosity was piqued. I think he handled her very well and he was delicate and lighthearted in his approach. Overall, I think she was good for the defense in one respect but had little value in the other respect.

She described her life with Dale and Marissa as tumultuous. That was clearly understood when she spoke of Dale and Marissa both having affairs with other people.

Rhiannon spoke particularly of Dale coming home smelling like other women's perfume and carrying lipstick smears on the side of his neck.

Of particular interest was when she spoke of violence in the household and I believed her.

We had a remarkable similarity in that I was the oldest in my family and understood when she said there were times that she had to protect her two younger sisters.

She saw both Marissa hit Dale and Dale hit Marissa while admitting that Dale hit Marissa more often.

I think all of us understood the personal hell she had gone through while living under that household. Violence permeates everything and becomes abundantly clearer when she spoke of using their dressers to block the door so that the violence wouldn't come in their room.

She believed that her parents liked to hold the façade of being the All-American family. I knew that feeling all too well and I believed I saw her being genuine and seemingly untarnished by the experience she had gone through.

She was asked about her relationship with Allen Flores and if she knew that he and her mom were having an affair.

"Of course, I knew," she said. "They would be kissing and holding hands in the front seat of the car."

"Did Dale know about Allen?" Mr. Basta, the prosecutor asked.

"Well, when he found out, he started crying," she said. "It was a 'No-No' to talk about it. We all knew better."

She was later asked if Dale knew that Marissa was going to Orlando with Allen and the girls. She responded that he had helped pack the car for the one week trip.

"Did you have fun in Orlando?" she was asked.

"Of course," she answered. "It's Disney World!"

There was another point mentioned by Rhiannon recalling a time when Dale got upset one Christmas because the presents from Allen Flores were better than the presents he had given her that year.

"Was Allen ever at the house?"

"Of course not," she answered. "It's common sense. You wouldn't have two men dating the same woman in the same house."

We learned from her that Dale worked but we did not learn how much money he made. It made me wonder again, where did all the money disappear to that Marissa borrowed from Flores?

The prosecution was able to draw some critical information out of Rhiannon.

This is how I pictured it from Rhiannon's story...

Rhiannon woke with a start. She looked at the red LED light on her clock and it stared back reading 2:37 in the morning. She wondered what kind of dream she was having as she rubbed her eyes.

For a moment, she remembered the night before when she and her parents had gone out for hot chocolate. She felt crappy for getting kicked out of school. She thought the whole thing was ridiculous.

How was it her fault that somebody wrote sexual stuff in her school notebook? At least her parents were being cool about it, she thought.

They hadn't been that cool when they found out she was having a sexual relationship with David, the son of her mom's boyfriend. They were pissed. She was grounded for a month.

She rubbed her eyes again. She couldn't tell if it was a dream. She thought she heard, "Dale, buddy, wake up. Stay with me."

Her room was dark as she went to her door and carefully opened it. She looked down the hall toward her parent's room but the door was closed.

Rhiannon crawled back into bed thinking she was having strange dreams. A little while later, she heard clanking and mumbling and something that sounded like wheels rolling on the tile floor in the hallway. She was just getting irritated when her door swung open.

"Are you okay?" a policeman asked.

"Yes," she answered. "What's going on?"

"What's your name?" the policeman asked.

"Rhiannon."

"How old are you?"

"Thirteen," she answered, still wondering why this man was in her room.

"I need you to stay in here with the door closed. Do you understand, Rhiannon?"

"Sure but what's going on?"

"Just stay here and we'll advise you later. Go back to bed, okay?"

"Okay," she answered. The door pulled closed with a click.

It wasn't fair that adults never told you what was going on.

She went back to bed, never knowing that her life would be forever changed from that moment forward.

The defense rested.

The first was her dream and who was telling Dale to wake up. At first, I thought it was the paramedics she heard and then I realized that the paramedics didn't get there until 3:14 in the morning.

I believe Marissa's phone call to emergency services was at 2:45 in the morning, which means that it was Stan Cook's voice she was hearing. The crying she heard could have been Marissa but it may have been Dale.

We finally had a time-line. We knew from Rhiannon's testimony that the attack was on or before 2:37 AM. We know the first call to 911 was at 2:45 AM.

What happened in the eight minutes before that call to 911?

There was a second unrelated item that was on my mind. What was the location of the hammer when Marissa said she used it to defend herself from Dale?

We saw the bloodied hammer on a table near the door when the police got there. But, I can't remember where in the room she claimed she was hanging a picture when explaining how the hammer happened to be there. I wanted to see where the picture was hung, because the hammer would logically be closest to that side. I thought she said this picture was hung on the other side of the room. I don't know why this bothered me but it did.

We were recessed for lunch and returned with the prosecution side lining up rebuttal witnesses and they were very strong.

The first on the stand was the returning Detective Mike Bishop whom we had seen before and always saw sitting at the prosecution table. He essentially exposed a couple of more lies.

The first he exposed was that there was never a protective order filed by Marissa against Dale. I think this was in the interrogation tapes, which we'll review later.

The second lie that he exposed was that she had never applied for the police department despite saying she had spent two months training and claimed to be a member of the Citizen's Academy.

Why wasn't I surprised? It seemed that everything she said was a fabrication.

The next witness was the attractive Dr. Janeen DeMarte.

She looked familiar. I couldn't figure out where I remember her from.

She was a psychologist who received her Doctorate training at Michigan State University. She had long dark hair and wore a very conservative gray ladies business suit. She looked like she was in her late twenties or thirty at best. She knew her terminology and one could tell she was well educated, spoke well and looked like she knew her craft.

She was a damaging witness in that, without her saying it, malingering had damaged Marissa's psychological tests so badly that they made themselves invalid. She spoke of the detail of the Minnesota Multi-Phasic Inventory 2, as if it had been rendered to garbage after Marissa completed the various psychological examinations.

She further spoke of the Personality Assessment Index and how that, too was rendered useless by further malingering. It looked to her like Marissa was purposely answering questions as to how she thought they should be answered as opposed to actual truth.

Dr. DeMarte certainly didn't help things for the defense when she said they were using outdated tests; which gave outdated results. Hence, their diagnosis of Marissa wasn't worth the paper it was printed on.

At this point, does it surprise anyone that she would lie on her tests?

The defense did not help matters any with this witness. Upon first approach, Mr. Tavasoli was asking her about her education.

"So you got your doctorate at the University of Michigan?"

"No," Dr. DeMarte answered. "It was actually Michigan State University."

Mr. Tavasoli chuckled. "Oh, I'm sorry. Big Ten school," he finished with a chuckle.

I'm not sure if that was a mistake or a calculated mistake. Was he trying to make less of her Michigan State education? If he was, it didn't carry as a good joke and probably irritated those of us from the Midwest. One should know that Phoenix has very few people who were born here. Only forty-three percent of Arizonians are actually from Arizona. I, being from Michigan, didn't appreciate the joke.

I kept looking at Dr. DeMarte and feeling like I had seen her before. At first, I was thinking that she had been an earlier witness.

I looked toward the gallery and saw Juan Martinez again, the prosecutor of the Jodi Arias trial and then it dawned on me. I had seen her testify in that trial about a year prior. It's funny but I remember trusting her then and I trusted her now.

The defense tried to play on the fact that she was young and therefore did not have a lot of experience as a certified Doctor of Psychology. I don't think it carried much weight. She had it together and there was a believability factor that I'm not sure Dr. Karp of the defense had.

The prosecution's last witness was Detective Scott Zuberbeuhler, the detective we had previously seen, who specialized in computer forensics and his testimony was clearly damaging.

He was able to say that on February 4, 2009, Marissa had done multiple searches for "using abuse as a defense in a trial". She had done this search four or five times.

I remember February 4th as the date when the confession letter was created for Stan on the very same computer.

It appears she was very busy that day.

The Judge told us at the end of the day that tomorrow would probably be the last day for defense rebuttal witnesses. The end was near and we were coming close to hearing closing arguments. One could feel the speed of the trial pick up in intensity.

This intensity was clearly present in the jury room. Wings took charge and asked Sydney, our bailiff, what the next steps were. She wanted to know because we all wanted to know when the lottery to remove jurors from the 'Island' was going to happen.

Sydney was able to say that she would be pulling the three numbers prior to the case being handed to the jury. Three of us would then be 'On-Call' for the duration of the next two stages of the trial in the event one of the remaining twelve would not be able to complete their task.

The end drew close as we realized that our duty was about to come into play...or not.

DAY 21

BOTTOM OF THE NINTH

Today was an incredibly short day with the prosecution bringing forward their final four rebuttal witnesses. That is not to say that the intensity didn't pick up ten times. It was on all of our minds after having an idea from yesterday that things were quickly drawing to a close. Specifically, I think most of us knew that soon three would be kicked off the island into the proverbial alternate sea and none of us wanted to be that person.

I was so nervous that my hands were cool and sweaty.

The first witness that Mr. Basta brought forward filled a gaping question in my head and I had to work for it. Guy Triesky and his wife, Harriet, were called separately and not in that order. They were Dale's employers at the time of his death.

Both husband and wife testified similarly that Dale had been with the company for ten years and he was a mechanical engineer that helped design machinery. They were the owners and Dale was a trusted employee who had never shown any sign of anger or violence in the full ten years he was there. They were a pleasant hard-working American family who had owned their business in Gilbert for the better part of thirty years. I found them trustworthy.

I detected a sadness in both of them, which told me that they had been victims. They lost not only a trusted employee but a close friend.

There was one thing that wasn't answered in my head and at the end of testimony, since it hadn't been asked, I simply asked on the jury questionnaire form and handed it to the bailiff, Sydney.

We, the jury, through the Judge, simply asked Guy Triesky, "Was Dale a full-time employee and what was his salary?"

Guy answered his question toward us, "Dale made $83, 000 a year. He was a designer for us."

I wasn't sure if I had missed it throughout the trial but I don't remember anything coming up about how Dale provided for his family. As a matter of fact, it is noted that you rarely hear about the victim except as they speak through the evidence. In this case, the only evidence that told us anything about Dale were pictures taken after his assault. We had images of his damaged body taken by those first on the scene, to the pictures of him lying in a hospital bed with half his skull missing and, finally, the coroner's depiction of him at autopsy. You really didn't hear from him through other evidence, in part because so much of it was Marissa's creation.

His salary determination gave him life. One could see that he didn't live outlandishly and he was providing for his family. That, then, begs the other question:

What was Marissa doing with the expenditure of a quarter of a million dollars in a span of two years? It doesn't make sense unless she was a gambler or a drug abuser. Where is the material manifestation of all this money? I don't see drug abuse but I remember Allen Flores giving her money for the casino aside from the night that she wanted to send Travis Tatro down there.

I'm just wondering if she did have an issue with gambling. I can't see where the money went otherwise and wouldn't Dale have noticed her buying lavish things? We're definitely delving into this in the jury room, provided we make it to the jury room after tomorrow's closing arguments.

I'm surprised that the prosecution did not point this out as being important.

At least we now knew that he was working and stable financially. Or, apparently so from what we have seen.

The next two witnesses were both friends of Dale's. One friend had known him for the better part of twenty years after meeting in high school. Again, they were both similar in testimony in that both said Dale was not violent.

There was a moment when Mr. Basta asked Dale's friend if he had witnessed violence against Marissa and the reverse if he had seen violence against him.

"I do remember one time around Christmas," he said on the stand. "We were all just hanging out and Dale cracked a joke and Marissa slugged him in the ribs really hard."

"How do you know it hurt him?" Mr. Basta prodded.

"We were all laughing and I heard her fist hit his ribs and you could tell it hurt him by the way he choked on his laughing," he said.

The prosecutor asked both friends, "Were you ever witness to any bruising's or marks on either Dale or Marissa?"

"No," they both responded at separate times.

The prosecution rested their case.

The Judge dismissed the jury and brought us back in moments later and handed us an eighteen-page Jury Instructions packet. He then informed us that closing arguments would be the following day. Furthermore, a final jury consisting of twelve jurors and three alternates would also be chosen. The alternates would be on-call for the rest of the process.

The Judge read out loud all eighteen pages. We read along with him but I can tell you that none of us was paying attention. We were all wondering if the process so far had been all for naught? We had also built a bond with each other that none of us really expected.

We knew we were going to miss three people and each of us hoped it wouldn't be ourselves.

I couldn't help thinking that the tension inside is so much like the feelings months ago, when we went through the first three steps of jury selection. It just kept going through your brain over and over, like the Gerbil wheel, hoping and praying that your name would not be pulled. Making deals with God so that you wouldn't become an alternate juror was the call of the day.

There is a commitment level in the head that is afraid to fully wrap itself around the potential journey of which you are to embark upon once you make the final twelve. The mind doesn't want to commit full responsibility until the figurative jury keys are handed to it. We don't own a responsibility until that happens.

I likened the situation to an AA mantra in that you are best to think only one day at a time. Just one day at a time.

The tension was certainly accentuated by the fact that you can't talk about the trial. In a lengthy trial, you learn the habit of not talking about it. Now that we are at the end of this phase, I find I really want to talk about it. I don't want to imagine sitting in the gallery as an alternate juror and still not be able to talk about this event until the end.

I couldn't wait to discuss this with the other jurors wondering what they thought of Marissa, Dale and especially, Travis Tatro.

It just occurred to me that the Judge has yet to answer my question about being the thirteenth juror.

I have to remember, "One day at a time."

At the end of the day, whether it's by lottery or by God's choice, we would know after closing arguments.

Whatever will be, will be and I don't think I'm going to get a wink of sleep tonight...

DAY 22

...AND THEN THERE WERE TWELVE

The first thing we did when we got in the jury room before the start of the day was to exchange phone numbers. I had collected a few throughout so that I wouldn't be in a panic on the last day rushing to get fifteen phone numbers. I only needed Wings, Lucy, Parker, Sunny, Butthead and Victoria. One didn't know whose journey would end today.

I sat in my usual spot in the corner next to Bruce. As always, he was dressed in a perfectly ironed shirt with crisp khaki pants. He was filling out a jury question form. After greeting him, I asked him if he was okay.

"This will be my last day," he said as he folded his jury question in half.

"What?"

"I went to the doctor yesterday and it looks like I have prostate cancer."

"I am so sorry," I said not knowing exactly what to say.

"We're getting a second opinion but it looks like we caught it early," he said.

It was if someone had told him he needs a new alternator in his car. It was just something that happened and he would deal with it accordingly. He was calm and level headed and I could only hope to be that way in the same situation.

It was a bizarre way to start the day.

The closing arguments were pretty much as anticipated with the prosecution beginning the day, followed by the defense closing argument, and then completed with the prosecution's last word in a final rebuttal closing. The arguments were much the same as the opening statements, and much of what was spoken will be delved into once this gets to the jury room.

I think what we wanted in the closing arguments is not exactly what we got. A juror goes into the reception of closing arguments knowing clearly that like opening statements, it is not evidence. In that, there is an expectation of a picture being drawn. We want to know what happened and how it happened in a clear concise way. We needed the evidence to make sense.

I respect both attorney teams and know that it requires a significant amount of education to be an attorney. Further, for an attorney to be part of a death penalty trial, experience is a given. Given there is mutual respect for both sides, I follow with what I think might have worked better or what did work well without going into the details of what was said.

I like Mr. Basta and how he handled witnesses throughout the trial. One did not feel vindictiveness, anger or emotions getting out of line. He had a strong ability to connect with any witness throughout the trial. He had a simple flair without being theatrical.

Mr. Basta was a very detailed attorney. He would have his notes at the podium and could always be seen holding a pen in one hand. He would question the witness in a series of questions and then walk back to the podium, click his pen and check something off his notes. It was very procedural and gave the feeling that he was extremely organized.

He handled the closing arguments in a similar manner by stepping forward to the jury, explaining a series of thoughts and then finishing by going back to the podium and checking a note off his list.

His approach was methodical as he walked us down the path of evidence without using all four hundred and thirty-six pieces that were in his arsenal. I think he only picked about fifteen that he thought important. The jury would be able to touch all the evidence so he didn't need to go deeply into it.

The best thing he did in his closing arguments is that he somehow managed to find each and every juror's eyes person by person. I didn't have to talk to the other jurors to know that he looked them in the eye. I think that act alone is the most powerful thing that a lawyer can do at this stage of the game. It shows honesty, conviction, engagement, and most importantly, lends itself to believability in the words a lawyer is saying.

I was sitting in my regular seat, which is lower front and far right as an end cap to the jury box. I always led the jury out when we were called back to the jury room. It would have been position eight if one were to count the jurors as they filed in. It is also probably the most difficult spot for an attorney to connect eyes with, yet Mr. Basta caught my eyes at least three or four times.

I wish Mr. Basta had painted a better picture of what happened just prior to 2:37 in the morning when Rhiannon saw her clock and first heard the event. I wanted Mr. Basta to put me in the bedroom and walk me through the attack. His presentation felt somewhat fragmented as if we still had a few pieces missing in a jigsaw puzzle and it was up to us to put it together.

I really wanted to know what happened between 2:37 and 2:45 a.m. in the minutes between Dale's attack and the first call to 9-1-1.

There was a pair of shorts that we saw early in the trial and Mr. Basta presented that these shorts had not been in their original position as to when the assault happened. I related to those shorts that Marissa had called ugly in her interrogation tapes. You see, I had the very same shorts at home.

Mr. Basta was able to point us in the direction of realizing that those shorts were taken off Dale just after he had been hit at least four times with a hammer. He was able to show the blood stains on the inside of the waistband pointed toward those shorts being pulled off Dale by someone, and it may have explained why he was lying on the floor with his head being juxtaposed next to the dresser. This was shown in the photograph taken by the first police responder.

The other thing he pointed out were the tissues found in the trashcan in the bathroom. I remember wondering what the significance was of the tissues a long time earlier in the trial. These tissues were found with Dale's semen. Mr. Basta pointed out that the whole of the bedroom and bathroom was a mess except that the trashcan held no liner with just the tissues lying in the can. It looked like this evidence was set up and was not consistent with the rest of the room.

This did paint an ugly picture. I picture Dale going to sleep on the wrong side of the bed when Marissa had just had sex with him. Was it possible that she had saved his semen on the tissue and placed them in the can to support her potential claim of his raping her?

I visualized Dale lying on his left side after having his head bashed in. Someone had taken those shorts off him while he was bleeding and I wondered if that attempt was done while the button was still closed on the waist. It would explain why he had what looked like shin burns. Is it possible that this was done in such a frantic haste that the shorts gathered around his legs causing the shin burns?

Mr. Tavasoli of the defense took an hour and a half to complete his closing arguments. I liked Mr. Tavasoli in that he had been very personal with witnesses throughout the trial. He had a talent for making people feel comfortable in what may have been an uncomfortable situation.

I speak with all due respect for his team and understand the incredible amount of work that must go into defending this case. However, I don't know that his closing arguments had the impact that a jury would have wanted. There were essentially two things that really bothered me.

The first was that his approach to us also seemed very fragmented. It did not draw a picture of what happened nor draw us a picture of who Marissa was and why this happened.

The second critical item had to do with his eye contact. I remember a long time ago in speech class where the teacher had advised that if you are really nervous, a good trick is to look above the audience you are speaking to and this will ensure that you don't become intimidated. I felt Mr. Tavasoli was doing that and it created a distance between the jury and his arguments.

Mr. Tavasoli didn't make eye contact with me once and I doubt whether he made eye contact with the other jurors as well. I know that the arguments are not evidence and I know it's not required that you look in your audience's eyes. I do know that it would have helped.

He did leave me with something to think of in our decision making process but I wasn't sure the evidence had been submitted for us to review. He spoke of Marissa and I believe he was alluding to sexual abuse prior to 1992.

My first reaction is that I didn't see any evidence in trial of it and my second reaction is that the defense didn't present a lot of evidence to stand on to begin with.

Sexual abuse would make sense in Marissa's case and might explain why she doesn't seem to have consistent relationships with partners. It feels like she is disconnected in some way and whenever she does have a relationship, she is looking to have another relationship. It might explain her cattiness in being a stripper three years after she was married. It may further explain why she didn't care that Allen Flores had recorded their sexual escapades, although I take anything Allen says with more than a grain of salt.

The afternoon was over before we knew it and the judge sent us back to the jury room for the final time as a group of fifteen. I had a pit in my stomach all day and it made it hard to focus on the closing arguments.

I was confident that I had a back-up plan in case I lost my full-time position as a juror. I figured that if was selected as an alternate, I would still come to court every day and sit in the gallery if that was legal. I would then contact the other jurors at the end of the trial to find out what happened in the jury room and how they reached their decisions.

We were in the jury room when Lucy said she had a dream that herself, Jarod and Butthead would be the alternates. I kept feeling that it would be numbers one, seven and eleven that would be selected as alternates. All my superstitions were alive and well as I hoped for the best.

Before we knew it, we called back to the jury box and we could see Sydney at the front of the courtroom as she reached into a box to pull juror numbers. I looked over and saw Cherie sitting with her fingers crossed. Tension and anticipation was on all of our faces.

"Numbers one, four and eleven are our alternate jurors," the judge said.

I said, "Thank you, Lord," to myself realizing that I didn't hear the number thirteen.

The judge asked the selected jurors to stand up and they were escorted to the back. Lucy and I had been very close in our expectations with Jarod and herself being picked as alternates. Bruce automatically became an alternate because of his pending surgery and his note to the Judge. The juror numbers were one, seven and eleven which was pretty close to my guess in the end.

We were dismissed to the jury room and as I walked by Sydney, I said, "Thank you for not pulling my number."

Sydney smiled and said, "You're welcome!"

I was sad to see the three alternates go as we had all developed a closeness that I don't think any of us would ever forget. I was especially sad for Lucy because her heart had been in this process the whole way and one could see that by the furious notes that she had taken throughout.

The three alternates would remain on call and would return when the next two phases of the trial resumed. They would remain as alternates unless one of the remaining twelve left their position. The worst part was that their book of notes throughout the trial would be turned into the court and subsequently destroyed. I kept thinking, "All that work for nothing..."

I couldn't believe it.

I was a juror and I was now a part of "We, the Jury."

WE, THE JURY

Eleven of us were seated in the jury room at 10:25 AM with deliberations scheduled to start at 10:30. We had decided on that time before we left court the day prior.

Sydney looked in and counted the jurors and looked at her watch. I looked around me and saw Jeebs, Parker, Annie, Butthead, Doc, Victoria, Althea, Cherie, Sunny and Wings.

"I'll be back in five minutes," Sydney said, shutting the door.

Two minutes later, Ted came in. It was warmer out so he no longer wore a hoodie but he still had the sunglasses. He found his usual seat.

"Sorry, guys," he said. "It took forever getting up the elevator. Butthead, you ought to call someone about that."

Butthead looked at him. I don't think he was amused.

Sydney came in a minute later acting as if nothing happened. She was in mother hen mode as she gathered our attention.

"I want to explain how this will work before you get started. The first thing that I want to explain is the evidence. The bulk of it will be brought to you in these two boxes," she said.

Two file boxes were sitting on the end of the jury table. One could see hundreds of plastic sleeves and another box had hundreds of photos.

"This is the evidence list," she said, raising a packet of paper about thirty pages thick. "Each item is on this list. Each item is in the order of the list. You may look at the item if the item's seal has been broken. You may not open an item if it is still sealed. If you want to see an item that is sealed, you will complete a jury questionnaire form like you have been using and the foreperson will sign it. Who is your foreperson?"

We all looked around the table, as we had not yet selected one.

"I nominate Cherie as foreperson," Wings suddenly said.

"Me, too," I said.

"Me, too," Jeebs said.

"I'm good with it," Parker volunteered.

"There you go," Wings said jubilantly. "Is everyone good with Cherie as foreperson?"

We all agreed.

"Are you sure?" asked Sydney.

We agreed again and Cherie was foreperson.

"Then, it's settled, Sydney said. "Anything that needs to be unsealed must be requested by all of you and Cherie will sign it before the request is presented to the court."

Sydney gave Cherie a folder with blank questionnaire forms.

"You may only look at one piece of evidence at a time," she explained. "Further, you are to place the evidence back where you got it. Whenever the jury leaves the jury room, the evidence is inventoried against this list. Are we clear on this?"

"Yes," Cherie said while we nodded in agreement.

"I will need the foreperson to give me a schedule of deliberations," she said looking at Cherie. "You are not to be late to deliberations and you must stay in the jury room except for the lunch hour. You may pick your schedule as you wish and submit it to me."

Cherie nodded and made a note.

"There are pieces of evidence that are not in here but are available to you. Again, you will submit an official request."

Althea raised her hand. "Are these requests made in open court?"

"Yes," Sydney answered. The Judge and both attorneys will be aware of your requests". Sydney opened another folder.

"These are your jury verdict forms. There is a form for 'Not Guilty' and one for 'Guilty'. The foreperson will sign and date this form. This form will then be given to me when the Judge requests it in court."

"I understand," Cherie said, taking the folder.

"You will ring the buzzer behind the microwave when you need me. You will ring the buzzer when you have a verdict. Nobody will be interrupting you," she explained.

"Does anyone have questions?" Sydney asked. "One more thing," she said. "If you request the gun, you may not have the bullets at the same time."

She looked around and opened the door to leave. She took the sign that was hanging on the door with the blank side out and turned it around. The sign read that a jury was in deliberations. She hung it on the hooks, smiled at us and we were by ourselves

Two large boxes of evidence sat at the head of the table stared back at us.

I took charge of one box when jurors requested to look at evidence and Parker took charge of the second box that contained mostly photos.

To say that this looked like a daunting task to begin with would severely understate what we felt within the first hour and a half. I think some of us saw this case in a certain way and were surprised to find that not all jurors felt the same way. We learned this in the very beginning by taking an anonymous poll of ourselves.

Cherie simply asked the question, "Do you think she's guilty?"

We then wrote our potential verdict on a slip of paper and put them in a pile in the center of the table. Cherie studiously gathered them up and went to the dry erase board on the wall and wrote a column for guilty, not guilty and undecided.

She tallied the slips and we were surprised to see that five of us saw her guilty, five of us thought she was not guilty and two of us were undecided. We were an even split.

I fell in the undecided category because the question was too general and did not specify first or second-degree murder although I leaned toward first-degree murder.

The question was simple. Why did Marissa hit Dale in the head with a hammer multiple times?

Cherie came up with the idea of writing a list of evidence that we needed to see to begin walking the path of understanding. She was concerned that we were rambling and didn't have direction when Jeebs piped in and said we should look at the law and it will decide the structure.

We were rookie jurors on a capital murder case. It took us some time to set our direction.

Each of us brought up items we wanted to see and they included the Stanley Cook confession that was referred to but never read, the insurance policies, photos of the crime scene, photos of the hammer and photos of Dale.

I was designated to read the confessions aloud and there was a pile of them, probably five or six confessions written by Stan and a couple written by Marissa. I should say, the confessions were 'allegedly' written by Stan and Marissa.

The confession of Stan was missing a lot of punctuation so the reading of it sounded almost fragmented and sounded like Stan a little. I don't think it carried believability as it kept focusing on how "Reese" was being unjustly accused and he couldn't understand why a black man wouldn't be believed. In Los Angeles, he noted, he would have been in handcuffs in a second.

We did notice and delve into the fact that Stan said he took the gun from his nightstand and ran into the room when he heard Marissa being abused. He later said the gun was in his pocket and that he took the hammer because it was there, to beat up Dale for every time he had hit Marissa.

I got home and was getting ready to write in this journal when I realized something about the confession letters of Stan and the letter of confession by Marissa who was saying that Stan did the attack.

There was something peculiar about the way Stan's confession letter was written aside from the missing punctuation. Throughout the letter, located in the middle of sentences, there were random words that were capitalized.

The letter that Marissa wrote explaining what happened that night had the same characteristics. At least I'm pretty sure they did and I would like to go back tomorrow and check if the same capital letter characteristic appears in Stan's confession as well as her written interpretation. I think I can get the jury to see that if they agree Marissa's words were hers on her letter then it goes to follow that she is the author of Stan's letter.

Getting back to Stan's confession, here are some of the points that didn't make sense to me: It didn't make sense that he ran into the room to defend her with gun in hand and then used the hammer. How did the gun get into his pocket? When would the gun get into his pocket? Did he stop and look at the situation of Marissa being raped and then put the gun in his pocket before selecting a hammer to protect her? It defies common sense.

We discussed the gun at length and talked about the gun going from Allen Flores, who had a written receipt saying he loaned the gun on January 13th to Marissa. It was that same gun that found it's way into Stan's hands. Stan had an SKS rifle and case in his closet so why did he need a gun in the first place?

It was also extremely odd than Allen would write a receipt for his loaning the gun. I believed that Marissa got the gun for Stan and thought at some point he would be able to shoot Dale and that plan fell apart.

We did agree that even though Stan suffered mental problems due to his accident, he surely knew the difference between right and wrong. We also agreed that Stan looked like a patsy in this whole deal and the reason he was brought into their home was to help keep an eye on the children. We further agreed that none of us could believe any of his testimony because of his memory problems and citing his answers such as: *'that could have happened'*, *'it apparently happened'* and *'he didn't remember'*.

All of us believed that Stan was not being forthright and knew a lot more than he led the court to believe.

We did not dispute the fact that most of us thought Allen Flores a scumbag. We took some time and looked at his and Stan's immunity agreement and noted that Allen's immunity was based in trade for child pornography charges.

However, upon reading the document carefully, it said that while there was a vast amount of pornography on his computer, by comparison, the amount of child pornography was relatively small. I don't know that it changed our minds on his untrustworthy character. It looked like he used Marissa as much as she used him.

We delved into the insurance policies of which we found two. I thought there was another. Dale initiated one policy in 2008, and Melissa took another out on Dale effective January 1, 2009. We also saw the document where Marissa changed the beneficiary from herself to Allen and noted this was done after she was charged.

Parker worked insurance as his regular job and we let him look through them. He didn't see anything as unusual, but I had a feeling that we would be going back to these policies as they had potential for speaking to the motive of the crime.

Ted was very good at knowing the association between evidence numbers and the actual evidence. We each had enumerated four hundred and thirty-six pieces of evidence throughout the trial. We quickly found out that it was pretty hard to find the actual piece we were looking for at beck and call. Ted had a surprising ability to remember what lined up with what and that was going to be a useful talent in keeping the train of evidence moving.

We spent some time looking at the blurry pictures of when Dale was first found lying on the floor, naked, with his head juxtaposed next to the nightstand. The more I looked at it, the more unnatural it looked to me.

He was lying on his side when he was attacked and that is supported by the multiple hammer blows to the right side of his skull just behind and over the ear. The question was how did he get to the floor? In one explanation, Marissa said she pushed him and in another she said he fell on the floor.

Neither scenario looked right to me. If he was pushed to the floor, I think he would naturally have turned over and would have faced away from the bed as opposed to his facing toward the bed. If he fell off the bed, he naturally would have rolled away. I could also see the blood smear move at a downward angle from the top of the nightstand and one could follow the blood to his head. The nightstand did not have a multi-directional smear which would indicate the natural result of his body rolling off the bed either from being pushed or pulled.

We looked at a picture of Dale's shorts and I mentioned what the prosecutor had said. He argued that Marissa removed the shorts just after the attack.

"Closing arguments are not evidence," Parker said flatly.

"If it's not evidence, then why did he bring it up?" I asked.

Nobody had an answer for that.

It was my belief that after Dale was assaulted, someone removed the shorts. The attacker would do this by grabbing the belt loop area of the shorts and yanking down quickly. I had an identical pair of these shorts and know that they bundle plus have the capability of scratching due to the sewn patchwork design. I believe when the shorts were first pulled down to his knees, the button was still closed. This would move the legs toward the edge of the bed and gravity pulled the legs down which caused the scrapings on his legs. The button then was undone as the legs fell to the floor and the body followed. This would explain the semi-circle arc of blood seen on the nightstand.

It made sense of the odd position that Dale was discovered in. Most importantly, I wanted to see the bloodied handprints that were seen on the sheet where Dale had been lying. I wanted to see if their directionality supported my removal of shorts theory.

Sunny commented that nothing in this murder was normal and I was beginning to agree.

PREMEDITATION AND INTENT

We made some mileage today in a lot of ways. The pieces were slowly attaching and at a slower pace than I had expected. At times, the day was laborious and there were other times that we started reaching common ground on the killing of Dale Harrell. It wasn't until today that I learned the correct spelling of his name.

Cherie opened our day of deliberations by asking if anyone had any thoughts the prior night about the evidence, trial or anything that had to do with our task at hand.

I was awake all night thinking about what I wrote yesterday and what I wanted to share with the jury today. I was nervous about it but I thought it was important and came in with my guns loaded, so to speak. I even brought in a pair of shorts in the event that we wanted to see how difficult they would come off a body. I was willing to lie on the jury table just to prove my point.

"This is about physics and everything that happened before the lawyers and police got involved," I said as I drew a rough picture of a bed on the dry erase board in front of everyone. I drew a nightstand next to the bed and asked if we could see the first two pictures taken on the scene. These two pictures were the first taken by an astute officer who arrived behind the second officer that was assisting Dale. The pictures were blurred but helped make the point.

"Objects are subject to the laws of physics. A physical object will act a certain way every time when force is applied to it. We all know that when we bounce a basketball, it will bounce back up every time. We also know a rock will fall every time we drop it out a window. A body will act the same way," I said.

"How are you an expert?" Doc piped in.

"Just hear me out. I am not an expert, however I am a California Certified Funeral director and have moved many a body in my life."

"Yeah," Wings said, "Those are dead bodies."

"That may be but let me finish," I said pointing to the bed on the dry erase board. "If we were to apply basic laws of physics to this," I said pointing to the picture of Dale lying on the floor with his head juxtaposed within the angle between the nightstand and the bed, "How do you explain his moving from the bed, when he was lying on his left side, to the floor with his face facing the bed?"

"I don't see where this is going," Parker said from the back of the room.

"Just follow me," I said. "How did Dale go three feet over and two feet down?"

"He fell off the bed," Ted said.

"How did he fall off the bed with his face facing the bed?"

"I don't know," Ted responded. "He just fell."

"What made him fall?" I asked.

"I don't know," Jeebs said. "I thought we heard he fell off the bed."

"Let me approach this in another way. How many of us believe that Marissa held the hammer with two hands and drove it into his head?"

Everyone started nodding.

"That's a good point," Cherie our Foreman said. "Let's write that down. We believe that Marissa held the hammer and hit Dale with it," she said writing it down on a flip chart. "Does everyone agree?"

Everyone agreed.

"Good," I said returning to my presentation. "So, if we believe that Marissa held the hammer and hit Dale with it, are we comfortable in saying that she was not being raped at the time of the hammer impact?"

There was some discussion and it turned out that everyone agreed on that point. This was a good segue into my next point.

"Based on that, we can say that Dale was not pushed off the bed because Marissa held the hammer. But," I pointed out, "If you take pushing out of the equation, we must ask if he fell out of bed. What would have made him fall? What force made him fall out of the bed? He had to go from Point A at the top of the bed to Point B on the floor. Something had to be the impetus or energy to make him move. Didn't the attending physician at the hospital say that he was paralyzed from the injury?"

Sunny answered in the affirmative.

"So being paralyzed, if he couldn't fall from his position and he wasn't pushed," I pursued, "then how did he get to the floor?

Victoria and Annie jumped in and said, "He had to have been pulled!"

"Absolutely," I said. "There is no way he could end up on the floor facing the bed unless he was pulled." I pointed to the photograph of Dale lying on the floor and pointed out a large bloodstain on his forearm. At the base of the bloodstain, one could see drip marks.

"This means that at some point, his body was vertical for a long enough amount of time allowing the blood to drip downward following basic laws of gravity. It would drip in the horizontal position he's in," I said, pointing at the stain.

"Where did the blood come from on his arm?" Butthead asked, looking up toward the front.

"I suspect that this could not have happened without the shorts being a part of the scene. There is no reason to move the body to the floor without the shorts, and it is because of the removal of shorts that he received the shin burns on his legs. It also explains why the blood changes direction. His body was moved not once but twice. The blood on his arm came about because Dale's head was in a somewhat vertical position as he came down the side of the bed."

I pointed to the picture of Dale and to the blood on Dale's arm. "This blood comes directly from his head as it drained onto his arm.

Then, Dale was pulled again which explains the angled turn of blood on the nightstand. Consider that his whole head would have been soaked in blood."

Parker was firmly against it. He felt that I wasn't a blood expert and there wasn't enough evidence to show that he had been moved twice. He did agree, however, that he was moved once since Dale couldn't move himself. "What's that prove, anyway?" he asked.

"It proves there was intent at the precise time of the event. It speaks to her having consciousness of guilt. She knew what she had done was wrong. I even go so far as to say her intent was malicious. She is not trying to resuscitate him or help him. She is moving him as a by- product of pulling the shorts off."

"Here are the shorts," Jeebs said, pointing to a picture of the bedroom that was photographed after Dale was removed from the scene.

The shorts were lying in a bunch underneath a dresser.

"Didn't a blood expert say they had been moved from their original position?" I asked. "The blood spatter on the shorts shows that they were moved after the assault."

"Maybe," Parker said.

"You said you had two things to show us," Cherie pushed. "What's the other thing?"

I brought out the letters that we had spoken of the day prior. I began with the letter, "The Night It Happened." that was written in first person and I thought to be written by Marissa. I pointed out the random capitalizations of letters. These words that were capitalized were located sporadically throughout the letter and did not have punctuation on either side of the word. They were just random capitalized words in the middle of sentences.

After showing everyone the letters, I asked, "Do we believe this was written by Marissa?"

Everyone was mixed on this point and we could not agree. Butthead and Parker, the resident computer experts, said that it is often a practice of computer programmers to make that signature type of random punctuation. Butthead mentioned it was a habit from writing computer codes that those in the industry developed unconsciously.

Although I was defeated on that point, I noted the same mistakes being made on the confession letter. I don't know that most of the jury had noticed that before but I noticed a lot of nodding heads.

"Can we agree," I said, "that these two letters are authored by the same person?"

"No," Doc said. "I will agree that the letters were typed by the same person," and everyone agreed to that. Cherie wrote it on the flip chart.

I sat down and tried not to show that I was a little frustrated. I think I expected everyone to see and understand my viewpoint.

Doc leaned forward and looked toward me. "Look I see what you're saying but it just doesn't look like premeditation to me. But that's just me. You can think what you want."

"However you get to premeditation is up to you," Annie said supportively. "We're all going to get there in a different way. It doesn't matter that we agree on each and every single point. There's enough evidence here to convince us one way or the other.

Some of us are going to take a different path to get there. Don't worry about it."

"Okay," I said but I did worry about it anyway.

"Are there any other conclusions we can write down before we move forward?" Cherie asked us.

"Yeah," Ted said matter-of-factly, "Marissa lies."

Everyone agreed that Marissa, Allen, Stan and Travis Tatro all lied or were no good as witnesses.

Parker pointed out inconsistencies in Travis Tatro's testimony regarding when Marissa first approached him about "taking care of Dale". I was surprised how different I had felt about Travis Tatro and leaned toward Parker's opinion fairly quickly. I still believed he didn't have reason to lie but his occupation and having worked at a strip club served to impeach him a little too much.

We spent the afternoon primarily listening to Compact Discs and recordings of the 911 calls to emergency services. It had been a long time since we heard them and they still sounded as creepy as they did the first time we heard them.

The 911 calls were broken into pieces as they were interrupted by hang-ups and it was clear that Marissa was disconnecting the phone and the disconnection was not happening from the emergency services end.

Her first obvious mistake happened in the second phone call. We replayed it countless numbers of times to make sure we heard it correctly. Essentially, Marissa says she was being raped and hit Dale with a hammer and then Stan came in and hit Dale with a hammer. This called would have been around 2:55 AM and only eighteen minutes after Rhiannon had heard Stan trying to comfort Dale or wake him up.

I think this stood out to all of us. Why would someone lie to 911 if they weren't trying to cover their tracks?

This point was further looked into because shortly after that admission or statement, the phone went quiet but one could still hear the 911 Operator asking for information.

"Marissa?" he questioned.

"Are you there? Hello?" he asked again.

The phone remained quiet on the other end, the end that Marissa was on.

Wings suddenly said, "She turned her phone on mute."

We all looked at each other and wondered. The phone was a 2009 cell phone and was remarkably antique compared to what we carry now and few of us could remember the features on the phone.

Victoria said it was easy to put those phones on mute. All you had to do was press the button on the right and at the top. Since all of us could not visualize it, we buzzed Sydney and asked if we could see the phone to clarify the simplicity of putting the phone on mute.

A short time later, Sydney returned with the phone in an evidence bag and gave it to us. We passed it around and saw how easy it was to put the phone on mute.

Sunny said, "One thing about people who lie is that it's hard to keep track of your lies when you start telling them. I personally think she caught herself in a lie and put the phone on mute to rethink the situation."

It was a good point and I think most of us agreed.

"I've got to ask you all" Cherie said, "I need to know how many of us don't think this is first degree murder?"

Two of us volunteered that they were convinced it was murder but they weren't convinced it was first-degree murder.

"I see some intent," Parker volunteered, "but I don't see the premeditation. I'm sorry but I want to think that this person is innocent until proven guilty and I don't see the premeditation."

"I want to sleep at night so I'm not convinced either," Wings said.

I think at this point there was a little frustration in the jury room between those who believed and those who didn't. At the same time, we wanted to be fair to everyone's thoughts so we wanted to continue onward with a focus at looking at intent.

The final part of the afternoon was spent listening to the phone calls from Marissa in the Buckeye jail to Stanley Cook. The calls were made collect and we were able to improve the sound with Butthead adjusting the bass out of the equalizer setting on the laptop.

We listened intently and repeatedly to those calls and it was becoming clear that Marissa was a manipulator and clearly upset when she heard that Allen Flores' computer had been seized with journals on them and one of them clearly identified that Allen had loaned her $7,000.00 for the unexecuted attack on Dale at the casino, an event that never happened but was testified about.

All these things were little pieces, little pieces that added up to one thing.

Tomorrow we decided we would listen and watch the five-hour video of Marissa's interrogation. I knew it would take a while to go through but we certainly felt that the interrogation held most of the answers since it had been recorded the same day as the assault.

All I remember about the interrogation is that it was filled with lies and fabrications. I wondered if we should keep a list of lies...

DAY 25

COINCIDENCE

It was completely uncharacteristic for Sunny to speak up at the beginning of the day. We had been watching the interrogation tape of Marissa and Detective Tomory. Many of us were squirming uncomfortably in our chairs trying not to show emotion. The first time we had seen the interrogation tape was prior to the prosecution presenting the rest of their case. We all knew we were watching a string of lies by the defendant and some of those lies just didn't have reasoning behind them.

We had just watched Marissa claiming that Dale wielded an overwhelming power over her and how often he abused her.

"Can you stop the CD?" Sunny suddenly asked.

"Sure," Parker said as he put the CD of the interrogation tape on pause.

"I want to say that watching her is really starting to piss me off," Sunny said.

"Okay," Cherie answered. "Can you tell us what is bothering you?"

"This girl is saying she was abused and I know the defense went to a lot of work trying to say she was abused and I just don't buy it. There is no way that someone who is abused would act that way."

"What do you mean?" Cherie asked. The room's attention was focused on Sunny.

"I'm sorry to say this but I know what abuse is in a marriage. My first husband beat the crap out of me and he had power over me. I couldn't go to the bathroom and take a pee without him knowing about it. To be sure, he would know if I was out stripping at night. Or, that I was having an affair with a guy like Allen Flores. What about the trip to Orlando? If Dale was so controlling, he wouldn't let her do any of those things and he would surely know about it," Sunny said. It was clearly heartfelt.

Annie spoke up next to me. "I agree with what Sunny said. If Dale had so much power, she wouldn't get out of the house. I know what it's like to be in an abusive relationship and thank God my second husband is not like that. My first husband had me scared all the time and I was wrapped around his finger. It was a horrible, awful relationship and what Marissa says doesn't hold water," Annie said vehemently. "She looks like she's pretending to be scared of him and I think she's a horrible actress. When you live under a roof like that, you don't attack. You're scared of the other person. What she did with the hammer makes no sense if she was really abused."

"I know what you're saying," I said to the group. "I, also come from a unique circumstance where the children were the abused. I come from a wealthy family and understand what it's like to live in an All-American family façade. My parents got in over their head financially and their fear of losing everything turned to anger. We weren't kids anymore but we were a financial responsibility that became almost too much for my parents to bear."

"Did your parents hit each other?" Jason asked.

"Oh, No." I answered, "They just hit their kids. At first it was sporadic but as my father lost more financial control, the anger was concentrated on the kids. I may have wanted to kill my parents at times but you never do it because at the end of the day, they are stronger than you. Instead, your reaction is to comply with their wishes at all costs or it is to run. The interrogation tapes piss me off, too," I finished.

"I'm so sorry that happened to all of you," Cherie offered.

"I am, too," Parker said, "but maybe she was abused. We saw the witnesses who said she had a black eye. We don't really know what her personal life was like…"

"Yeah," Victoria jumped in, "we don't know, but all I can see is a black eye. It doesn't explain all the crap she was doing with Allen. I also think that she attacked Dale when he was sleeping. I don't think he was up and about."

"I agree with that," Althea said. "Even if she was abused, what does that have to do with the moment she picked up the hammer?"

Wings volunteered, "There's no evidence that he was sleeping."

"There was evidence that he was lying down," Butthead offered.

"Maybe she just freaked out," Wings said. "I hit my husband with a telephone book once and maybe it's the same thing. You don't know how you're going to react in any given situation. I never thought I had it in myself to hit my husband but it was there." She added, "But he deserved it, though."

"I don't know anything about that stuff," Parker interjected. "I've killed people before and I've had Post-Traumatic Stress Disorder and I've had complete blackouts. I killed as part of my job and I know what it did to me. I came from a good family so I never saw abuse. I know about blacking out and maybe that's what happened to her. Maybe she really doesn't remember."

"Watch the video," I said. "If that's the case the why is she lying? Lying is usually done to protect oneself. I think if a person is innocent and in a situation like this, they wouldn't lie repeatedly. She lies to cover up and she lies because she thinks everyone is stupid."

We spent a significant amount of time talking about intent, premeditation and coincidences. I suggested we make a list of coincidences such as when she got the gun from Allen, the effective date of the insurance policies and the availability of the hammer even though the gun was in the room.

The gun was the smoking gun that wasn't. It was interesting that a gun was in the room but never used. Many of us believed that Marissa got the gun to Stan in the hopes that he would fire the weapon. This also got us on the train of thought that she had planned the murder but it didn't come out the way she planned. We knew from the video she was scared of guns and at the same time we knew that Stan knew the difference between right and wrong and could not fire the gun at Dale even though that's what Marissa wanted.

The trial and deliberations were weighing on all of us and created an interesting dynamic. There were those of us who had made up their minds and it was becoming obvious that they had made up their minds. It came out in subtle signs such as sighs when we wanted to continue watching the interrogation. Some were playing games on their iPads. Still others were starting to close their eyes.

The IT guys in the room were getting irritating because they kept wanting to play with the controls on the CD laptop by adjusting volumes and trebles on the equalizer of the player. We all knew it was an IT thing but the adjusting was driving us nuts.

I think the hardest thing was watching the interrogation tape and watching Marissa lie more and more often. We could see that she was adding details to make her lying seem more truthful. We noticed how many times she would say, "Uhhh," while thinking and this looked to us like she was manufacturing her story to fit with what the interrogator, Detective Tomory, wanted or what she thought the detective wanted from her.

The biggest thing that was bothering everybody was her affect or countenance throughout the interrogation. She would giggle randomly. She would smile a lot. You would see moments where she wanted to act like she was crying but no tears came out. She would crack little jokes and sarcastic comments as if she were 'best buddies' with the interrogator. One could even see that her personality was affable but with directions of manipulation.

I couldn't count how many times we would replay the pieces of the interrogation when the detective would step out of the room. She would literally change before your eyes and become her real self. At one point, it sounded like she was rehearsing a script when we heard her say: "Push, Shove, Fall". This looked like an outline she had created herself.

Parker pointed out that these things were not enough to consider. He also said again that just because someone lies, it doesn't prove they are guilty of first-degree murder. Although we agreed, we also said that this goes to her character and her character is consistent with having the capability to kill.

We were looking for a smoking gun and I didn't think we were going to find one. I wondered if we could prove Dale was lying down and not attacking Marissa. In the event of that moment and in consideration of the insurmountable mountain of coincidences, there did not seem to be a reason for Dale to be struck with a hammer, unless he was worth a lot of money...

I thought it interesting that it was so difficult to answer the question, "Why did Marissa hit Dale with a hammer?"

Cherie thought it time to poll the jury on anonymous pieces of paper.

Ten of us believed Marissa to be guilty of first-degree murder. Two of us were undecided.

I noted that the two outside the group said they were undecided as opposed to 'not guilty'.

The jury was moving forward...

DAY 26

SHADOW OF A DOUBT

Here's what I liked about Cherie as the foreperson. She had an amazing ability to draw people in and keep us focused at the task at hand. She allowed people to speak without fear of retribution. Cherie was an astute listener who could listen without showing bias to either side. The other thing that I liked was that she offered a platform to anyone who had thoughts the night before and wished to share them prior to commencing our task.

The first thing that Cherie did was to walk up to our new Post-It flip board, the sheets had the ability to be pulled off and stuck on the wall without tape, and list four things on the board. In black Sharpie, she scribbled the words "Cells", "Crosstalk", "Respect" and "Focus". We watched as she scribbled like a professor in front of his students.

She pointed the Sharpie toward the word, "Cells".

"Sydney told us that we are to have our phones off when we come back here and we need to follow that." she said. "We can't be playing games on our iPads. I know that many of us have made up our minds but we can't share that with the group. Whether it's obvious to you or not, we have got to respect those that have not made up their minds. We have a lot at stake here and we need to respect the process, the accused and we have to respect the deceased. Is everyone good on not using cell-phones and showing respect?"

Everyone nodded their heads in agreement and the guilty parties looked down knowing she was speaking of them.

"When someone is speaking," Cherie continued, "let's stay away from cross talk."

"What's that," Linda asked.

"It means when one person is talking, there shouldn't be other conversations amongst each other. It distracts those of us who are listening to whoever is speaking, and some might call it rude. So, please, respect each other and stay away from it."

We all agreed.

"Finally, I know this process is long and tedious and I want this to be a good experience for everyone."

"We want to sleep at night when we're done, too," Wings volunteered.

"You're absolutely right," Wings," Cherie confirmed. "We do want to sleep at night so we need to remain focused at the task at hand. So, I got to thinking about the smokers in the group and those of us who don't need a lot more convincing. The process can get tiring and laborious and we want to keep the door open for those who need to decipher more evidence.

Remember, we have four hundred and thirty-six pieces of evidence available to us and we have barely touched the tip of the iceberg," she said leaning down to a paper bag she had at her feet. She reached in and pulled out some items and put them on the jury table.

She pulled out a chocolate cake and put it in the center of the table. We started laughing when she pulled out little plastic eggs of silly putty and rubber spiny balls with LED lights inside.

"I made the cake myself and this is for some sugar to keep us focused. I hope you like it. We have to use a plastic knife to cut it. They wouldn't allow my butter knife to come through security even though they saw the cake," she said, referring to the security downstairs that we went through daily.

Everybody scooped up the silly putty and rubber balls. It was a great idea in many ways. It served to keep people off their iPad games and kept your hands busy. For the smokers, these little play toys got the smoking urges off your mind.

There was a point in time when we had to buzz Sydney, the bailiff, for an item. I knew she was coming to the door and Jason was sitting across from me. While he wasn't looking, I quietly got as many balls and Silly Putty eggs that I could find and I pushed all the toys onto his folder in front of him.

The door cracked open with Sydney peeping in. Mind you, we have to cover all the evidence we are looking at before she enters, as it was a rule for no one to see what we were looking at. This made it easy for me to put the toys on Jeebs folder so when the door opened and he turned to look at her, I was quietly laughing as he noticed all the toys in front of him.

"Look, Jeebs has got all the toys," I said.

He blushed red when everyone looked at him and started laughing.

He pushed the toys off his folder. "I don't know anything about them," he said.

Sydney looked at him curiously and shut the door.

At least it made us smile.

We decided that against most of our wishes that we needed to continue the interrogation tapes. The interrogation tape of five and a half hours was probably the most damaging evidence against Marissa. It told us a lot about her as a person and none of us could ignore the fact that she was blatantly lying throughout the interview. We thought Detective Tomory was brilliant in her handling of the questioning.

We would pause the tape continuously to ask what she had said or to discuss why Marissa was saying something else. There was a time stamp on the tape that showed it began at three o'clock in the afternoon. We were three hours into the tape when Victoria asked us to pause it again.

"Did you notice that she doesn't ask about Dale once in all this time?"

"Oh yeah," Althea answered. "She doesn't ask about her kids either."

"If my husband was lying in the hospital after getting his head caved in, I would be going crazy," Cherie said.

"But you don't know how you would react in that situation," Parker countered.

"We have to look at it as a reasonable man would," Jeebs said. "If you think how you might react if your wife was in the hospital, wouldn't you want to know how she's doing? Even if you did it, you would want to know. It's natural."

"It would be natural if you're innocent," Ted said.

Parker nodded his head and went back to taking notes.

I knew by now that the two people who had not made up their minds were the two computer specialists in the room being John and Butthead. I didn't think they were being unreasonable in holding out. The way I looked at it was that their world was very black and white and they wanted to see this situation in the same manner. It was almost as if they wanted a sign that said, "I did it," before they would be convinced. At the same time, knowing I am a reasonable man, I knew the evidence spoke for itself and it came down to two key segments.

The first damning piece was the interrogation tape and we had all commented that it was surprising that she didn't ask for a lawyer. I believed she didn't ask for a lawyer because Marissa seriously under underestimated her position in the assault. I think she honestly believed that everyone would buy her story of abuse and that if showed she were a nice person, everyone would think she couldn't have committed such an awful act without provocation.

The second piece was directly the blood spatter and the forensic science behind it. This evidence placed Dale in the bed, probably sleeping, and showed that she attacked from behind. The spatter put Marissa over Dale and it was clear she held the hammer. The spatter put Stan Cook in the room and we all decided that he must have shown up at the last blow to Dale explaining the limited amount of spatter on his person.

The problem with the case and the things that made us walk slowly was the existence of the gun; it's not being used and the fact that most of the witnesses could not be trusted to have told the truth. Even my favorite witness, Travis Tatro, was discarded due to his profession or lack thereof.

"I just think that it's awful that no one can speak for Dale and that it's always about trashing the victim," Cherie offered at one point. "If you think about it, all anyone can say is that Dale had an affair. He doesn't get a chance to speak here."

"I think he is speaking," I said. "He is speaking through the wounds he received. I bet we can see him sleeping on the bottom sheet when he was attacked."

"What do you mean?" Cherie asked.

"I wonder if we can request the sheets. If we laid the bottom sheet across the jury table, I bet we see a void pattern where he was sleeping. We would see that he is faced away from Marissa. Also," I continued, "I would like to see the shorts again as well. We know there's blood spatter on the shorts and it is only on the left side."

"What's that mean?" Butthead asked.

"Well, if Dale was wearing the shorts, the bottom sheet around him will show blood spatter. There would be a pattern of clean sheets where he was located when he was hit. It would show us that he was lying down and wearing the shorts at the time of the attack."

"Let's just finish watching the tape," Parker said.

I knew John was the Doubting Thomas but I also knew that one could not ignore the drone of Marissa's lies. We'll worry about the sheets later, I thought.

The interrogation tape played and Marissa dug herself in deeper. She should have gotten a lawyer in the very beginning but she couldn't get a lawyer because she had to make everyone believe her biggest lie of all, that she was being attacked.

Marissa picked up the hammer and hit Dale in the head at least five times.

We knew from the blood spatter expert that the first blow could not create blood spatter and it is from the second blow forward that the blood is careened to the walls and the ceiling with each subsequent impact.

Marissa described Stan striking Dale in the head after being raped by Dale. She said that Dale was choking her and she had just awoken from unconsciousness to see the first hammer strike to his temple.

She described in vivid detail how she recoiled when the first round of blood splashed to her face. She couldn't understand what she was seeing. She had the 'grey fuzzies', she said. The blood woke her up on the first impact and she tried to move away.

Unfortunately for her, blood does not spatter until the second blow.

Cherie polled the jury again at the end of the day. We jotted our words on a torn piece of paper and threw them into the pile at the center of the table.

Doc read each potential verdict aloud while Cherie tabulated the count on the Dry Erase board.

Eleven slips in a row read, 'guilty'. One slip said, 'not yet.'

We all knew who it was and we all knew that we would reach a decision in its proper time...and we wanted to sleep at night.

DAY 27

AFFECTATIONS

A tap at the door interrupted the interrogation of Marissa by Detective Tomory. Marissa looked up and stopped speaking. She was wearing a light colored zippered hoodie with the hood over her head. Ted called it a 'cone' hoodie saying he hated hoodies like that. He was the professional in the room since we had nicknamed him 'The Unabomber' for his always wearing a hoodie and sunglasses.

"I just wanted to give you an update on what's going on," Detective Sy Ray said to Marissa. She looked interested and leaned forward in her chair while Detective Tomory sat next to her in silence.

"We've got your kids with your mom and she's at a hotel in Glendale so the kids are okay," he said. "As far as Dale goes, he is stabilized in the hospital. It looks like they got there just in time, as one of the principal doctors was able to handle on Dale pretty quickly.

"Can he speak?" Marissa asked.

We all thought that was a pretty bizarre question to ask. One would have expected a question directed more toward his physical condition. Further, none of us could ignore the fact that she had not inquired about his condition once in almost five hours of interrogation.

"At this time, the best the doctors can say is that he is responding to prompts especially on his left side. He can move his fingers and leg upon our speaking to him. I wouldn't say he's going to be okay as it's too early to tell, but the good news is that he is responding to stimulation. We will have to find out over time what kind of improvements he will make," Sy Ray said. "He's pretty lucky to be alive."

Marissa nodded her head but did not appear to respond. Some of us noticed that the lack of response was detrimental to her. It did not feel like this was a normal way to respond given the condition of her husband of ten years. It also appeared that the wheels in her head were spinning especially for those of us that leaned toward her guilt.

The problem with believing in her guilt was that it was akin to watching a house of playing cards collapse because they were so ill supported. It was as if each piece of evidence was lining up against her. One couldn't walk down the road of presumed innocent because she didn't look innocent anymore.

"Marissa," Sy continued with a pause, "I understand you've been through eight years of abuse and I think there's evidence to support it. Domestic violence cases are taken seriously and are successful as a defense."

Marissa nodded her head.

"But," he said pausing again, "we need you to be straightforward with us. Things will not go well for you in the long run if we find inconsistencies in your recollection of what happened. I'm not saying you didn't have a bad marriage or he didn't abuse you because we weren't there. But we've had people who are experienced in scene reconstruction and they are saying the evidence doesn't line up with your story. Do you understand that?"

"Yeah," Marissa said as she looked at the backs of her hands as if to check for fingernail imperfections. She seemed curiously distant which could have been from her being up since three in the morning or she was thinking how to adjust her story. Like I said, once the house of cards was leaning toward first-degree murder, it was hard not to read her actions as further support for premeditation.

"We want to give you every opportunity to think about what you're saying and maybe bring this closer to the truth. We want to help you but we can't help you unless we know what happened," Sy Ray finished. "So, I'm sorry to interrupt but I wanted to give you an update."

Sy Ray stood up and stepped out of the room letting the door swing closed.

Marissa leaned forward with her elbows on her knees as she faced Detective Tomory. She appeared to be mulling things over as silence filled the room.

"Let's go back to the moment the incident happened, Marissa. Tell me what you remember. Where was Dale?"

"Dale was on the bed and he was facing the computer toward the wall. I went to the bathroom and on the way back in the room, I just picked up the hammer and hit him," she said as she started crying. "I took both my hands and wrapped them around the hammer and hit him again and again. I kept saying, 'You don't own me' and I hit him again!"

We paused the tape at a point and you could hear a pin drop in the jury room. As soon as the CD stopped, Cherie said,

"That's premeditation. Ignore, for the moment, all the insurance policies and everything else we have heard. Dale was clearly lying down, probably sleeping, when she decided to pick up a hammer and drive it into his head. Does anybody else see that?" she asked.

Everyone agreed that she was not being threatened in any way and that she decided to pick up a hammer. We also agreed that this was the only story that matched the forensics we had seen.

"I don't understand why she changed her story back to Stan with the confession letters on February fourth," I said. "If she knows she's caught in the interrogation, what makes her change it?"

"The insurance," Parker answered. I was surprised he jumped in because only days before he seemed so much on the side of her innocence. "If she killed Dale, she wouldn't get the insurance. If someone else killed Dale, she would get the insurance."

"Did the insurance get paid out?" Sunny asked.

Ted looked at the evidence log and then started digging through the files until he found a document showing that the insurance proceeds went to the courts in a separate fund. "They had to pay it out because of what Parker said. Even though he was allegedly murdered, that was covered by his policy."

We nodded our heads. It made sense but I thought it was awfully dumb of Marissa to try and go back to her old story.

"Everything she's done is stupid," Althea said. "If you ask me, she didn't plan this out very well but it's clear that she planned to do it."

"I agree," Victoria said. "It's as if she thinks everyone is dumb but her."

We made a list of further evidence that we wanted to look at especially in regards to Marissa's shirt and Stan's shirt. Although photographs of the blood-spattered shirts were available, we thought it would help to actually see the items.

Sydney brought in the plastic wrapped items as we requested and we inspected them. Marissa's blood soaked t-shirt drew our attention because of the tear in the shirt. The front of it had been torn across the center. Marissa claimed it happened when Dale attacked her and a finger got caught in a pre-existing hole in the shirt. That reaction caused the tear.

Butthead looked at the cardboard supported shirt. "The evidence says there's blood on the inside back of the shirt."

"What's that mean to us," Wings asked.

"It means it was torn before she attacked him," Butthead said. "If the shirt wasn't torn, the blood could not be on the inside."

"Meaning she tore the shirt," Wings said with understanding.

"Not necessarily," Parker said. "We don't know who tore it but we do know it was torn by finding spatter on the inside."

"Yeah but who else would tear it?" Ted offered as if he was stating the obvious.

"Remember she lied about it," Doc said. "But, then again, who can believe her? All she did was lie."

We looked at Stan's gray t-shirt with the minimal amount of spatter on it and agreed he had to have come in right at the time of the last blow. There was clearly spatter but it was minimal at the same time. We noted that the comment said, 'I'm right and you're wrong' as said by Grumpy, the Snow White dwarf. Somebody also thought it weird that the dwarf was holding an axe in the picture.

Cherie pursued the persona Marissa carried when she was being interrogated and how she would appear to change when the officer left the room. At one point, Marissa called someone to get an attorney and it seemed her façade had changed from grieving to business.

There was another point in the interrogation after Detective Tomory left the room that Marissa called her mother. We thought it interesting that she lied to her mother saying she was being arrested for attempted homicide because she 'moved to the wrong side of the room'. This was entirely untrue.

"I would lie to my parents if I was being arrested for something like that, so that doesn't tell us anything," John said.

Marissa then called Allen Flores during a break in the interrogation and made it a point to emphasize that they had to set their boundaries. She also asked for bail money. Then she asked that Allen come down to the police station and pick up her plastic bag of papers and cigarettes at the front desk.

"It's always about Marissa and what she wants," Annie said. "Did you notice that?"

We all noticed.

Cherie pointed out that one of the biggest things that bothered her was the change in Marissa's affectations. She could be one way one moment and completely change gears in a second.

I thought Marissa was like a chameleon. She could fit into any situation and be who the people around her wanted her to be rather than being one person all of the time. I believed this came from her being shuffled around as a child and believed she learned how to be a chameleon just to survive in her changing home circumstances. I didn't think it qualified her for an unprovoked murder.

I thought being a chameleon had a very dangerous quality about it especially to those around her. She could fade into her surroundings and take what she wanted. She was a chameleon with Black Widow tendencies.

I have a feeling that we were close to reaching a verdict, probably by the end of the days' business tomorrow.

DAY 28

MURDER IN THE FIRST DEGREE

.   It took us six days and twenty-four total hours to reach a verdict. I'll always remember those days as ones that left you feeling like your head wanted to explode. It was a combination of frustration and the long, twisted journey we took to the depths of a problem. Your mind never stops thinking about it throughout the process and reminders seem to show up everywhere.

I had a hammer on my front porch from doing some household maintenance projects and it was lying innocuously on a table. I will never look at a claw hammer the same without thinking of Dale Harrell and the brutal attack he suffered.

Doc came into the jury room today and gave Victoria a king-size pack of Reese's Peanut Butter Cups. Victoria looked at it and back at Karen who was smiling mischievously. "Is this supposed to mean something?" Victoria asked.

"Thought you might like them," Doc said, pretending to be innocent.

"I see where this is going. Thanks for the Reese's Cups," Victoria said, shaking her head.

Certainly, none of what had happened was funny by any stretch of the imagination. At the same time, we were twelve strangers taken off the street and asked to make the most difficult decision of our lives. We were human and we were good people. Humor is a Band-Aid for the soul.

The process of our reaching a mutual decision was a long road and we were happy to reach the end of this phase. The tricky part in the whole process is allowing each individual to make up their own mind by using the evidence alone and not being prompted by other jurors. We felt that if we hit a roadblock on the way, then we would if necessary look again through all four hundred and thirty-six pieces of evidence if necessary.

"All right people," Cherie said pointing toward the wall. The walls were virtually wallpapered with Post-It brand large sheets of paper. Butthead had brought them in for us. The sheets had outlines, lists and conclusions that we had collectively decided upon. Cherie directed her attention to the outline of an evidence list that we had been going through the prior five days.

"Are there any more pictures that anyone needs to see?" she asked.

"I want to see a picture of the bed and pillow," I said.

"Jeebs?" she asked. "Will you find that for us?"

"Yep," he said, accustomed to his role as evidence finder. He pulled out a picture and put it in the center of the table.

I picked it up and showed it to my fellow jurors including Cherie. "I wanted to point out the bloodstain on the pillow. Why is there a big space between where the first glop of blood is on the left side of the pillow and the glop of blood on the right side of the pillow?"

I kept thinking about this all last night. It was odd how a picture can show in your head and how well you can remember it. The picture of the pillow was full of blood except where Dale's head was. That specific area was free of blood spatter and thick dark areas of blood were located on either side of it. The dark blood was much darker than the accompanying blood spatter. It was almost black in color.

I showed the jury that the second area of dark blood did not make sense if Dale was not moved. I surmised that this blood was darker because it had been mixed with dura mater or the gray matter that surrounds the brain. It would make it thicker and probably congeal differently than straight blood. If one could, picture being hit by a hammer while lying down and that hammer hit just above your ear, it would decompress, and the blood would flow out of the head and downward. This was consistent with where he was hit.

I also made a point that the forensic pathologist had concluded that Dale could not move after the first blow. I was concerned about the deep blood splotches located about six inches from his nose and it could only be dura mater mixed with blood.

Additionally, while his shorts were being taken off, his body was turned toward his face. When that happened, it accounted for the six inches of blood void in front of his face. His head turned into the pillow and then the blood and dura mater came off the right side of the face and landed on the right side of the pillow.

I know I'm not a medical examiner but I wanted to make sure I got everything off my chest before a verdict was reached."

"I see your point," Parker said, "but it's not in the evidence so we can't consider it."

"I know," I said.

At one point on the outline we were checking off, we were able to look at the Driver's License, Social Security Card and Birth Certificate of Dale Harrell. These items had been found at Allen Flores' house in February after the murder.

We thought it curious that all the items were at Allen's house and we found it interesting that Dale had a twin sister. Another fact not known until recently was that when twins are born, a notation is made on the birth certificate designating it as a twin delivery. That birth certificate exposed another of Marissa's lies when she had said she had birthed twins. We saw her daughter's birth certificate and there was no twin designation.

The last items on our outline were some documents that were sealed in the evidence bag and had not been marked 'Opened'. The rules were that we had to get the court's permission so we submitted a request to Sydney to forward on to the Judge. We were told that it would be available after lunch.

We had a half-hour before lunch and Cherie decided to poll the jury. We all knew to write our verdict on a piece of paper without using jury numbers and we placed the folded slips of paper in the center of the table.

"Wait," Wings said, "shouldn't we wait until we see that last piece of evidence that we requested?"

We looked at her realizing she was probably right when Doc said sarcastically, "maybe it'll be the smoking gun and it will change all of our minds."

Cherie just shook her head but agreed with Wings that we should wait. We left our votes in the basket and we departed for lunch on Phoenix's first ninety-degree day of the year. We were all grateful that this trial had not been held in the middle of the brutally hot summer that was soon to come.

We returned from lunch refreshed and ready to see the last piece of evidence before the votes were counted.

The unsealed bags featured Marissa's last Will and Testament that were found at Allen Flores' residence. The will was made on December 10, 2008 and only a mere month before Dale's attack. We all understood the significance of the date because Marissa appeared to be busy getting affairs in order during that time period.

We couldn't help noticing that Marissa willed the care of her children to Allen Flores, a person she had known less than two years. Nothing was willed to her husband, who was living at that time.

Marissa made a point to make sure that her mother did not get the children and it was apparent that there was discourse between the two and none of us knew the details except to conclude that it existed. Marissa also stated that she wanted to be cremated and have a Weeping Willow tree planted where her remains were buried so that people could reflect and talk to her.

I had a visualization of Marissa's ashes in a flowered porcelain urn. The sun would be shining on the green grass except where the branches of the Weeping Willow blew in the wind and created a soft shade for one to sit and reflect. The wind would blow softly as one reminisced on Marissa's life. The branches rustled.

It was ironic and odd that she picked a Weeping Willow to be her tree, as they aren't seen very often in Phoenix. . I was familiar with the Weeping Willow tree. When we were young, my mother would rip off the thin branches, strip back the leaves, and then she would whip us with them. Their strikes upon the backs of the legs stung like a thousand bees. They yielded a greater pain than a thick belt.

A Weeping Willow shading her flowerless grave would be something I would never forget.

Marissa further explained that she wanted her kids to go to the International House of Pancakes to honor her in the event of her passing, and the children could have all the toppings on their pancakes that they desired.

It was nauseating.

I also thought it ironic that this was the last piece of evidence that the twelve of us would see before rendering a verdict.

Parker began pulling slips of paper out of the basket while Cherie stood at the dry erase board and tallied our votes. He read each piece of paper.

"Guilty" was repeated twelve times with twelve tallies on the board in the same column.

There was a sense of relief that everyone had reached a verdict.

"I'm proud of us," Cherie said. "I think we made the right decision and we respected each other's wishes throughout the process. I want to let you know that I appreciate it and I appreciate all of you."

She proceeded to fill out the verdict form provided by the court and read it aloud to all of us.

We all agreed that Marissa DeVault was guilty of first-degree murder.

"Ring the buzzer," Cherie said to Wings. Wings walked over and rang for the Bailiff who appeared only minutes later at the door. We told her we had reached a verdict and Sydney told us that it would take forty-five minutes to assemble the court and we waited.

The court had been darkened throughout our deliberation time and we saw it every day as we passed it on the way to the jury room. I knew that the lights would be turned on in that courtroom and people were scrambling to get into place. I imagined attorneys and news people gathering their things. I imagined people rushing to fill the gallery before it was full.

I imagined Marissa waiting in a holding cell.

Meanwhile, we helped take down the multiple sheets of paper signifying evidence that was posted on the walls. We knew that our decision signified the next phase of the trial and the returning alternates were not allowed to see what we had discussed. We piled it all in a corner.

The forty-five minutes passed quickly and we were filed to the jury box. Our seating order got screwed up because the last time we had been there, we had fifteen jurors. Their absence was apparent in our random seating.

The Honorable Judge Roland Steinle, III was in his usual perch and the gallery was fuller than I had ever seen it throughout the trial. Although it was always silent upon our entry or departure in the past, it was eerily silent when we entered. One could almost cut the tension in the room.

I remember focusing on not wanting to look at the defendant. I think it was because I didn't want the verdict to show in my eyes should our eyes connect. I saw her momentarily as she looked toward us and I felt like she was smiling in friendship toward us. It really looked like she was more than hopeful, and probably expecting, we would have a verdict in her favor.

Cameras were in the courtroom and I remember hearing the click of a camera when the verdict was read. Time sped up for us while I bet time slowed down for Marissa. I didn't look at her when the verdict was read.

We were filed out and told to return in the morning and to expect the return of the alternates.

Sydney escorted us out of the jury room and directly to a private elevator adjacent to the courtroom. She even walked us to the front doors of the courthouse ensuring that no one spoke to us.

We slid past the multitude of cameras and reporters who were posted outside the front door of the courthouse.

We walked in a group toward the parking garage. I remember a reporter saying, "We can't talk to them," referring to us as we walked by.

We dispersed into the city back to our homes and we were all confident that we would sleep well that night.

I said a prayer for Dale.

DAY 29

AGGRAVATION

Our moods were upbeat as we entered the jury room in preparation for the newest stage of the trial. I think we felt forward progress by reaching a verdict in the first phase and gave us a sense of unity.

Sydney led us into the jury box and passed us a new packet detailing the procedure of law for this phase of the trial. As we sat, we saw that the gallery was only about half-full which was somewhat of a surprise after seeing a full courtroom the day before.

I half-expected that the defendant would be in an orange jump suit after her first-degree murder conviction. Instead, she was dressed in a black coat with a blue blouse underneath while wearing her glasses. I remembered the day before and except for the first day of jury selection, it was the only day Marissa had not worn glasses throughout the trial.

Seated next to Marissa was a blonde-haired lady who had been there throughout the duration of the trial seated to the left of Marissa from my viewpoint. One of the jurors had commented that they thought this person was a paralegal. I think this person was a mitigation specialist who is assigned to death penalty case defendants, so they may confer throughout the duration of the trial. I'm not sure how I knew this but I suspected I was right.

The Judge explained at the commencement of the day's proceedings that we were now entering the 'Aggravation' stage of the trial.

He carefully explained that there were two questions that the jury was to answer at the conclusion of this stage. He further explained that we would see opening statements from both sides and each side would have an opportunity to present evidence. He reiterated that opening statements were not evidence but a pathway to understand evidence.

The first question that we were to answer was, 'Did the defendant, Marissa DeVault, commit the murder in the expectation of anything of pecuniary value including money or property?' Thankfully, the Judge explained what pecuniary meant as I had never heard the word before. He explained that pecuniary meant anything financial. He also explained that money or property need not be the sole motivation for the murder and we must connect the motive to the killing as money or property.

At the time, I thought this would be an easy answer for the jury to answer because I don't know that we saw another motive aside from money.

The second facet that we were expected to answer was the circumstances of the murder. We had to decide if the manner in which Dale died was in an especially cruel manner. We had to consider if the victim suffered unusually great physical and/or mental pain and distress due to the defendant's actions combined with the fact that the defendant knew her actions would cause great pain or suffering.

That, too, seemed like a pretty easy question to answer.

Michelle Arino presented opening statements for the aggravation stage and her confidence level was significantly different than when she had presented her opening statement at the beginning of this case. Where her voice had been nervous and quiet, it was now confident and heard with clarity. Her outline was direct and focused. Her suit was pressed and sharp in grayness and she looked in everyone's eyes as she spoke.

"Ladies and Gentlemen," Michelle Arino began, "As we told you in the beginning of this case, this case is about the defendant's love for money. This defendant had 1.25 million reasons to kill Dale Harrell and that's exactly what she did. She loved money and lots of it. Consider that she was able to get more than a quarter of a million dollars from Allen Flores. You have seen the ledgers and her love of money speaks for itself."

"Marissa DeVault was always behind on her bills but she made sure that the life insurance payments were paid no matter what. It didn't matter to her that the electric, water and gas were not paid in time. It didn't matter that she was behind on her house payments. She had Allen Flores and she had insurance policies that were effective only two weeks before her brutal first-degree murder."

"The evidence shows that the defendant used Stanley Cook to take the fall. You have seen the confession letters. She designed these policies with Allen Flores who has said he was an expert in insurance. She knew that these policies wouldn't pay if she were discovered to have been the perpetrator. Allen would have told her that. The money is the reason that Stan Cook had to be the killer. Listen to the Buckeye jail tapes after she was incarcerated, she emphasized.

Michelle painted a picture. "The defendant calls Stan at home and she knows every password to every life insurance account. She knows what windows to open on the screen even though she is locked up in jail. The reason Marissa knows is because she spent a considerable amount of time on the screens making sure that the insurance would pay out upon Dale's death."

"She couldn't pay her bills and she couldn't properly take care of her children because she was busy planning Dale's death and planning on the money she would receive. It is all in the evidence, Ladies and Gentlemen," she said, pausing.

Michelle Arino did a very good job of making eye contact and also didn't hide behind the podium as she spoke to us. She would step to the side of the podium instead of behind it, which created the illusion that there were no barriers between her and the jury. Periodically, she would step behind the podium to check her notes and then step away from it when she spoke which helped drive her points home in a very effective manner. She must have learned this technique from Eric Basta.

"You are also asked to answer the question as to whether the defendant suffered and if it was especially cruel. You were picked as a jury because you represent what a reasonable person would do if they were in the defendant's shoes."

"Marissa DeVault was especially cruel by the nature of this crime. She used a hammer. She could have used a gun. The evidence shows that Stanley Cook was standing only a few feet away and had a gun in his pocket. Let me remind you that this is the same gun Marissa got from Allen Flores only a week prior to this attack. Wouldn't a reasonable man choose a gun if they were intent on killing someone?" she asked.

"Picture a household hammer. We have all hammered a nail and missed, hitting our thumbs. It doesn't feel good. It hurts a lot, doesn't it?" she asked. "Now I want to remind you of what the forensic pathologist told us. She said that Dale Harrell was hit in the temple at least two times, probably more than five times and it was hard to determine how many more times he was hit due to the destructiveness of the injury. Imagine getting hit in the head with a hammer and understand that all of us know that a hammer will cause cruel and excessive damage," she emphasized.

"Dale lived for twenty-seven days with his jaw wired shut. He had a tube down his throat and numerous tubes coming out his body. Dale knew something happened to him. The doctors have told us he was conscious and if he was conscious, he felt the debilitating pain. Dale felt the pain of trying to live every day with the wounds he had suffered. Dale's injuries were cruel and excessive and the defendant knew as any reasonable person would, that her actions would hurt him greatly."

Michelle Arino paused again, "Remember that Dale's orbital bone over the eye was crushed. Imagine the pain in your eye due to a hammer. I want you to remember the blood that was spattered on the bed, the walls, the ceiling and as far back as the closets. Imagine that you were sleeping and didn't know this was coming," she said poignantly.

"This injury was caused by Marissa DeVault and she had choices in her premeditation to kill. She chose how to kill him and she chose a hammer when a gun was only feet away. Thank you for your considerations," she concluded as she walked confidently back to the prosecution table.

I thought it interesting that so much of this trial was about a gun that had nothing to do with the murder except that it wasn't used. It was curious.

Mr. Tavasoli handled the defense argument against cruelty and financial gain. He looked sharp and ready to tackle the task at hand by being genuine and forthright in an attempt to speak to our common sense. He was certainly at a disadvantage due to our conviction the day prior. As a juror, we were told that we had to hear this argument as 'Proven' or 'Not Proven' when it came time to deliberate this section of the case. He spoke carefully and did do a better job of making direct eye contact with many jurors than he had done in closings.

"We have asked you to do a difficult job and we respect your service," he began. "This case is about emotion and red herrings. The State's case is based purely on emotion and I ask you to look at the evidence in this case. Note that Marissa called 911 shortly after the event. If she wanted her actions to be cruel and unusual, she would have left him where he was after the attack."

"You need to understand that in this phase, you are looking at aggravation and aggravation means to make something worse. She did not make anything worse. She used a hammer because it was there. If she wanted to make it worse, she would have used the claw end of the hammer and the evidence clearly shows that it was the ball of the hammer."

"I also want you to consider that all death is suffering. Dale suffered, but it was because he stayed alive in the hospital. He survived because she didn't wield killing blows and it would have been especially cruel had she done that. I want you to note that all the blows were to one part of the body and there were no marks on the rest of his body. If she wanted this to be cruel, she would have hammered him everywhere and there is no evidence that happened."

Mr. Tavasoli walked back to the podium, glanced at his notes and returned to the front of the podium. "Let's talk about red herrings. The insurance policies are red herrings. They aren't meant to make us look in that direction but when we look, there is nothing there."

"I grant you that the effective date of the policies is suspect in that they begin at the start of the year and Dale was attacked two weeks later. We have learned that the defendant is intelligent and we know that Allen Flores was an insurance expert. Common sense would tell us that no one would kill as a beneficiary only two weeks after the effectiveness of the policy. Further, Allen would have told her that she could not collect if he was murdered by her."

"I want you to consider that this couple was having marital problems and that two people would want their life insurance policies updated prior to divorce proceedings. Allen Flores didn't know about these policies."

"We learned that Dale Harrell was making eighty-three thousand a year which is more than enough to support their family and that is combined with what Marissa made working part-time at Macy's and so on. She didn't need this money and there is no evidence that she was behind on bills and needed this money."

"Ladies and gentlemen, I submit to you that Marissa killed Dale with a hammer because of the domestic violence that was prevalent in their marriage. The forensics suggests that a rape was involved. Remember that Marissa said she hit him and said, "You don't own me." This is why she killed and she never collected a dime on insurance proceeds."

"Take the time necessary to reach the right conclusions," Mr. Tavasoli said as he returned to the defense table.

The Judge asked if the prosecution wanted to present any evidence. Mr. Basta declined.

The judge than asked if the defense had any evidence to present and Mr. Tavasoli responded in the negative.

We were excused and sent to the jury room to deliberate.

It was clearly not as easy to answer those two little questions as we thought it would be.

Cherie polled the jury on both questions before we left for the day and we learned that we were exactly split down the middle on both questions.

It felt like we were back to square one as we left the building for the day.

MIGHT BE A DUCK

All of us had spent the night before thinking about a hammer. I remember coming home and seeing it lying on my patio table and picked it up. I looked at the roundness of the ball of the hammer. I felt the razor sharp sides that surrounded the claw. I raised the hammer in the air and then remembered that she had held it with two hands. The second hand added to the throttle of the handle made it feel purposeful. It felt directed and controlled. The weight carried it quickly as I let it fall in the air.

I thought of the weight that a girl could put into it as she drove it into someone's skull.

The thought that it went into Dale's skull at least four to five times brought the matter home to me in my mind. She knew what she was doing with each blow she slammed into his head. It was on purpose and she knew it would hurt. It's hard to understand how someone's mind can allow a person to believe that this is a plausible solution to any problem. It makes you wonder about the presence of evil and at what point it stepped into her soul.

In that, I had decided that murder was done in an especially cruel manner and that the defendant knew that he would suffer. Although it was significant that he lived for twenty-seven days after the attack, it was more significant that the instantaneous pain upon impact would cause great suffering.

The day began with Cherie spear-heading the conversation about the violence of the attack. We wanted to answer the question regarding the cruel manner in which Dale died. She went so far as to say that she almost requested the hammer from evidence, which was in a clear plastic sealed box and had decided against it probably thinking it may have been too prejudicial.

We spoke of the difference in dying from a rubber mallet to a knife to a gunshot and all of us agreed that a gunshot would have been the most humane given the circumstance of having a gun available. It was quite bizarre imagining yourself in a position to murder someone and making a choice between death tools.

It crossed my mind that I believed she moved the body to remove the shorts. Since it wasn't admitted as actual evidence, I couldn't consider it as part of my belief that Dale died in an exceptionally cruel manner.

We discussed the pros and cons of death by a hammer and decided that anything beyond the first or even the second blow had become an especially cruel way to be attacked and, ultimately, die.

Cherie asked that we poll ourselves anonymously to see where everyone stood and we needed to reach a conclusion on that answer. We had a choice of answering that it was proven, not proven and a column for could not agree. We threw our pieces of paper in the center of the table and Cherie created a tally board on the dry erase board while Parker read the results.

We were surprised that all of us agreed that it had been proven that Dale died in an exceptionally cruel manner or words to that effect. Once again, we felt a unity and we felt confident that we were making forward progress in the deliberations.

The second question is the one that divided us throughout the afternoon. We were to decide if it had been proven that Marissa had committed the event in expectation of pecuniary value whether it is money or property.

"The question we have to answer is whether that she did it for money, right?" Annie asked.

"Yes," Cherie answered. "It can be money or property."

"Personally, I think she did it for the money in the life insurance policies and I don't think you can change my mind on that. She had the policies all lined up and she owed Allen Flores a lot of money. She was behind in her bills and needed the money. That's what they said in closing arguments. Plus, all the policies happened to be effective on the first part of the year," Annie explained.

"My family has insurance policies and they all start at the beginning of the year. That doesn't prove she killed him for the money," Wings interjected.

"Did you consider her phone calls from Buckeye jail to Stan Cook? She sure knew how to dance around all the computer screens without being in front of the computer. It shows that she was checking on those policies all the time," Wings countered.

"I can do that," Wings said. "I check on my policies, retirement accounts and my stocks all the time. I can do that with my husband over the phone. Those phone calls don't prove anything except to say she was checking up on her accounts. She's in jail and doesn't have any money. I might be looking, too."

I jumped in the conversation pretty confident on where I stood on the issue. "What about her relationship with Allen Flores? Their whole relationship was based on money to begin with. I think it's possible that she hooked into him because of his experience with insurance. She certainly didn't sleep with him because he was a good-looking guy. I don't think she loved him. I think he was a cash cow to her," I said.

"Do you think she wanted him for his money and that would be 'pecuniary' value?" Tamara asked.

"I hadn't thought of it that way. I think she realized that the gig was up when he found out that Dale wasn't dead from being hit by a tire iron. He would want to stay far away from her so she would have to act fast to execute her plan," I said.

"I think the prosecution wants us to believe things that really aren't in the evidence," Parker said. He did not speak often but when he did it always commanded our attention because he was levelheaded and very black and white. "The defense has their story and the prosecution has their story and it's our job to figure out which is closest to the truth. To be honest, I don't think either side put up a very good argument."

"I agree," Ted said. "What's up with not giving us any evidence to work with?"

"They gave us over four hundred pieces of evidence," Parker corrected. "I think they wanted to throw as much as possible at us to see what would stick and all it created was confusion."

"Amen to that!" Victoria said.

"There's a lot here that neither side is telling us so we just have to go with the facts in front of us and I don't believe the prosecution proved their case," Parker said carefully.

"Explain that," Cherie directed.

"Well, for instance, the prosecution says she was behind on a whole bunch of bills and that's why she needed the money. We looked at her bank statements and I didn't see anything out of the ordinary. We didn't see bounced check fees and we didn't see any of her bills introduced as being late, behind or in default, Parker explained.

"We didn't see her collect any money. We also didn't see that she got a quarter of a million dollars from Allen Flores. I agree that he might have kept a ledger but where's all the money that he says she received?" Parker asked.

I nodded my head on that as I wondered why she was driving a ten year-old crappy car when she was supposedly swimming in money from Allen. I was still convinced she did it for the money but had to acknowledge that Parker had a valid point.

He continued, "Just the fact that she has insurance is not uncommon. The fact that she needed money is not proven and the fact that she did it for the money isn't proven either."

"You might have a point, Parker," Wings said. "The thing that gets me on this is the rage involved. I think she wanted him dead and it was because of things that happened in their marriage. Something pissed her off to do this. If she just did it for the money, she would have used a gun."

"If she didn't do it for the money," I presented, "then why did she do it?"

"It's not our question to answer," Parker offered. "We'll never know why."

I was not content with that answer. It seemed to me that too many coincidences lined themselves up and it was our job to connect the dots. I didn't see any other motivation except for the money. If Dale had been awake and facing Marissa, my feeling would have been drastically different. However, he was sleeping and faced away from her and couldn't be a threat. If he wasn't a threat then why did she kill him?"

"It seems we're divided on this issue so what evidence do we need to see to come to a decision?" Cherie asked. She was a smart negotiator.

"There's no evidence to see," Althea said. "We just need to make a decision."

"I don't see what there is to discuss," Ted said. "If everyone has made up their mind and there's no evidence to see, why don't we just tell the judge that we could not agree on that point?"

"He might have an idea," Cherie said referring to Ted. "Let's ask the court what we should do if we can't agree. Is everyone okay with that?"

We were okay with that and Cherie submitted the question for the   judge.

In less than an hour we were somewhat surprised when Sydney came into the jury room and told us to assemble for court as the judge was waiting.

We filed out to our usual spots and saw the whole court had been assembled with both the prosecution and defense tables staffed. The gallery was almost half-full and we saw Marissa at the defense table dressed in her usual black attire complimented with a light blue blouse. It looked like she had been crying and I dismissed that observation quickly knowing that this segment of the trial was not about sentiment or empathy. We were there to understand if we could leave our decision in the category of 'cannot agree'.

The Judge explained that it was acceptable to reach that type of decision if we felt it was our final decision. Just as quickly as we appeared in court, we were sent back to the jury room.

"Do we want to deliberate more?" Cherie asked.

"I think we know where we're at," Doc said. "I'd like for this trial not to last until Christmas."

A lot of jurors nodded their head in agreement. It felt like the trial would have no end at times and tempers were starting to flare at times in irritation.

Cherie decided to poll the jury and the results surprised the daylights out of me when nine jurors claimed they felt the motive for financial reasons was not proven.

"Let's submit that we couldn't agree and move on, Cherie," Althea offered.

"Sounds good to me," Ted volunteered.

"Whatever you want to do," Butthead said, "is good for me."

I was surprised into indecision. I respected the jurors around me and I know that our orders said that we weren't to be influenced by what other jurors said but I had to stop and take a second look. It seemed to me that everything had been about the money including her relationships but I had to consider some of the points that Parker brought up.

"Is that our final vote?" Cherie asked us.

Everyone readily agreed that we had decided that we could agree on the cruelty of the death but we could not agree that it had been done for financial reasons.

I didn't want to submit to that final vote much to everyone's consternation.

"I'd like to see her bank account and the ledger from Allen Flores before I'm comfortable making a decision," I said.

I wanted to rethink my position because I respected the other jurors and what made them think it wasn't for the money. I wanted to see the money trail and see if the prosecution was correct in saying that she was behind on her bills. I wanted to see how much she had in her bank account when the insurance checks were written. I wanted to see evidence of overdraft fees. If the finances did not line up in the manner that the prosecution purported, then I would jump to the other side.

A quarter of a million dollars disappeared and I wanted to see where it went.

The room didn't take well to my suggestion that we look one more time. I could not rest easy without knowing I had made the right decision as to whether the prosecution had proved their case or not.

"Aw, come on," Doc said seated behind me. "If we have to see more evidence, I'm going to punch somebody."

That ticked me off and I responded that no one was going to punch anyone.

"Listen up, folks," Cherie interceded. "We are not going to rush this trial along unless everyone is comfortable. Just because some of us have reached a decision, it's not fair to force anyone else into a decision. Here's what we're going to do," she commanded.

She dug out a jury question form and requested the evidence I asked for.

"Let's break for the day and come back Monday. We're in for the long haul and we need to finish this correctly. Is everyone in agreement on this?" she asked.

We all agreed and were a little surprised at the tension that had built in the room that day. We respected each other and had become more than accustomed to each other but one couldn't ignore how long we had been going through the process and the tension was understandable.

We had the weekend to think about money, Dale and Marissa. It was hard to enjoy the spring sunshine with the weight of decisions on our minds.

It was really hard to look at a hammer.

I was starting to change my mind and had the weekend to reconsider.

I just wanted to sleep at night with no regrets.

DAY 31

PECUNIARY EXPECTATIONS

I spent the weekend thinking about the connections between Allen Flores and Marissa DeVault and shared the same opinion as the rest of the jurors: that they used each other. For a moment, it was interesting to think that Allen Flores was a pecuniary gain himself but one could hardly imagine her wanting him for that price. There was money there to be sure. However, many of us thought the money train had pulled to a screeching stop upon discovering that the 'late' Dale Harrell was actually alive and well.

That had its own issue because few of us thought that Allen was a threat if she didn't pay him back. In other words, we couldn't see him as the impetus for hurrying up to kill Dale just so she could pay him back. He may have owned a gun but it was hard to see him using it in a threatening way. He just seemed too wimpy.

There is another question that has been difficult finding an answer for. Why did Marissa pick that particular day to commit the murder? I didn't see why it couldn't have been another day. It would seem to me that it would take a lot for a person to pick up a hammer and put it into someone's head without having a reason for the day they are doing it.

This creates a problem when the links to the pecuniary reasons are muddled with the possibility that something set her off that night. There was a lot of rage in the blows and an apparent lack of planning for picking that day. This creates a shadow of a doubt in my mind as far as the motive being financial.

We went into the jury room after a long weekend and everyone felt refreshed and was quite cordial and even laughing with each other. The tension had dissipated and was replaced by many of us bringing in donuts, peanut butter bakes, cookies and a host of other things. It looked like a buffet in the center of the table. Even the Judge had restocked all of our goodies including peanut butter stuffed pretzels, Red Vines and Lindt Chocolates. We enjoyed our company again.

The only evidence we requested was the item of Marissa's bank account and Allen Flores ledger where he claimed to have loaned her over $300,000 over a two-year period. I wanted to match the dates of the money he said he loaned her to her bank account to see if they would match.

We lined the documents next to each other and started checking bank balances especially near the date of Dale's murder. A couple of overdraft fees appeared on the fourteenth of January but we wondered if she would have even been aware of it. It did not look like impetus for a sense of urgency in murdering Dale.

I looked at the top of the bank account statement and saw that it was the shared account that he had created for her since he felt she wasn't good with money and this would help discipline her in finances. It was clearly apparent that any deposits were directly from Allen and that she rarely used the account except for a few automatic check payments for household utilities. This also told me that it was worthless.

We needed to see her bank account to know where all of Allen's money was going. Further, the prosecution had said she loved money but few of us could see what she liked about it. If people love money, they like to buy things and show it off. We didn't see any purchases except for household family and the infamous trip to Orlando with Allen. It still killed me that Dale had helped pack the car for her to go with Allen to Florida.

We looked at Allen's ledger and few of his transactions went into the joint account and it made Allen's ledger suspect. Maybe he was using a ledger to keep control of Marissa. He could have been holding it over her head and who is to say he wasn't making up figures in the document? Certainly, anything to do with Allen Flores was suspect, and foggy and clouded in dirty mysteries beginning with the video camera taping of his sexual escapades. . He also had child pornography on his computer, although it was said to be a comparatively small amount.

We dug through the evidence in hope of finding bills that were overdue and none were to be found, be on our table or on the evidence list of four hundred and thirty-six pieces.

I had changed my mind based on these things realizing that my basic premise in believing she killed for money was seriously flawed. It was based on Allen Flores and it was based on the fact that I thought she needed money. Without bills or her bank account records, one can't say that this segment of the case was proved beyond a shadow of a doubt.

"I'll tell you what I think," Wings offered while eating half a blueberry muffin. "I think she planned to kill him but it wasn't supposed to be that night. Something set her off and she did it. Hitting him five times tells me she had a lot of rage and that isn't how she planned to do it."

"I think that's possible," I said. "I also think she put all the pieces in one room together and hoped it would just come together. It seems poorly planned if it was supposed to go down that way."

"That's what I'm saying, "Wings agreed. "She didn't plan to hit him five times and I think she was going to use the gun but something pissed her off."

Wings had a good point and whether it was right or wrong, it was my tipping point to say the prosecution had not proved that Marissa killed Dale for pecuniary or financial reasons. I think she did and we all think she did but without direct evidence to link the overwhelming circumstantial evidence, it became the shadow of a doubt that made me change my mind.

Cherie arranged a jury poll on the question and we dropped our torn yellow pieces of paper in the center of the table, each piece had our final decision on it. Ted read aloud as Cherie polled and we finished with two jurors saying the case was proven while ten of us said the prosecution had not proved that the deed was done for pecuniary reasons.

We notified the court that we had reached a verdict and we were in the jury box only forty-five minutes later with the court assembled.

It was speedy in its formalities. We saw the defendant dressed in a black sweater wearing glasses as she was seated with her defense team. The gallery featured very few people and the prosecution team waited silently with Mr. Eric Basta, at the end of the table.

The Judge's assistant read the two verdicts for the court to hear with the first verdict being on the death being tied to financial value. One of the jurors saw that the defense team looked happy upon hearing that we could not agree on the verdict.

The next verdict was read in regards to Dale being murdered in an especially cruel manner and that our decision affirmed that the case was proven.

Judge Steinle III informed the court that the defendant had met the criteria for the third stage. Furthermore, the jury would begin proceedings for the final stage of the trial first thing in the morning.

.

Marissa DeVault had just been qualified for the death penalty in the State of Arizona because the jury had determined that at least one of two conditions existed.

It was up to the law to tell us what to do next...

Tonight featured the phenomenon called the "Blood Red Moon" over the Arizona nighttime sky from the first of four lunar eclipses this year.

It seemed a foreboding of things to come.

DAY 32

MITIGATION

Judge Steinle opened the day with a discussion of the final phase of the trial of which we were about to embark. As he always did at the beginning of a new phase, he read aloud the jury instructions and the rule of law regarding this phase. This was called the penalty phase of the trial and sometimes referred to as the mitigation phase. The jury had each been given a packet and read silently as the Judge read aloud for the court. I believe this was also done so that it would be on record via the court reporter.

It was explained to us that our role would be slightly different from a normal criminal prosecution in that we would be making the decision on the penalty whereas a typical trial had the judge handling the sentencing.

The presentation order we had been used to with the prosecution speaking first, followed by the defense with a prosecution rebuttal would now be reversed. The defense would present opening statements first and finishing with a defense rebuttal, while the prosecution would present statements secondly. This phase was expected to last throughout the middle of next week with closing arguments expected on Monday after the presentation of witnesses.

Mr. Tavasoli presented his opening statement first. He was dressed in a light gray suit with a matching gray tie and complemented by a soft pink shirt. His blue eyes were focused and were successful in making eye contact with the jury. He also seemed more relaxed than at any other time in the trial.

"Ladies and Gentleman, I'd like to thank you for the time you have spent deliberating and, although the result is not what we wanted, I wanted to thank you for your diligence."

He paused and glanced at his notes and then came to the front of the podium and faced us. His words were deliberate and unfaltering for the most part.

"This stage of the trial is different than the stages that you have already experienced. As you know, the jury handles the sentencing of the defendant, and not the judge, and that is a great responsibility. This is no longer about reasonable doubt and you are no longer weighing the value of evidence."

"This is about legal liability versus moral culpability. You must reach a decision based on your own moral assessments and individually reach a decision. You have the right to believe or not believe what you hear and you now must look at things as being more probably true than not probably true," he said

He moved closer to us. "I know it's a different way to look at things than you are used to. I also caution you to make sure you respect each other when you ultimately go through the deliberation process," he said walking back to the podium, checking his notes.

He came around the podium and acted as if he was telling a story. He began slowly and carefully, drawing our attention. "I want you to consider John or Jane Q. Public. John or Jane is married and they are contributing members to society. They work hard, they pay their taxes, they go to church on Sunday and, if all goes well, they raise some kids and have a nice family. They stay in the same home and go to the same school while they're growing up. John and Jane have good parents who steered them right in their upbringing," he said stopping to rub his eye. He straightened his tie and continued.

"John and Jane have given their kids stability." He looked toward Marissa and back at us. "Marissa didn't get to have the luxury of a stable family that John and Jane got. You heard in the testimony of an earlier phase that Marissa was a stepchild in a strange home at eight years of age. Marissa didn't know who her father was and her mother was an alcoholic. There was abuse in her family and alcohol contributed to it. At the age of twelve, possibly younger, she was sexually abused by her first stepfather who not only took her panties off but made her touch him as well. As much as we don't like to think about things like this, he had sex with her, as well." He stopped and looked at his feet and then surveyed us with his eyes and began speaking again. One could have heard a pin drop in the full courtroom.

"We will be presenting expert opinions as to the effects of being sexually abused and what it does to a person. It is not an exact science but it will show behaviors consistent with the abuse she suffered. This abuse is what made her warped. These experiences ultimately influenced her behaviors later in life and ultimately contributed to her act of murder. She did not have control of these experiences and they are what made her today."

"We know that Marissa has lied but you need to understand that this is a survival pattern because to survive in an un-protective world, one learns to survive by keeping secrets and she had a lot of secrets she was ashamed to share with anyone."

"Let me ask you, would John Q Public have found himself in the same position she was in had he been sexually abused and lived in an abusive family? I sincerely doubt it. The next question is should John Q Public have the same moral culpability as Marissa and the life she suffered through when she was a child?"

"The way we are raised defines our behaviors as adults. Whether we like it or not, it impacts our decisions later in life. The way we are raised defines who we are and those who are raised in a morally defunct family are at a great disadvantage to those who are raised the way we are supposed to raise children. Children are not supposed to be touched in that way. Abuse should not happen but it does. When it does, it creates a mitigating factor that you cannot ignore."

"The damage of abuse forever alters us the rest of our lives and is ultimately why Dale died. If Marissa had been raised in a stable environment, I guarantee you that she would not have ultimately been led down this path."

Mr. Tavasoli paused again and looked at Marissa. "This experience has changed Marissa. She has had therapy for her issues. She tries to contribute positively to her environment and she helps other inmates. I want you to understand that this phase culminates with the feeling in your gut and your feeling should be that she deserves life in prison. Thank you for your time," he said stepping back to the defense table where Marissa sat.

Mr. Basta for the prosecution was next to present his opening statement. I had grown comfortable with his style and looked forward to it when he spoke. He had a subtle sense of humor of which he used sparingly but was effective in making us comfortable. He did not attack with vengeance but rather drove home his points stating the evidence speaks for itself. He was careful, focused and detailed when he spoke. He was always confident in spite of the occasional admonishment from the judge that we had seen throughout the trial.

Eric Basta always presented himself in a crisp clean suit that was stunningly free of wrinkles including those often seen on the tail of a man's coat after driving to work. Today he wore a light yellow shirt with a sharp checked pattern tie complimented with a tan suit. His shoes, however, always drew my attention because the leather of the tie-up shoes was well worn and unpolished.

The shoes of men always told me something about the person. A rubber-soled shoe told me that the person was more into comfort than fashion. A perfectly polished shoe told me that person wants to make an impression and is not afraid to kiss some ass along the way. A worn and scuffed shoe told me that this person was not afraid to work, did not care a lot about fashion and didn't want to kiss anyone's behind. I didn't think it negative at all and the work involved in prosecuting this case was a testament to that.

Mr. Basta began his opening statements and did something I hadn't seen very often. He spent most of his time behind the podium with his hands on either side of it as if it were a lectern. I didn't get the message we were being lectured, but rather as a subliminal sign that the State of Arizona stood behind its case. This subtlety, although probably not intentional, gave the message of strength.

"We, too," he began, "would like to thank all of you for the attention to detail in this case and the amount of time that you have put into it. I know it's been a long haul and we recognize that," he said, pausing to reflect on his notes.

"Remember where we are in this case. The defendant has been convicted of first-degree pre-meditated murder with the aggravating circumstance of an especially cruel death in which the offense was committed. You have seen the evidence and you need to remember it for this phase of the trial."

"The burden of proof is on the defense to show a preponderance of evidence that will mitigate the aggravating circumstance of this case. In other words, you must look at mitigating factors that will reduce the defendant's moral culpability in this case and that is up to each of you to decide. You have to ask yourself, "Do mitigating circumstances reduce her responsibility for the way in which Dale was murdered?" he asked us.

One could see his eyes darting randomly across the jury's faces. He even caught my eyes twice.

"As a jury, you will look at mitigating factors through witnesses. You decide if witnesses are credible. Does their testimony reduce the cruelness of the crime? I need you all to keep an open mind. I want you to ask yourselves if: 1) the mitigation factors were proven, 2) if the defendant is less morally culpable and 3) are the proven circumstances greater than the mitigating factors? Thank you," he finished, stacking his papers in quiet finality on the podium. He stepped back to the prosecution table.

Mr. Basta then brought two victim impact statements to the stand and read them aloud to the jury. The first statement was from Dale Harrell's twin sister, Mindi and was followed by a statement from her daughter.

These were hard to listen to as they described Dale as a fun loving guy who loved to build things. They spoke of a love lost and never to be returned. The letters spoke of the hell and guilt they went through from losing a brother and uncle unexpectedly. They spoke from the heart and I thought of Dale as my eyes welled up.

The defense presented Dr. Neil Websdale, a child abuse expert whom we had seen the first day that the defense presented their case.

He spoke with an English accent, and was sharp, both in his demeanor and dress. He had authored a number of books and was an expert in this field. He was also the doctor who had mentioned the term "Murder of the Soul" in his earlier testimony and I remember thinking that it was a little too far-reaching for a term.

He had a strong credibility when I had last seen him but I remember being confused at his purpose, as his testimony had not tied directly to Marissa. He had been there as an educational witness in my mind and I remember taking notes like crazy but it was like plowing through the testimony.

There is nothing negative about that except that the inherent problem with a witness like this is that so many of their results and conclusions seem to be based primarily on how Marissa responded on psychological examinations. Most of us felt that since she was an adept liar, it would be logical to assume that she was a liar on her examination answers.

She could fake good by responding to a question as if she's an angel and she could fake bad by responding on a questionnaire that she was the most abused child in the world. In other words, she was a master malingerer.

Given that the premise for conclusions is faulty, it makes taking notes of the testimony like plowing through mud. You know that the testimony is tainted because Marissa is doing the tainting.

We heard what we had speculated in the jury room. Most of us had felt that she had been sexually abused at a young point in her life and it did impact how she behaved later in life. The problem remains that is that it is hard to believe or qualify her justification for first-degree murder. I remember Mr. Basta asking a witness if there was ever a link made between abuse and homicide and the answer was negative.

This question is difficult and I wonder how deep we will have to go into it in the jury room. It made me think of my past and how it would influence my decision-making. But, just because I was abused, it didn't give me cause to kill. I am still in the middle on this but I can feel the question looming.

The Judge admonished us that we were not to speak to each other or anyone else about the case until we were back to deliberation. We are now at twelve jurors with two alternates and were happy to be re-united with Lucy and Jarod.

We learned from Jeebs that Bruce's prostate cancer had become aggressive and the doctors wanted to be aggressive in their approach to it. It was not good news and I've included him in my prayers.

DAY 33

GRAIN OF SALT

We had two days of psychologists and my opinion is better than yesterday. I think there was some frustration in that this science doesn't give concrete proof of many things. It is not as simple to interpret as forensic evidence. In forensic evidence, one sees an item in black and white and it's as if you can touch and feel the item when it used for deliberating.

Psychology, on the other, is sometimes vague and shrouded in terminology. It carries the 'iffy at best" quality about it when used in deliberation. One cannot trust it completely especially when the basis of results uses self-reporting and we know the quality of Marissa's word. A flimsy premise means it won't stand five minutes in a jury room.

My question is why do we only see psychologists and psychiatrists after something happens? Their inherent value would be before something happens. I realize the stigma still attached to seeing a therapist but I think they are highly under-valued in what they can do to prevent tragedies and steer people in the right direction.

The testimony of the two well learned psychologists created a visual of Marissa as a child. I realize that most of the information comes from interviews of Marissa but it was somewhat verified by interviews with her stepsister. I know that at the same time, I must not speak toward empathy or sympathy.

Marissa Suzanne DeVault was born November 6, 1977. She had an alcoholic mother, an alcoholic grandmother and did not know her true father. She thought Daniel Carlson was her biological father until the age of seven when she learned that he was her stepfather.

Marissa learned to lie at a very young age. She lived in a somewhat tumultuous but controlling environment. She learned quickly that it was better to lie to avoid a spanking and run the risk of getting caught. Her parental guardians believed that spanking was a form of discipline and it was acceptable whether it left marks or not. Marissa learned from her mother how to use make-up to cover bruises before she went to school. She learned what it felt like to be slapped, hit and have her hair pulled. She felt her mother was serious when her mother told her she was worthless and wished she had never been born. The violence was a secret in the family and the make-up was used on a regular occasion.

She was molested three times before she was seventeen. Of particular interest was a man named Eddie that had raped her when she was sixteen. He molested someone else later and it made Marissa jealous.

Marissa was put in a new home at eight years of age and she experienced what she felt was abandonment. She was a stepchild who had to survive in a strange family and she learned to fend for herself by the use of lying, sex and manipulation. To make matters worse, she was molested by this stepfather between the ages of twelve and fourteen. This fact is taken with a grain of salt but would help explain her dissociative behavior later in life. This would also explain why she liked to harbor secrets and how she learned to lie so often. When one lies a lot, it becomes habit and it was a learned habit of survival from a very young age. She got a new stepfather around the age of fourteen, Michael Wright.

Marissa was pregnant with Rhiannon at seventeen years of age and married to Dale by the time she was nineteen. Marissa felt the pregnancy with Rhiannon was death to both the daughter and herself. By the time Marissa was twenty-three, she was a stripper.

Her life feels like a train that was never on the rails. I don't speak of this with pity but I do understand much of what she went through from my own home environment.

There was a piece where Dr. Jon Conte spoke of her being interrogated by her parents when she did something wrong. I know these interrogations because my father was relentless about them. I remember standing for hours in one spot while my father would ask questions while he ate his dinner. It is a different kind of torture. The best response in those situations is to apologize a lot, lie a lot and use the excuse that you forgot. These learned responses sometimes kept situations from escalating into full-fledged beatings.

Much to the chagrin of the Judge, we learned that Marissa had digital sex with her stepsister at age fourteen.

Dr. Conte explained that this is natural at this age and most kids at that age do 'exploration' and that was okay.

The end result of his testimony did not show it to be an excuse by any stretch of the imagination in the death of Dale. It did show to me that she was not set up for success. It is this issue that I will take back to the jury room with the other jurors. I believe in my heart that abuse existed in her family when she was young and she carried those same learned habits into her adult life.

It was always in the back of my mind for two days of testimony. Is this enough evidence to counter the heinous way in which Dale died?

At some point, we learned that Dr. DeMarte was coming back to testify for the prosecution. I certainly remembered her for being the very attractive psychologist from Michigan State.

I also knew, that I may as well put a big X in my notes over the last two days of testimony. I nicknamed her "Psycho-Killer" due to the damage she had done to the same psychologists in the first stage of the trial. In that, I expected total destruction of testimony and it may just cancel each other out in the end. Her success was her knowledge of terminology and her ability to point out the inconsistencies in the self-reporting segment of the defense experts. I knew what to expect.

The thought that crosses my mind is whether we all understand the damage it causes when we raise our hands to our children. Do we do it once or does it become habit? When it becomes habit, do we understand the damage it causes to the brain and the soul of the victim? It shapes our choices and we survive in a world that we have learned to be untrustworthy and feared. We carry these experiences and some of us live, some die, some choose to die and some choose to kill.

The defense presented a battery of witnesses that took us by surprise in the emotional weight that they would carry. The next three witnesses were like the shards of glass left on the tile floor after a glass shatters. They were the debris field left in the wake of the death of Dale and how he died.

They were also the witnesses who slept in the adjacent rooms as Dale was slaughtered.

Rhiannon was re-introduced as a witness. She was the oldest daughter and stepchild of Dale who was now eighteen years of age. She looked cautious and delicate wearing a pale pink dress with a white sweater and sandals. She tenuously sat herself in the witness chair. Somebody assisted her with pulling the standing microphone close to her. We all remembered that she had a soft voice.

I noticed the cameras had been removed from the courtroom as was similar the first time we were witness to her testimony.

Andrew Clemency of the defense handled the questioning. He wore a gray suit with a white shirt and red tie. He always reminded me of Sarge from Gomer Pyle with his brush cut and gravelly voice.

"Did you see violence in your house when you were growing up?" he asked Rhiannon while looking at the jury.

"Yes, I did," she answered in her soft voice. "It happened all the time."

"Did you ever see your father hit your mother?"

"Yes."

"Was this a rare thing or did it happen more often?"

"It happened a lot. We knew we had to hide when he would get mad."

"Did he ever hit you?" he asked. He put his hands on his hips and looked at the jury knowingly.

She looked down and then up again. "Yes, he did. I was bad a lot and I would get punished."

"Thank you," Mr. Clemency said as he went back to the defense table.

Mr. Basta got up and stood at the podium.

"Can I get you anything, Rhiannon? Do you need water?" he asked.

"No, I'm fine," she answered seeing the pitcher in front of her.

"Let me ask you, and I know this is hard to talk about, but did your mother ever hit you?" Mr. Basta asked.

"Yes."

"How did she hit you?"

"She would slap me or kick me."

"Did it ever leave marks?

"Yes. My mom showed me how to use make-up to cover it up."

"Thank you, and did you lie a lot?" he asked after a pause.

"Yes. I don't anymore but I used to."

"Who taught you how to lie?" Mr. Basta asked.

She looked a little confused at the question. "I taught myself how to lie."

"Did you ever see your mother lie?" he asked pointedly.

"She lied all the time, although it was mostly about Allen."

"You had a sexual relationship with Allen's son, didn't you?"

"I did," she answered quietly.

"His name was David and he was your age, wasn't he?"

"Yes," she answered.

"How did your parents feel about this?"

"My mom said I couldn't see him anymore and Allen said the same thing. They were both pretty mad at me."

"I see. Didn't you continue to go Allen's house with your mom even though you were told to stay away from him?"

"Yes," she answered.

"No further questions," Mr. Basta said leaving the podium.

Mr. Clemency got up and asked Rhiannon one question. "Did Dale ever call you names or demean you in any way?"

"All the time," she answered softly.

"No more questions of this witness," Mr. Clemency said.

The court was silent as the next witness was lead in by her attorney. The attorney was very protective and handled her with obvious kid gloves as she led her thirteen year-old witness to the witness stand.

There was no denying that this witness began our downward slope on an emotional roller coaster. The witness was introduced as Marissa's second daughter who was now about twelve or thirteen. Her name was Khiernan and she was dressed in a loose fitting tan dress with a small black petticoat, black patent leather shoes and thick glasses. She struck me like a newborn fawn in unfamiliar territory. The courtroom must have seemed large and intimidating to her and one felt like it took enormous strength for her to be here.

She read a typewritten letter that had been retyped by the defense after certain items were taken out. Her speaking was soft and faltering and all of us felt the pain that she had inside.

It was everything I could do not to cry. I suppose if someone looked at me, they would just see a man brushing something casually away from his cheekbone.

Her letter recalled the times that Dale would hit his mother. She was sad about everything that happened and was sad that she lost both her mother and father. She spoke of a steak knife that was stuck in the ceiling of her room and knew that Dale did it when he got angry. She spoke softly of all her toys getting destroyed when he was mad.

It was hard to concentrate on what she was saying because it was starting to really sink in that Marissa's damage stretched far beyond what she had done to Dale's skull. These children were victims of her violence and no matter the result, they would carry this with them the rest of their lives. They looked fragile and damaged in their demeanor and one could only hope that they would get a chance at a decent adult life.

It struck me how selfish Marissa's act was in the face of the life of her daughters. It was as if her hammer had damaged everyone in her reach.

I looked at the defendant and she was clearly emotional. I didn't feel sorry for her. I felt sorry for the wreckage of a family that once was.

Khiernan stepped from the witness chair and was led out of the courtroom.

The next witness brought the courtroom to its knees.

The doors behind the gallery opened. Diahnon Harrell came to the stand with the same attorney that had accompanied the prior child witnesses. She was a heavier lady who could be mistaken for a den mother if one didn't know she was an attorney. Diahnon looked small as she was led to the steps of the witness stand.

Diahnon was about eleven or twelve years old wearing a flower print dress complimented with a green top and black shoes. Her hand clutched a letter. She looked like Michael Jackson's daughter, Paris, when she had spoken at his funeral.

She sat on the witness stand with her lawyer behind her. The lawyer stepped forward and slid the microphone closer to Diannon's mouth.

Diahnon looked toward the courtroom and then looked at the jury. She looked at her piece of paper and one could see her hands shaking with nervousness. She began to read her letter aloud as the court listened silently.

"I am so sad that my mother and father are gone. I never experienced true sadness until..." she said with her voice trailing off. Suddenly she broke down crying and all of us felt it simultaneously.

Diahnon's attorney requested a break for the witness and we were quickly dismissed to the jury room.

It was one of the few times that our entrance to the jury room was marked with complete silence. We busied ourselves with getting a drink of water or grabbing a snack. We didn't talk to one another, as we were lost in thought. I think many of us were trying to control the painful emotion that was inside each of us. We couldn't talk for risk of showing this emotion. It was raw and deep as one saw the true damage of the hammer swing.

The court's composure was regained as we were led back to the jury box. It had been decided that the eleven year-old witness could not finish reading the letter and that her attorney would complete the reading aloud of her letter to the court.

Diahnon spoke of the sadness that was with her every day and how her grandparents could not replace what her family once was. She spoke of her mother having her bones broken by Dale and how she still did not know how her life would begin again. She missed her mother and wanted her back despite what everyone thought of her.

The conclusion of the letter led to the dismissal of court for the afternoon. It was none too early for many of us as we could feel the weight of our eventual decision growing heavier upon us.

I drove home thinking of all we had witnessed and I couldn't help thinking of the many years ago when I took my parents to court.

My brothers and sisters were in the same age progression as the family of the victim. I imagined how hard it would have been had we taken the witness stand against our parents. I also realized at the same time how implausible it was that we ever would have been on the stand given my father's position in the community. I think I understood why the Judge would not have allowed that to happen. It was a true Catch-22 with no winners in the end. If the Judge had allowed my siblings on the stand, it would have ripped apart the family. However, he did not allow them on the stand and it ripped apart the family anyway. It just took a longer process to do it.

This stage of the trial had turned dark and sad. It weighed on the mind and infected your dreams.

I wondered if the defendant would ever take the stand.

ANGUISH IN ALLOCUTION

The first witness of the day was featured via a connection with Skype and was heard by the court much like a conference call with Mr. Tavasoli asking questions to a sound box.

The person on the other end was Jeanine Carlson who was Marissa's stepsister and had grown up with her from age five through their teenage years. It was explained that Jeanine could not be here in person because of medical reasons. She had just had a baby by cesarean section and it temporarily limited her ability to travel.

Jeanine's voice resonated as calm and well put together. Her answers felt honest and gave us a decent picture of Marissa's childhood living with her mother Samantha. Jeanine stayed in

Marissa's household every other weekend and every other holiday to make both families happy.

Jeanine painted a picture of a very tense household and did not remember a lot of pleasurable times except those times she would spend alone with Marissa as sisters. Their relationship had been close.

Unfortunately, much of the contact with her stepmother, Samantha was painful as the mother did not make a pleasant environment. It was clear that alcohol played a role in some negative events. It was also clear that their lives were filled with unpredictability and bouts with physical violence. Incidents that included belts on bare bottoms, hair pulling and mouths getting washed out with soap.

The two girls lived with tenseness and interrogations. There was an incident where a granola bar disappeared from the pantry and the mother noticed it. They were both interrogated and told to stand for hours in one spot until a confession was made. No confession was ever made but the memories held the incident intact.

Jeanine spoke of the verbal abuse that included being called sluts and tramps. They were told they were stupid and dumb. They were ugly and didn't need to be around. They never knew what would trigger the rages that Samantha went through, but they knew the results would be damaging to them one way or another. She mentioned a time when she and Marissa were exploring digital sex.

The minefield of their lives in that household continued for years and Jeanine always looked forward to going home with her real family, and felt bad for what Marissa had to go through. She also noticed that Marissa had learned how to lie and how it got them through many situations that could have been worse had Marissa not lied.

Jeanine was helpful for Marissa in a lot of ways as it helped us understand a little more why Marissa became the way she did. It certainly did not provide excuses or resolution but it did give a pause to think of Marissa as more human than the person who had committed the crime.

The next witness for the defense was the most stunning of all and as unexpected as a June bug in a blizzard. The witness introduced by Judge Steinle, was the defendant, who had a right to make an allocution statement. The defendant had a right to speak as well as not to speak.

We saw a rustle by the defense table as Marissa stood up and picked up a packet of papers and walked toward the podium in front of the jury. She looked behind her at the defense table as she made her way fifteen feet to the podium. Time seemed to slow down as we took in the fully unexpected sight. I remember thinking that it was about time that we heard from this murderess. I also remember the conflicted feelings I had when looking at her.

She stood in front of us wearing almost all black including her shoes which looked like dance slippers. She looked small like a wet rat in the rain.

She placed her hands on either side of her document and looked tenuously toward us. She began speaking and I remember thinking that we could not trust the words that came out of her mouth. I remember wondering if we would see the evil that had taken Dale's life. Mostly, I was looking for tears and expecting lies.

Marissa spoke in broken fragments. "She struggled to read her prepared speech but it no longer applied as she realized her audience, the jury of fifteen, was looking for something that could not be conveyed in the words she had written."

She had to bare her soul in front of the jury and she had to be honest, something we truly doubted we would see. She had to show us her soul and she had to show remorse. We did not want to see remorse because of the punishment. We wanted to see true remorse for the crime she had committed.

"I did this," she began looking to the jury, "I am so sorry for the untimely demise of Dale. If I could rewind the tape and play it back, I would do things differently."

At that exact moment, I felt anger at the softening of how Dale died. For a second, it reminded me of Jodi Arias when she referred to the death of her slaughtered boyfriend as having "passed away."

They didn't *"pass away"*. They were brutally murdered at the hands of the defendant and I was incensed that it would be put in any other term of reference but murder.

I had to keep an open mind and searched her eyes for truth or lies.

Marissa looked around the courtroom and it was as if she suddenly realized that everything was about her and what she had done. The court was silent as they waited expectantly for her continuing words. It was as if she was in the center of a vortex and the court surrounded her. She became small and significant at the same time.

She stopped reading and spoke in real tears. She removed her glasses and wiped at the wetness on her cheeks. She looked at the jury and realized these were all the moments wrapped into one as she stared at the jury.

She realized that these were the words that may or may not save her life.

"I am so sorry I did all this. All the lawyers who are here are here because of me. I see the pain I have caused my family. I took Dale and he was a wonderful," she said, breaking down and crying.

The court remained silent, watching her.

She took her glasses off and wiped her face. Her hands were shaking. He eyes looked around furtively like a condemned man might look prior to be stoned. She was afraid. She looked toward the ceiling.

"If there was anything I could do to undo what I have done, I would do it. I live this nightmare every day and it is my fault. It is my fault. There will be generations of people in my family, people who are not born yet who will have to carry the weight of my actions and I am so sorry," she said crying again.

"Objection," Mr. Basta, the prosecutor suddenly said from his table.

Judge Steinle III just glared at him and then looked back at the defendant.

She looked at the Judge as if she wanted to know if she could continue. The Judge nodded his head for her to continue.

Marissa looked back at us. "I could help inmates and I could do some good. I really could," she said in a pleading voice.

"If I could do anything to get Dale back, I would. I am so sorry," she said.

She looked toward us and down at her paper on the podium. She put her hands flat on the podium and the then raised her fingers and hand on both hands while her wrist stayed touched the podium. Her palms were raised vertically and it looked like she was in a telephone booth pressing her hands on the glass. It then looked like she was trying to push away. She was in the center of the vortex and there was no one there to blame but her.

For the first time in the duration of the trial, I saw true fear in her eyes. I remember thinking that I could not show sympathy in any way and had to look straight ahead.

One could not show a tear even though they were welling up. I don't know who the emotion was for, whether it was for Dale or the children or this defendant in front of us. It was a soft realization that she was begging for her life and it was a difficult position to be in when one looked back at her.

The emotion that enveloped her face was raw and guttural. She was almost ugly in her pain. Blue veins pushed out of her forehead as tears ran down her face. She looked alone, frightened and lost. There was no one there to help her. She had orchestrated the show and the reason for everyone behind here. She cowered in front of us. The pain seemed to pull from her deepest regions of her body and came out as primitive. She stepped back, afraid of us and afraid of everything she had done.

The whole time, I wondered if she was telling the truth or if she was putting on a show like we had witnessed throughout the trial.

Marissa took her papers from the podium and ran to the guard that was seated near where she usually sat and said,

"Take me out of here."

She crumpled up her speech much like a spoiled girl might do when not getting her way. She looked almost pathetic as her cries turned to heaving wails.

"The defense rests," Mr. Tavasoli said standing.

"We are in recess," the Judge answered. "Please take the jury."

We were led back to the jury room and none of us looked at each other although I saw many of us wiping our eyes quickly so the others wouldn't see us. One was not human if one did not feel the emotion that had exploded in the courtroom.

The prosecution began their case after lunch with the reading of a letter from Samantha, the mother of Marissa. It was eerily distant in its tone and made me think that this is something my parents would do if my life were on the line. I would have expected such a close familial person to appear and instead we had a letter to listen to as if the mother had washed her hands of Marissa.

We listened carefully and heard of a grandmother who had taken three girls and was somewhat resentful of the responsibilities that she had acquired. At one point, she commented that in a mere twenty years she would be seventy-five and it was a shame that she had to take care of kids when she should be relaxing in retirement. I know that isn't exactly what she said but her absence seemed to speak volumes of her distaste of Marissa. I suppose it is understandable on one hand but it is also cold on the other.

Samantha spoke of taking care of three girls who would be forever damaged because of Marissa's actions. She spoke of taking them to school, bathing them and taking them to therapy. She detailed that each had nightmares and all the nightmares were different to each child and she was weighted with taking care of them and their needs. Those needs and nightmares would not be there except for Marissa's actions.

When Samantha spoke of all of them being robbed of peace, she was careful to note that Rhiannon was buried in guilt. . Rhiannon felt that being expelled from school the day before the attack had somehow caused Dale's death. This misplaced guilt had buried the family in therapy and none of the family would ever be normal again.

It was all because of Marissa and one could feel that the mother truly wished she had never been born.

The day finished with the computer expert, Detective Scott Zuberbeuhler, speaking for the prosecution. He was asked about a computer file that was saved and printed from Allen Flores' computer on January 14, 2009. This document was printed at midnight, only hours before Dale was attacked with the hammer.

I didn't remember seeing this in evidence and was surprised that we were hearing about a document from the same night. It would be the first thing we would look at when we got to the deliberation stage. I made sure to mark the evidence number so we could request it later.

The document was called, "There Is Something Odd Going On."

Detective Zuberbeuhler also detailed that there was a search on the computer for engagement rings about a week prior to the attack. Presumably, these were the rings that Stan had spoken of when he thought Marissa and he might be getting married. There were no divorce papers ever found or drafted on any computer.

I wondered about the document, "Something Odd Going On," and was it the smoking gun that would mitigate the value of the testimony of Marissa's childhood life.

It was too bad that Dale had nothing to mitigate the value of his life except the smashed and damaged skull that would live in our memories until we went to our graves.

Sydney led us back to the jury room.

"I swear, I'm not talking about the trial," Wings suddenly said after Sydney left.

"What?" Cherie asked.

"What in the world is digital sex?"

I remember looking at Jeebs and he was shaking his head. He looked back at me.

"What are you guys hiding?" Cherie asked.

"Nothing," Jeebs answered.

We busied ourselves gathering our things to leave.

Wings wouldn't let it go. "Well? What's digital sex?"

Jeebs blushed. "Finger sex," he said quietly.

Wings got a funny look on her face. "What is it?"

"It's finger sex," I said, not wanting to see Jeebs tortured anymore.

"Oh my God, is nothing sacred in this trial?" Wings said with exasperation.

Apparently not, I thought.

DAY 35

PSYCHO KILLER

I spent the weekend seeing the ghosts of Marissa's allocution statement. I could see her hands and wrists on the podium as she pushed the jury away by raising her hands to face us. I could see the wetness of her face as she cried. I remembered the way she had exited and had asked the guard to take her out of there. I also remembered the echo of her cries as we were escorted back to the jury room.

I couldn't help thinking of the three young daughters who had testified in defense of saving their mother's life. The sounds of sadness made me sad when thinking of a future that their mother had made uncertain.

I thought of Dale and the justice that he deserved. It was sad that he would never see his daughters grow up. It was awful that he would not walk this earth again because of someone's selfishness. It was horrible that he lived for almost a month in a torn and tattered condition while Marissa walked free. I do not think she even visited him in his dying days even though she was free.

I felt the weight of this responsibility in our eventual decision. I could feel it in the pit of my stomach and prayed to God that when our time came to decide, that it would be the right decision. This was not the first time that I thought that there were no winners at the conclusion of the trial. There would only be more ancillary damage for all parties concerned.

Mr. Basta once again presented board certified, clinical psychologist Dr. Janeen DeMarte. She wore a black dress-suit with a white top and fashionable necklace. I remembered her as the Michigan State Doctorate graduate, and given her young age is 'well-versed' in her science. Her testimony as a psychologist killer was entirely expected.

The prosecutor handed us a single sheet of paper for us to look at while Dr. DeMarte testified. It contained the "Criteria for Anti-Social Personality Disorder". The testimony that followed was a description of how Marissa fit this diagnosis.

"Can you explain how the defendant fits this diagnosis specifically in the area of lying and deceitfulness?"

"The defendant has an abnormal proclivity for lying as evidenced in such things as her interrogation tapes with the police and her phone calls from the jail where she was incarcerated," the doctor pointed out confidently. "In the interrogation tapes, we hear Marissa lie about such things as having a son that died in childbirth. She lies about her relationship with Allen Flores. She also lies about Stanley Cook having committed the offense."

"You said she lies in tapes from the Buckeye jail. Can you be more specific?"

"In one phone call, she calls Stanley Cook and tells him how bad her mother is. Yet, in another phone call to her mother, she tells her the complete opposite. At another point, she claims she knows nothing of the finances in the household yet she is clearly named on household bills. Further, she claims that she was not aware of how much money Dale made and that is clearly a falsehood. This is a regular pattern of deceitfulness and lying."

"Another trait of those with Anti-Social Personality Disorder is stated to be consistent irresponsibility," Mr. Basta noted as he pointed to the sheet of paper in our hands. "Can you explain that more in depth for us?"

"Certainly," Dr. DeMarte responded. She brushed her long dark hair back over her shoulder. "Miss DeVault said she was always two months behind on her bills and this is why she engaged Allen Flores' help. She also shows bad credit on standard credit reports documenting irresponsibility in paying on time. This is further evidenced by her many short-term jobs. Finally, her neighbor said her kids were always dirty and not well-taken care of."

"Very good," Mr. Basta said as he checked something off his list. "This document states that people of this disorder show a failure to conform to social norms by repeatedly committing unlawful acts. What evidence did you see that supports this?"

"This can be readily seen in such things as her abuse of the Access System, a state welfare program for mothers who need assistance, by accepting money when she was not qualified to accept that money from the state. She was having an affair with Allen Flores while she was clearly married. She was also a known stripper while she was married clarifying her inability to conform to what we know as acceptable social norms," Dr. DeMarte said. "Another example would be the violence of the premeditated murder of her husband and her attempt to make Stanley Cook take responsibility for this act," she said seriously.

"Are there any other acts which support your theory?" Mr. Basta asked.

"Yes," Dr. DeMarte answered. "She tried to cover her crime by having her roommate beat her with a sledgehammer only days after the assault to make it look as if Dale abused her."

"Was there concern raised when you saw the document titled 'Something Odd Going On"? He asked.

My attention became more acute than it already was when I heard this. Maybe we would finally figure out what that document was that had been printed hours before Dale's death on January 14, 2009.

"I read that document with particular interest as it was written by the defendant's lover and boyfriend. Although she had lied about the frequency of their sex, I learned that she was having sex with him almost daily," she said almost as if it were from a journal. "Allen Flores speaks of being afraid for his life because of the manipulation and deception that the defendant showed him. It was readily apparent that they were very close, and he felt violated in that she was not paying back money she had promised. He was also concerned that she stated her father was dead, yet he learns that the father is still alive."

"Was there anything else that concerned you?" Mr. Basta asked.

"Well, yes," she answered. "Allen Flores was scared for his life when he learned that the defendant had feigned the violent death of her husband only to find out he was alive. He foreshadowed a vision of himself being murdered by her and began documentation in the event he met an untimely death by her. Their closeness suggests he was truly afraid for his life after he realized the length of manipulation and lies she had endeavored to make him do what she wished. He realized that she was a dangerous woman," the doctor said.

I memorized the evidence number, as this was a document I thought we missed when we had looked at evidence in a prior phase of the trial. It sounded fishy and intriguing at the same time. Hopefully, it would be able to answer those unanswered questions that bothered each of us.

"Thank you," Mr. Basta said returning to his outline on the podium. "The document then states aggression and impulsivity are data points for Anti-Social Personality Disorder. Can you explain that for us?"

"The defendant regularly showed aggressiveness. Her meeting with Allen Flores was based on money when she solicited him on a website. Many people in the stripping profession show these signs. She was aggressive with Stanley Cook by sleeping with him when she was out on bond. Another example would be the spending of almost two hundred and fifty thousand dollars in her relationship with Allen Flores. This is clearly impulsive spending and money not spent for the benefit of the children."

"Earlier, you said that people with this disorder are said to have a reckless disregard for the safety of others. Do records, interviews or documents of the defendant support this behavior?" Mr. Basta asked.

"They do. I spent a lot of time looking through evidence and saw countless examples of her disregard for the safety of others as is consistent Anti-Social Personality Disorder," Dr. DeMarte answered as she glanced at her notes. "One could consider the reason we are here as a great example of her disregard for the safety of others. The victim was murdered with premeditation. We also see her try to put Stanley Cook in harm's way by manipulating him to take responsibility for the murder. In regards to the children, I saw that her oldest daughter had sexual contact with Allen Flores' son, David. The daughter was told to end the relationship yet the defendant continued to see Allen Flores and put the daughter in harm's way by having her accompany her back to the home where David was," Dr. DeMarte pointed out. "She put her in a dangerous position by regularly exposing her daughter to future sexual abuse."

"Is there further evidence that you saw?" Mr. Basta asked.

"She has been described as belligerent and angry by neighbors," Dr. DeMarte answered. "She also involved Stan Cook by making him injure her after the incident. This is further evidenced by her removal of the victim's shorts after she brutally attacked him. This is a very dangerous woman," she emphasized.

"Objection," Mr. Tavasoli said jumping up in his chair. "That is not a scientific conclusion!"

"Over-ruled," Judge Steinle said in response.

Mr. Tavasoli sat down clearly irritated by the ruling.

Mr. Basta continued. "The last item on this list reads that the defendant shows a lack of remorse. Can you explain that?"

"The defendant has a history of lying and then absolutely no remorse or acceptance of responsibility for her actions. Consider that even her mother, Samantha Carlson, was surprised at the complete lack of remorse that the defendant showed after Dale Harrell's death. The mother told me that Marissa had been lying consistently since she was two years old to get out of trouble.

There was an incident where the defendant was caught having sex with her stepsister yet Marissa continued to lie about it. There was another incident where Marissa claimed her stepfather, Michael Wright, approached her for a sexual favor. The mother was able to sit down with the two of them and learned there was a partial truth. They were able to discuss it and clear the issue yet Marissa claimed further abuse," she said with conviction.

"She showed no remorse even after she admitted killing her husband and continued to pursue Stanley Cook as the person who did the murder. I also saw a document about a civil suit brought against Marissa for damages in the death of Dale Harrell. Marissa held the cremated remains of Dale as ransom so that the family would drop the civil lawsuit," she said. "It was also noted that in her jailhouse recorded phone calls that she was laughing about the death of her husband."

Mr. Basta nodded in an affirming manner. "You are comfortable in your diagnosis of Anti-Social Personality Disorder as applies to the defendant?"

"Absolutely," the doctor answered.

The afternoon was spent with Dr. DeMarte knocking down the walls of the defense psychological experts, Dr. Karp and Dr. Conte. As far as DeMarte was concerned, their age and experience worked against them as experts, as she believed that they were using old and outdated materials. Their time had gone and DeMarte's recent experience and training had shown that their diagnosis was completely wrong as it was based mostly on self-reporting. In other words, we were expected to put an "X" through the testimony that they had given us. Her knowledge was undeniable and her firmness in position was respectable.

The defense interrogation was successful in showing that Dr. DeMarte's diagnosis was exceptionally one-sided favoring the prosecution. There was a discussion that Dr. DeMarte had stated that the use of an alias was a sign of Anti-Social Personality Disorder. The defense pursued the use of an alias by Marissa and learned that Dr. DeMarte thought the name 'Reese' was an alias.

"Is a nickname an alias?" Mr. Tavasoli asked.

"It can be," Dr. DeMarte answered.

"I see," Mr. Tavasoli responded sarcastically. "Reese is an alias and not a nickname?"

"It could be interpreted either way," Dr. DeMarte answered.

"I see you take the interpretation that the prosecution would like you to have," Mr. Tavasoli poked.

"Objection! The witness is not on trial," Mr. Basta stated.

"I'm sorry, Judge," Mr. Tavasoli said before he could be admonished. He continued with the witness.

"Is Psychology an exact science like chemistry?" Mr. Tavasoli asked her.

"It has gotten more specific over the years."

"That is not what I'm asking. I am asking if it is an exact science. For example, if someone shows the character traits listed to have an Anti-Social Personality Disorder, does it mean they have that disorder?"

"Usually," Dr. DeMarte answered.

"Can I say that sometimes instead?"

"I can't answer that," Dr. DeMarte said. "It depends upon the individual."

"So, it is not an exact science. One can't say that all people who have these traits have Anti-Social Personality Disorder," Mr. Tavasoli pointed out.

"Yes, you can say that," she acquiesced.

"Very good," Mr. Tavasoli responded. "Let me ask you; is it typical for people with this disorder not to have a criminal record?"

"It's not typical but it happens. They can be undiagnosed but eventually will get caught committing a crime."

"All people who show traits of this disorder will always commit a crime. Is that what you're saying to us?"

"No, I'm not saying that," she answered defensively. "I'm saying that people with this disorder will usually have a criminal history and if they don't, they eventually will. There's no way to tell if all people with this disorder will commit a crime."

"Are you aware that the defendant has no criminal history?'

"Yes," Dr. DeMarte answered somewhat smugly.

"Where does one get this Anti-Social Personality Disorder?" Mr. Tavasoli asked.

"It can be both from their environment of which they were raised and it can be genetic."

"Genetic?" Mr. Tavasoli queried. "Is that to say it is inherited?"

"Yes," Dr. DeMarte answered.

"Does the mother display the same characteristics?"

"I don't know," she answered.

"You don't know? Didn't you interview the mother to see if she displayed similar characteristics in your evaluation?"

"No, I did not," DeMarte answered. "My goal was to assess where the defendant fell on the scale not to find out where it came from."

"Isn't that important to know in case you are making the wrong diagnosis?"

"It could be," she answered. "I think there is enough evidence to show I have a correct diagnosis. I can't be expected to turn over every stone."

"I thought that was your job. Isn't your job to investigate every resource available?"

"I investigate multiple resources to make my diagnosis."

"But you don't investigate all sources?" Mr. Tavasoli prodded.

"No."

"Did you interview Marissa DeVault's stepsister to get additional information?"

"No, I did not," the doctor answered.

"Did you evaluate Dale Harrell to determine the environment that Marissa lived in?"

"He was dead. I could not interview him."

"Did you talk to his friends and family to get a better idea of her circumstances?"

"No. My assignment was Marissa DeVault and not Dale Harrell," she answered firmly but somewhat defensively.

Mr. Tavasoli picked apart her limited experience noting that book experience is not the same as real life experience. We learned that she was paid three hundred dollars an hour for court and two hundred and fifty dollars an hour for administrative and research fees. I don't think that was a concern to me because it is pretty much well known that many professional witnesses are paid a fee. Time is money and their experience should be duly compensated.

It seemed like hours before Dr. DeMarte was finally excused from the witness stand. My hands were sore and cramped from furious note taking. She was a psycho-killer but we found out that she and her science were not perfect.

"The prosecution rests," said Mr. Basta with both hands on the table in front of him.

"Is there anything more from the defense?" Judge Steinle asked.

Mr. Tavasoli stood up, "No, Your Honor."

"Tomorrow, we will hear closing arguments from both sides. I expect we will hand this to the jury tomorrow."

We were relieved to be dismissed and excited that we were reaching the end of a long and emotional legal road.

I drove home with an ache in my stomach as I realized that in twenty-four hours, the crime and the future of Marissa DeVault would be in our hands. I was nervous about the responsibility.

Did Marissa really sleep with Stan?

Everything Marissa did had an action followed by a reaction for a selfish result.

I think she slept with Stan for the confession letters.

FOR LIFE OR DEATH

We assembled in the jury box for the final time as fourteen jurors. Lucy and Jarod held the position of being alternate jurors and Bruce was now done with his service. We all hoped and prayed that Bruce would recover from his latest challenge.

In the meantime, final arguments were to be presented and we knew at the end of those arguments that we would lose Lucy and Jarod and we would be sent to the jury room for the final time.

It was interesting that while most of us took notes, Lucy and Jarod drew pictures. They knew they were lame ducks at this phase.

The arguments ran in reverse of the way it ran in the beginning of the trial. The burden of proving mitigation factors fell to the defense so they would present arguments first, followed by the prosecution and then completed with a closing argument rebuttal. In the early stage of the trial, the prosecution had presented first since they had the burden of proving guilt beyond a reasonable doubt.

Mr. Tavasoli stepped to the podium that now faced the jury instead of facing the witness stand. He wore a dark gray suit with a light green shirt and a patterned tie. He placed his notes on the stand and began his argument.

Marissa DeVault is not a cold-blooded killer, he told us. The forensics in this case point to rage. The forensics also suggests that her development and the experiences she went through affected her decision-making ultimately in the killing of Dale.

Mr. Tavasoli pointed out that Marissa is a damaged person. She suffered the effects of Post Traumatic Stress Disorder, and there was no ignoring that she was not only physically abused in her childhood by her mother but that she was sexually abused by her first stepfather. It was a combination of those abuses that made her the person she is today.

She was a stripper and Dr. Conte had determined that many people in that industry are sexually abused.

The abuse that Marissa suffered affected her personality by making her an untruthful person. Her being sexually abused put her in compromising positions later in life by giving her a misguided perception of reality. She learned that sex was a way to receive love. She did not recognize that she was abused and saw nothing wrong in her behaviors.

He quickly pointed out that we were not giving Marissa a free pass by not giving the death sentence. A life sentence was more than appropriate for the crime she had committed. She would be punished and she would never walk the streets free again.

However, we should consider abuse as one mitigating factor and there were many others to take into consideration.

Mr. Tavasoli put a PowerPoint presentation on the front wall of the courtroom and began detailing the list of mitigating circumstances outlined for us to see.

We were to consider the childhood sexual and physical abuse she suffered. In that category, we should also consider the abusive marriage of Marissa and Dale.

He wanted us to consider that Marissa had no prior criminal history and she had cooperated with police to some degree. She had not asked for an attorney during her lengthy interrogation. Her intent was always to cooperate with police.

Mr. Tavasoli directed our attention to Marissa's allocution statement and how it was a true sign of remorse. He pointed out that she had a realization of the damage she had done and was willing to do everything it took to make restitution.

Marissa didn't choose a lot of things in her life and was at an unfair advantage. We were to look at the fact that she didn't choose to be born from a one-night stand of her mother. She didn't choose to learn that her father was not her father in reference to Dan Carlson. She did not choose to be sexually abused by him when she was twelve years old. She certainly didn't deserve to live in chaos and uncertainty. It was a compilation of the above factors that have left her damaged and affected her decision-making abilities.

The children supported allegations of consistent abuse happening under the roof of that household. Rhiannon had spoken of putting dressers behind doors to protect the siblings from violence. Diahnon had spoken of looking under the door to see Marissa's arm being broken and Khiernan had spoken of the same behaviors present. These girls needed an opportunity to have at least one parent.

It was horrible in the way that Dale was killed and Marissa would pay with her life behind bars. This punishment fit the crime. She did not deserve to die and it was up to each of us to draw our own moral assessment.

Mr. Tavasoli took a moment to scan the eyes of the jury in silence and then he sat down.

Mr. Basta handled the prosecution closing arguments. He wore a conservative blue pinstripe suit with a white shirt and red tie. He pushed his glasses up on his nose before he spoke and had his signature pen in his right hand, presumably to check off his list while he made his arguments.

He told us that Marissa *was* a cold-blooded killer. This was clearly evidenced by her behavior directly after the murder. He pointed to the removal of Dale's shorts to stage the crime as a rape. He spoke of the countless lies that she had told in the police interrogation tapes on the same day of the murder.

Mr. Basta was quick to point out that Dr. DeMarte had diagnosed her with Anti-Social Personality Disorder and this disorder was consistent with those who committed brutal murders. He noted that Dr. Websdale, Dr. Karp and Dr. Conte based their opinions on self-reporting and that any opinions were faulty because Marissa had made the statements from which the diagnosis was created from. A faulty premise equaled a faulty diagnosis and we should disregard their testimony.

He directed us to look at two exhibits when we got back to the jury room to deliberate. These two documents would show that Marissa admitted falling off a horse and broke a scapula and that her scratched cornea was not inflicted by Dale but was an accident that she admitted to as well. The defendant was manipulative and had proved herself a liar again and again.

This defendant had lots of choices even if we assume some abuse happened. There is no concrete evidence it happened, he explained, but we could assume some happened. She had a choice to leave. She could have called the police. She could have called other family members for help. She says she was close to Jeanine and her sister would have undoubtedly helped.

The problem with her story of abuse is that Dale was sleeping and he was not a threat to her. He noted that she told Allen Flores about the killing before he was murdered. If Dale was not a threat when she attacked him, then she should be morally culpable and fully accountable for his death.

We should consider that Dale lay on his pillow bleeding as seen by the amount of blood on the pillow. We should consider that she pulled his shorts off while he desperately needed medical attention. She then pushed him off the bed to stage a rape scene. We couldn't miss seeing the wiped tissue with semen on it in the trashcan fresh without a liner. The staging of the scene showed she was a cold-blooded killer.

He spoke of the childhood and sexual abuse allegations that she said she experienced as a child. There was no proof that happened and the only reason we think it happened was because of her self-reporting on psychological examinations.

Mr. Basta asked us to take careful note that she was a stripper and a prostitute and she was driven by personal gain. We were to consider that she had even asked for help in the killing by speaking with Travis Tatro. Further, she also told Allen Flores she had hired Travis to kill him. She was driven to kill for personal gain and that was consistent with her behavior for her entire life.

Marissa did not show remorse after Dale's death as evidenced by her casual behavior during the interrogation. She was heard laughing on jail phone calls to Stanley Cook after her incarceration. She even told Dr. DeMarte when they first met that Dale had died of natural causes.

She was still not taking ownership of the crime and she had showed no concern for Dale throughout.

Marissa showed a surprising lack of concern that her lover, Stanley Cook, would be taking responsibility for the crime. If it were up to her, Stanley Cook would have been on trial.

Mr. Basta continued his assault by saying that Marissa had put her children in danger. Who was to say that she could not have killed her kids if Stan had not come into the room?

He also pointed out that Marissa continued to see Allen Flores even after she knew her daughter had been sleeping with Allen Flores' son. She continued to visit with Rhiannon in tow and consistently put her own daughter in danger of being sexually abused.

Child abuse was not linked to the cruelness of the murder and we should pay close attention to the fact that they cannot be connected by any evidence or testimony. He mentioned that her mother Samantha admitted to using a 'heavy hand' but that could not be construed as child abuse. It was merely discipline.

Marissa was greedy and loved to spend money. She saw people as assets in striving for her goal of getting a lot of money.

Mr. Basta clarified that all murderers have issues and that the defendant is no different. Her issues did not give her a right to smash Dale's head in with a hammer multiple times. She had made choices for her personal gain at the cost of Dale and his daughters.

He asked us for justice in giving the defendant the sentence of death.

The defense stood for the final time after lunch with their rebuttal. We knew the case would be handed to us at the conclusion and there were butterflies in my stomach. We knew the question we had to answer and I don't think anyone looked forward   to   it   with   relish.

DAY 36: PART II

LAST RITES

The courtroom was eerily silent as Mr. Tavasoli took his place behind the podium for the last time. He laid his notes down on the top of the podium and straightened his tie. One could barely see him take a deep breath as if to grab ahold of the tension in the air and then let it out slowly. He looked over the jury at nothing in particular as if to gather his thoughts.

We all knew it was our final time hearing testimony in the jury box and it was hard to believe that we were finally looking at the end of the road. We looked at the gallery and it was full with a large camera peering over the back of it taking in the courtroom.

The defendant sat in her seat without showing a lot of emotion. We were used to seeing her in black. Her hair was tied back. Her face was pale and framed by the glasses she regularly wore. At one point, she pulled them off to wipe her face and one could see dark circles under her eyes.

I probably would not have slept well the night before either, I thought.

Mr. Tavasoli began slowly and thoughtfully. His voice was soft as if he were speaking at someone's bedside. He looked at us one by one throughout his defense closing, something we were not used to prior to this stage. We watched and listened, many of us with legal pad in hand taking notes.

I was completing my eighth full legal pad of notes. As I would complete each legal pad throughout the trial, they would be three-hole punched and put in a three ring binder. It was an impressive set of notes and it was sad that all would be incinerated at the end of the trial. Hopefully, the bad memories of certain aspects of the trial would be incinerated as well but I highly doubted it expecting some of these images to be ingrained in my mind forever.

"Marissa DeVault is a damaged person," he began. "She was damaged by years of child abuse as a child. She was damaged by being sexually abused by her stepfather in various ways. She was further damaged in a marriage that has been proven to be mutually abusive. This does not give her a free pass in any way. She is still getting life in prison for what she has done with a minimum of twenty-five years. This is punishment that fits the crime based on who she is."

Mr. Tavasoli glanced at his notes and looked at us again. "The prosecution presented you with Dr. DeMarte who agreed that Marissa suffered some sort of Post Traumatic Stress Disorder. The question is; what was the trauma? Was it the relationship with her husband? Was it from her sexual abuse? Or was it from the 'heavy handedness' that her own mother spoke of when raising her?" he questioned.

"Dr. DeMarte's testimony is suspect and can't be completely trusted because she only interviewed the people the prosecution wanted her to interview. For example, the Doctor interviewed the mother, Samantha, but did not interview the sister, Jeanine. I find it curious that the Doctor would not interview the person who can support claims of child abuse. The abuse was there and she chose to ignore it for the benefit of the prosecution," he said.

"There's another item that you should consider to show the one-sidedness of this witness. Did you all hear that all strippers have some sort of Anti-Social Personality Disorder? It is unfeasible and unrealistic," he said. He took a drink of water from a plastic bottle and slowly screwed the cap back on tightly. He wiped his lip with the back of his hand and continued his closing.

"I have spoken of this from the beginning. The defendant had a gun in the room but chose not to use it. We think she planned on using the gun that she had received from Allen only weeks beforehand. But," he pointed out with his forefinger, "she did not use it. The reason she did not use it was because something else set her off. It may have been the fact that she had discussed a divorce with Dale the night before. It may have been that she told him she was staying with Allen. We will never know, but the cruelness of the crime shows rage outweighing the premeditation aspect. Right?" he asked us rhetorically.

Mr. Tavasoli had said that word 'right?' in a questioning tone periodically throughout the trial. It was slightly irritating and I don't think connected with us except to note it felt irritating. It felt like we were being reminded of our responsibility and we surely didn't need reminders as it had weighed on us for many months.

"I want you to pay special attention to the children in this stage of the trial. Consider that each of these children noted abusive behavior against Marissa from Dale. Each child said they were afraid and that it existed. This supports the theory of rage being involved in the attack. A spur of the moment attack, even though she had been planning an attack. The prosecution has theories as well as we have theories and I don't think anyone will know what went through Marissa's head at the time of the attack. It is this kind of 'shadow of a doubt' that should convince you to give her life instead of death. The prosecution is focusing on the crime but not her as a human. They are doing their job," he said pointing toward their table.

"Marissa DeVault is human. Her children are human. They have no control in this. If we sentence her to death, what happens to the children?" he asked us with a pause. "Haven't they been through enough?"

Mr. Tavasoli went back to his notes and his statements resonated in my head. I had not thought of the children in that light and looked forward to discussing it once we got back to the jury room.

"Marissa DeVault was not in control. Consider Allen Flores. He says he loaned her hundreds of thousands of dollars. Where is it? The prosecution wants you to think that she loved money and that's why she killed him. Where's the money, I ask you? Where? If you can't answer that, then you have to question the motive. If you question the motive, then you cannot comfortably put her to death. There is enough to cast a shadow of a doubt and to give her life."

He brushed his hand through his hair and pressed onward. "We saw remorse in her allocution statement. She told us that she was sorry for everything she has done. She is willing to help other inmates. And, " he pointed out, "she has been in years of therapy because she is remorseful. She will continue the therapy that she should have been afforded when she was eight years old."

Mr. Tavasoli walked in front of the podium and did his best to catch our eyes although he had a habit of looking above our heads. "We have asked you to make the ultimate decision and it is a difficult decision. We appreciate everything you have done but you have one more critical step to take. You will need to balance the mitigation factors against the aggravating factors and it is not an easy decision. But I ask you, the defendant asks you," he said pointing toward Marissa, "to give her a chance at reconciliation. She deserves leniency to give her life in prison. Thank you for your time and service," he finished.

Judge Steinle III went to the business of handing us the case and dismissed the alternate jurors with the admonition that they not speak to anyone about the case. Lucy and Jarod stood up and were escorted out the back of the courtroom.

The Judge looked at us and asked that the foreperson give him the deliberation schedule as our first order of business. Cherie nodded in agreement and we were sent to the jury room.

The first thing we did was to set our jury schedule. We knew we would do one poll and then we had to be off the day after tomorrow as one of the jurors had an outstanding commitment that the court was aware of. Cherie filled out the form and we knew we had the next day to deliberate before we would be off for four days. She submitted it to the bailiff, Sydney.

Cherie pulled out a legal pad and tore bits of paper for each of us to place out vote. The choices would be death, life and undecided.

Each of us put our current vote on a piece of paper. I scrawled 'Undecided' on my piece, as I knew I was on the fence. The papers were placed in the center of the table.

One by one, Parker read the vote and Cherie tallied them on the dry erase board. At the end, five of us voted for life in prison, five of us were undecided and two of us made the decision for death.

We were split and I hoped we wouldn't end up as a hung jury.

DAY 37

LADY JUSTICE

I think everyone came in with a heavy heart. It was a weight on our backs that clouded our mind in its sadness. We were there to answer the simple question of whether the defendant was to live or to die. Our decision had to balance whether the mitigating circumstances outweigh the aggravating circumstances. In other words, do the factors of her life outweigh the cruelness of the crime?

Everyone in the room knew the seriousness of our decision however no one looked forward to the discussion. We knew it would become laden with detail and filled with emotion and I knew no one looked forward to the discussion. We had seen this play out the prior two times in the deliberation phase and this time was no different except that the stakes were as high as they could be.

We wanted to be able to sleep at night the rest of our lives.

Cherie was the last to appear in the jury room. She had to take care of some work business, which had put her behind but not late.

She put her purse and lunch down and made herself a cup of tea while we all turned off our smart phones.

"The first thing we should do is take a vote and see if anyone has altered their vote overnight," she said, stirring her tea.

We went about the business of turning in our votes while Parker read them aloud and Cherie recorded them on the Dry Erase Board. The vote had changed overnight with eight calling for life with two undecided and two voting for death.

She moved to a Post-It flip chart and wrote 'Aggravating' on one sheet with 'Mitigating' on another sheet.

"The first thing we will do is come up with whatever things we need to go onto each of these lists. The bad things go into the "Aggravating" category while the reasons we should save her life go into the "Mitigating" category. Is everyone clear on this?" she asked.

We all agreed and were happy to have some direction in reaching our goal.

"Good," she said. "Let's start with aggravating circumstances. Ted? What can you think of?"

Ted looked up a little surprised that this was being treated like a classroom. "Well, she used a hammer and hit him five times or more," he said.

Cherie scrawled the word 'hammer' on the chart.

"Next?" she asked.

"The kids should be on the list," Doc volunteered.

"Why?" Cherie asked with her pen upraised.

"She knew that when she killed the father that she would ruin the kids' lives. She put them in danger by killing their father while they were in the house"

Cherie nodded in agreement and wrote it on the chart.

"She did it for the money," Victoria said.

"We can't use that," Parker said. "We were never able to agree on that so we can't use it. All we can say is that she did it with premeditation and it was cruel."

"Then why did she do it?" Victoria asked.

"We don't know," Wings piped in. "We think there was a rage from abuse but that's still speculation. We'll never know what set her off."

"We could put premeditation on the list, couldn't we?" Jeebs asked. "We know she planned it."

"Good one," Cherie said scribbling the word on the chart. "What else?" Cherie prompted.

"I wish we could consider the shorts," I said. "I know she ripped them off him after she hit him with the hammer."

"You can't use that," Parker said as expected.

"I know," I responded. "Did you notice that Mr. Basta brought it up again?"

Cherie wrote on the board. "Anything else?" she asked with an upraised pen.

"She didn't show any remorse," Sunny said.

The room blew up at that point with jurors saying that she did show remorse in her allocution statement. I agreed on those lines but the argument was intensified by the fact that she showed no remorse within the first five years after the murder. It was further emphasized that her interrogation video was the most damning piece of evidence in that it was done a mere twelve hours after the attack on Dale and the lies were overwhelmingly directed at taking the responsibility away from her.

This conversation precipitated our 'Mitigation' list, which became significantly longer. Ironically, remorse ended up first on the list because her allocution statement was felt to be genuinely true, sort of.

We all knew that anything said by Marissa was probably a lie, but the emotion involved with that day told our hearts we were probably correct in spite of everything previous. She had apologized and admitted guilt which is something not often seen in a court of law. It carried a great weight but did not excuse the defendant's actions.

"We should consider that she had no prior criminal record," Parker said. "I think this would be a very different scenario if she had a history of killing people."

Cherie dutifully wrote it on the list.

"We should consider that there was child abuse in the family," Althea said.

"That's ridiculous," Butthead volunteered. He had been a surprisingly quiet juror as of late. Maybe it just wasn't noticed because we weren't seeing dirty looks from the court reporter. "I don't think child abuse has anything to do with this."

"I disagree," Wings said. "I don't think young kids are going to lie on the stand. At least I don't think these kids were lying when they said there was abuse in the family. Even the mother admitted to being heavy-handed as it was part of their generation."

"Heavy-handed means they were beating the crap out of their kids," I said. "The abuse I went through would be qualified by my parents as being 'heavy-handed'. Anything that leaves a mark is abuse and the stepsister said there was abuse."

"That's not what I'm saying," Butthead said. "I don't see how child abuse made her swing a hammer."

"It didn't directly," I answered. "The child abuse she went through affected all her future decisions. If one is raised in a stable family, one has the opportunity to grow into a law abiding and well-rounded citizen. She learned to lie to avoid punishment. I truly believe that. The fear of abuse is the damage of abuse. She was brain-damaged psychologically from going through abuse and that should be a factor."

"I still don't agree," Butthead said.

"Does anyone believe there was sexual abuse?" Cherie asked.

"Absolutely," Parker said. "The mother admitted that she had to talk to the stepfather about a sexual favor he had asked about from Marissa. I don't believe for a second that they sat down and talked about it after one occurrence. The fact that the mother knew about it is evidence enough for me that it existed."

All of us agreed except for Butthead.

Cherie added sexual abuse to the list.

"Here's my biggest issue," Sunny said.

"What is it?" Cherie asked.

"The kids," she said. "I know we already talked about them but I feel like we're sending them to the death chamber with her. I'm wondering if they haven't had enough. I don't know how long it takes to kill someone on death row but I'm sure that it takes at least ten years."

She thought before she spoke. "Those kids are going to have to suffer through that decision process and it feels like we could be taking away their life and potential to grow. They will be going to death row with her no matter how long it takes," she said vehemently. Her face was reddened in emotion and one could see that further discussion could make her cry.

The room was silenced as we thought about this particular part of the problem. In all the time of the trial, I had not even considered this aspect.

"Screw the kids," Doc said. "She knew what would happened if she killed her husband. She knew there would be consequences and it was her responsibility to protect those kids. I feel bad for the kids but this is about Dale and how he died. He'll never get to see them off to their first prom. He'll never see them graduate from high school or get married or even have the opportunity to be a grandfather. She stole that from him and she stole it from the kids. I don't think she deserves a shred of decency," she said.

This sparked debate from everyone and it really became the crux of an issue that we knew we could only answer by reaching deep into our hearts. We wanted to speak for the victim and the cruelness of his death, but got trapped by the children. It was Sunny's greatest moment in deliberation because it showed the other side of the needle and the further damage it might cause to the kids.

Many of us discussed the fact that these kids had to have been incredibly damaged by the murder. They would struggle the rest of their lives with the fact that their mother did this to their father and it was the greatest of the abuses that had occurred.

We wondered about the welfare of the children. We knew they were with the stepmother and had been assigned there by the State of Arizona. We didn't know what would happen to them after the trial and could only assume they would be safe. The question was, how safe would they be mentally if they had to face the prospect of watching their mother awaiting her execution on death row?

The question was so serious that we decided that it was time to submit a question for the court.

"Can the welfare of the children be considered as a mitigating factor?"

Cherie had Wings ring the bailiff with the typical two rings to signify a question or a verdict. Sydney appeared at the door moments later and took the question for submission to the court. She told us that it would take forty-five minutes to assemble the parties for it to be answered in court.

"Isn't it interesting that this whole thing is about a gun that was never used. I've got to ask what would have been different if a gun had been used?" Jeebs mused aloud.

"That's not evidence," Parker said.

"In a way, it is," Jeebs noted. "Remember the first day of jury duty when we were in the box and they handed the gun around?"

"Yes," Butthead said.

"It's like the smoking gun because it was never used."

We were called back to our jury seats and the Judge read the question aloud in court. He then made us refer to the law and mitigating factors saying that a mitigating factor is any factor, up to each individual, that stands to call for leniency against the death penalty.

Well, that answer did not bring us any closer to the truth as we deliberated throughout the rest of the afternoon. We were torn for a variety of reasons and there was a realization that there was no true good outcome for the actions that Marissa had taken.

All we knew was that we did not want to hang and we wanted to make the best decision possible without causing more damage either to the victim or to our mental state as we would carry this in our hearts the rest of our lives.

Cherie executed one more vote before the end of the day. Ten of us voted for life in prison while two of us voted for death. Although progress had been made toward one decision or the other, we hoped that the next four days off would give us respite from the weight of the decision while at the same time, give us time to reflect all the matters on the table.

I was driving home that night and thought of an image that I remembered from college. The image was of a Greek or Roman goddess dressed in robes to her feet. I think her name was Themis and she was the representative symbol of justice. A blindfold covered her eyes while her braided hair flew in the wind. In her left hand, she welded a mighty sword while her right hand carried an old-fashioned balance scale.

The jury and our final decision were representative of that scale. Had the mitigating factors outweighed the aggravation factors?

I felt like I understood Lady Justice and the items she held in her hand. The lengthy sword was representing the punishment of justice, the blindfold representing the Judge as we deliberated in secrecy and the scale representing and weighing factors of accountability.

At long last we had reached the end of the road. Unfortunately, it looked like we had a good chance of hanging, similar to what had happened in a similar trial with nastier elements.

I now understood how a jury could hang and it made me feel no better for it.

POINT OF CONVERGENCE

The return to court after a long weekend was almost welcomed because we were so close to the end. Thoughts of the trial and the decision we had to make had not left my mind and I was looking forward to the day when we would no longer have this burden.

There was a peace that developed after reaching my decision. If I looked at the trial as a whole, I realized that it had, ironically, afforded me another peace that I had not foreseen.

The most important thing about being a juror is honesty to your own self. A decision like we had on our plate required that we reach deep into the moral character of our soul to find the answer that we could live with the rest of our days. It is not an easy journey by any stretch of the imagination and I cannot imagine walking down this road another time in my life. However, while on this road, I could only give the best that my heart told me.

I drove to the courthouse like usual. The day was going to be hot and I know all of us were grateful that this trial had not happened in the unrelenting heat that was sure to make the summer miserable in its intensity. I parked my car on the street across from jury parking as I was tired of driving six levels up in the parking garage. I waved at Phillip, the jury bus driver, as I began my eight-block walk to the courthouse. Phillip was dressed in a green silk shirt with his regular tie and looked more like a lawyer than a bus driver.

I stopped in the smoker's area of the courthouse and was a little surprised that I didn't see Althea, Doc and Annie sitting on the concrete bench smoking. They would always sit in a row and I was always curious to see their perfectly manicured toenails lined up in unison, each pair of feet adorned with a different colored sparkle polish.

I finished my cigarette after giving one to the usually expected homeless person that would walk by and ask. I walked through the doors of the courthouse and went through security after unloading my keys, wallet, tie clip, belt and pens into the clear plastic Lexan containers provided. I was metal free except for the two wheat pennies in my burgundy loafers.

I retrieved my items and went to the elevator while putting my belt on and made my way to the thirteenth floor. I was excited that this might be our last day and looked forward to committing to a verdict.

I rang the security bell meant for juror access and knew that something was wrong right away as no one answered my multiple spaced out rings.

Finally, Sydney came to the door and told me that deliberations had been cancelled due to a juror emergency. Deliberations would resume the next day at one o'clock pm.

I drove home and picked up Rocky, grabbed his dog bag and made my way to a local dog park. He had been resilient and patient as I had gone through the process the prior three months and deserved a night out.

I unhitched him from his leash and let him run free with the other dogs as he ran around sniffing and peeing on any standing object.

I thought about the trial and how it had impacted me in ways that I could not have foreseen. I thought about the decision I had made regarding Marissa's fate and realized that I could trace it back to a spring day in 1976.

I come from a wealthy family having been raised in multi-million dollar homes with a father who was a well-respected professional in my town. One could hardly meet a person on the street without their having met my father through some sort of dental surgery whether it was for a root canal or a check-up. He was at the office seeing patients when the incident that would change my life forever happened.

I was outside playing in the cul-de-sac of our driveway. I cannot remember if I was playing with Hot Wheels or flying balsa wood gliders to pass the time on that Saturday afternoon. It wouldn't surprise me to have been doing either one.

My brother was in the house along with my sister. I was fourteen at the time and they were eleven year-old twins. At the time, I did not know that my mother was interrogating my little sister.

"Louise?" my mother asked while Louise was sitting at the kitchen counter. "Why don't you tell me what you and your brothers do while we are square dancing?"

"We don't do anything," Louise answered meekly. "We stay in our rooms like we're supposed to."

"It's okay. You can tell me," my mother prompted. "Why don't you have one of these donuts while you think about it?"

My brother was listening at the doorway of our bedroom and knew something was up. Our mother never gave us sweets outside dessert after dinner. His palms were sweaty because he knew what our mother was after.

Louise readily took the donut. Our mother knew she was easy to manipulate because she had always been referred to as 'slow'. If one were really nice to Louise, she would crumble like a sandcastle at the first whiff of kindness.

"Go ahead, Louise," she pushed, "go ahead and tell me."

"Sometimes, we come out of our rooms and play," she said.

"Oh, you do?"

"Yes, Momma."

"What kind of games do you play?"

"I don't know," Louise answered. "We just play."

"Do you play Chinese Checker's or play Battleship? What do you do?"

"Sometimes, we go outside and play."

"What do you play outside?"

"Well, we just play. Sometimes we play hide and seek."

"What else do you play?" Momma asked.

"We played doctor once," Louise offered.

"How do you do that?"

"We pretend we are hurt and then someone plays doctor," Louise answered innocently.

"Do you ever get hurt in your private parts?" she asked.

Louise paused and my brother listened outside the bedroom door knowing that we were in big trouble.

"Sometimes," Louise answered.

At that point, the game changed. My mother dropped what she was doing and went to find me. The violations in her mind were beyond reproach. The first reason was that I had violated direct orders not to leave our designated rooms when they were out of the house.

The second violation was incredibly severe. We were raised devout Catholics and sex was never to be discussed in the house.

I remember her calling me from the garage door to the laundry room, her voice echoing across the yard where I was playing. The incident that Louise had spoken of was the farthest thing from my mind on that sunny day.

I ran to the garage door at her beckoning and was suddenly grabbed by the hair and yanked into the house. I remember being slapped a hundred times while her other hand held me by the back of the head. I was kicked relentlessly and realized that this was becoming the worst beating I had suffered at her hands. I remember the spittle coming out of the sides of her mouth as she screamed at me that she wished I had never been born.

There was a point in time that my defenses made me lose sense of where I was as I tried to stop the rain of blows that fell on me. I fell and felt my mother grab me by my hair and ears as she repeatedly slammed my head against the cement threshold that bordered the house and garage. White-hot flares of pain shot behind my eyes as I cried and screamed.

The next thing that happened was her screaming at me to take off all of my clothes.

"But, but," I whimpered.

"I will not have you running away again! " She screamed at me.

I had run away from home four times prior and all had yielded no results except to be returned back home to a house that had been inundated with violence.

She handed me a bucket and sponge and told me to scrub the kitchen floor by hand, naked as a jaybird.

"When your father gets home, he's going to kill you!" she said storming up the stairs to the master bedroom.

I was in a panic because I knew that every word she had said was true. I didn't care that I was naked and beat. I knew that the worst was yet to come.

I waited until I heard her go into the restroom and took my opportunity to run as fast as I could out of the house. I grabbed a towel from the guest bathroom, wrapped it around me and made my way to the garage as quickly and quietly as I could, shutting the garage door quietly behind me. My hands shook uncontrollably as I found my bicycle and snuck my way out of the back door of the closed garage.

I took one step on the pedal when I got to the driveway and pedaled out of there as fast as I could. Like the wind, I made my way to my best friend's house. I knew I would be safe at Robbie's, as I had told him of the many relentless beatings we had suffered and he offered his house in an emergency. In my mind, this was an emergency enough.

I hid in his basement for a period of three days and was forced to leave because he knew his mom would figure something out with missing food and so on. I went to the only other place that I knew and that was to my babysitter's house, Mrs. Thill. She did not know what was going on but I felt I could trust her. We always stayed at her house when my parents flew overseas for vacation. She was my only shot at safety. I ran across town taking side streets so that I wouldn't be seen.

When I got to her house, I was greeted with concern. She had not known that my parents were abusive until she saw the little pin dots of blood in my scalp from my hair being pulled. She saw the razor-like scabs under my arms where I had been grabbed by sharp fingernails. She tenderly felt the swelling at the back of my head from having it banged furiously on a cement threshold.

I had only known this portly lady as my babysitter. I did not know that she worked for the Department of Social Services. I learned this when she began taking Polaroid pictures of my multiple wounds. It was not long afterwards, after an endless number of interviews with strangers at the Department of Social Services, did I learn that I would be taking my parents to court.

The State kept me hidden for a few months before the impending trial. I was never so scared and full of doubt in my life. I didn't know whom to believe and I no longer had anyone that I could trust implicitly. I was determined to prove that what my parents were doing was wrong. The many other times I had run away were from being scared and had yielded no results. The police had brought me home and my priest had brought me home back to the same environment, even after hearing my terrifying stories of abuse. This time would be different. Someone was going to die unless someone spoke up. The secret needed to be out so that it would stop.

The much anticipated court day arrived. I was dressed in a suit and escorted into the courtroom by Mrs. Thill. I saw my parents standing with my brother and sister and my father had a sinister and angered look on his face. My brother and sister looked scared. Two lawyers chatted under their breath with my father as I waited for court to start.

It seemed hours later when a uniformed officer approached me and asked me to come to the Judge's chambers. I looked at Mrs. Thill and she nodded that I should follow the officer. I followed him to the Judge's chambers.

A large man sat behind a desk as I sat in a maroon leather chair facing him. The leather squeaked as I sat down.

The Judge looked up from his paperwork and took off his glasses. He rubbed under his eyes and then looked through the lenses to see their clarity. I watched as he pulled out a handkerchief and blew steam onto the glass. He started rubbing furiously. He looked through the lenses again and, satisfied, he put them back on his nose. He looked over the rims and across the desk at me and asked a question.

"Do you know what perjury is?" he asked.

"Yes," I answered.

"What is it?"

"It's lying, Sir," I answered.

"Son, I know what it's like to be fourteen. We all lie at that age to get what we want. You have levied charges against a man who couldn't possibly do what you've said he's done. In that, for the commission of perjury, you will be sentenced to a juvenile delinquency home for a period of one year," he said picking up his phone.

I remember being speechless and even more surprised when a police officer came into the Judge's chambers to place me in handcuffs. I was escorted outside and kept my eyes to the ground as I was placed in a police car. I tried not to cry but couldn't help it.

It was peculiar that the ensuing summer would be the best of my childhood.

I watched my dog get into various amounts of dog trouble with other dogs as I let my mind remember a period a long time ago.

I don't remember the beating as much anymore and I think little of my juvenile home sentence. What I do remember is feeling that justice was denied and I could do nothing about it.

Today I realized that I no longer had to carry my head in shame. It was not a badge of honor to be abused but rather a mark of the strength of my desire to survive despite the worst of circumstances. I had learned from Dr. Conte that exploration at that age was okay. That it was natural. I had also learned that the impact of the abuse we suffered stretched far into adulthood and my alcoholism was shrapnel damage from an abusive environment. I had learned that I had been brain-damaged psychologically and it was understandable.

I thought about the trial and why it seemed important that I learn something from it. I thought of my position as a juror and how we were asked to decide the fate of Marissa based on factors that mitigated the cruelness of her crime. What were those factors that somehow made the cruelness of her crime less?

Suddenly, I realized that this was the same situation I was in with my remaining parent. I had been waiting for over thirty years for someone to call to re-unite and I realized with stunning clarity that it was never going to happen. I realized that I had a choice to make. I had to choose whether I wanted a relationship with my mother or not should that opportunity arise. By her telling me I was no longer welcome home was her still exercising control. The doctors on the stand had said that control and abuse go together.

I thought that if Marissa were convicted of murder, I would never consider having a relationship with her. I wouldn't consider it because she's a criminal.

My parents were guilty of 'aggravated child abuse with malice', a criminal act, repeated over multiple occasions, and it made my parents criminals just as Marissa was a criminal. Although never convicted for it, I know the truth and that makes them criminals. It was clear that once this was looked at in legal terms, I was under no obligation to have a relationship with my mother.

If I were to answer the question about having a relationship with my mother, I would have to balance those factors that made the cruelness of what they had done to us and those factors that may have caused her to be cruel.

I pulled out a pen and some paper from my dog bag. I do not know where it came from except to say that forty years seemed to come together in one fell swoop. As I wrote, I cried. As each stroke of the pen scribbled onto the paper, it was as if I was tearing away at the cloth that had covered my shame. It was the first time that I felt the understanding of the truth setting one free.

"Dear Mother,

I am writing this as the oldest brother to my sisters, Susan and Louise and my brother, Larry. I am also writing this for all children, no matter the age, who may have found themselves in a similar situation.

I want to thank you for giving me this precious thing called life. I want to thank you for clothing us, feeding us and keeping a dry roof over our heads. I want to thank you for readying us for school and helping us to tie our shoelaces. I want to thank you for giving us a moral compass.

And...these thirty five years have taught me that family is the most important thing in life.

I forgive you for allowing domestic violence in our home. I remember the day clearly when it first arrived on a spring day in 1971 or 1972. We had just returned from church and I was 10, Larry and Louise were 8 and Susan was 7 years old. A sponge got trapped in the washtub in the laundry room and, since Larry and I had just washed our hands there, we were responsible for the flooding that occurred from the water coming from the washing machine.

I forgive you for allowing our father to beat us for hours while cleaning up. I forgive you for keeping us out of school to hide the markings of our injuries. I forgive you for the many hours that you spent putting make-up on each of us so the teachers would not know. I forgive you for the notes you gave our gym teachers saying that we had a medical condition when you wanted no one to see the bruises on our bodies.

I forgive you and my father for the beatings you rained down on Louise beginning when she was only eight under the premise that she would not learn, or Dad lost his temper, or that we were having financial problems or that Daddy drank too much.

I forgive you for hitting Louise with a metal Spray 'N Wash can and cutting her head open. I forgive you for lying to the doctor, telling him that Larry had hit her with a rubber thong. I forgive you for removing her head bandages on the drive home because she looked like a 'nincompoop' and you did not want dad to know.

I forgive you for putting Louise in an institution for the developmentally disabled, when she is really a victim of prolonged and severe aggravated child abuse with malice.

I forgive you for putting your oldest son in a position where he was forced to take his parents to court for child abuse in 1976 at the age of fourteen. He did this because he believed the abuse would inevitably have led to the death of himself or one of his brothers and sisters. I forgive you for making my brothers and sisters clean a child's blood out of the back seat of your car before you went to court so that no suspicion would be aroused. I forgive you for lying to Social Services, the Police Department, the prosecutor, your defense attorneys and the Judge when you were asked if you had ever hit or abused us. I forgive you for saying you never laid a finger on us. I forgive you for watching me being led out of court in handcuffs to serve a sentence of one year in a juvenile delinquency home for perjury, a crime I did not commit.

I forgive you for repeatedly telling myself and my brother and sisters that you wished we had never been born and that we were lying, cheating, bratty kids that would never amount to anything.

I forgive you for 1987. I was twenty-six years old when I learned that my father was dying of colon cancer. I spent that night writing you an eight-page letter and told you I was ashamed for what I had done. I had been wrong and I wanted to come home. I forgive you for writing me back and saying that Larry and I were no longer welcome in the family, and we were not to have any contact with 'your' family. I forgive you for allowing my father to die and denying us the opportunity to make our peace.

If I were to search for the good in all of this, I would get a simple message to all families:

1) Your children are a special gift from God and you are their caretaker and protector until they find what God put them on this earth for.

2) The line between discipline and abuse is very thin. If you hit a child and it leaves a mark, it is 'child abuse'. If you hit a child with an object such as a belt, broomstick, paddle or the branches from a Weeping Willow tree and it leaves a mark: It is considered 'aggravated child abuse'. If you hit a child with an object and it is prolonged or it is done with the intent to cause great bodily harm, it is called 'aggravated child abuse with malice' and one can be sentenced to prison for twenty years.

3) Domestic Violence is progressive like alcoholism. Once in, it will only get worse. It will sneak in under the premise that "Daddy had a long day", "I drank too much", "Mommy has too much pressure" or "We just want the best for you". The road to hell is paved with good intentions. There should never be a reason to hit a child, pull their hair, yank their arms, kick them or speak to them in any way that can cause psychological damage. The physical injuries may heal but the soul of a child never forgets. Yield good will and good results will follow.

4) The three most important words a human being can say to another: "I love you." Don't forget to tell your children every day.

I remember the first day that domestic violence came into our home. I also remember the walk we took together at Wall Lake in Detroit. Our bodies were sore from a beating that had lasted the better part of the afternoon. You and my father made a promise that it would never happen again. But, it did and the promise was broken.

I will always love you, Mother.

You have lost your right to be in a relationship with me, and now I choose not to have a relationship with you.

May God be with you always.

Your son, Paul"

I felt the weight of shame lift. It lifted from deep in my chest. Although I was sad that a child must say this to their parent, I felt better for the strength I did not know I had inside.

I wondered if the children of the murderess, Marissa DeVault, might find that a similar letter may free them from the pain they must surely feel.

A juror learns throughout the long process of a trial like this that there are many times that all will not agree on the path they took to a decision. My path can be traced back to the Voir Dire questionnaire, given when we first were called for jury selection and I realized how important that question on domestic violence would be. One cannot reach a decision without referencing one's personal history as it may apply to a case.

We all get there in our own way.

I made my decision based on the childhood and sexual abuse Marissa suffered, with a large emphasis on the sexual abuse from the same age that I had experienced my trauma. I think she was set up for failure from a very young age.

I made my decision because I knew the children could never grow until they found resolution.

Yet, no matter what path I took in making this decision, I realized there were all the reasons in the world to give Marissa life in prison but there weren't enough reasons to give her death.

I think everyone's point of convergence begins with childhood and it begins the first time that we make a decision to hit a child...that kind of psychological brain damage can be irreparable.

I will vote for life in prison and the children are only a part of the reason. In the end, I suppose they are reason enough. The cycle of violence needs to stop.

I realized why the defense had wanted me from the beginning and it wasn't for the reason I expected.

I pressed my clothes for tomorrow remembering it might be our last day. I selected a long sleeve Ralph Lauren Blake shirt and matched it with a Jerry Garcia tie, ensuring the color logo of the horse matched the tie. I had worn a different Jerry Garcia tie every day for court and new any tie I chose might be the last.

"Desert Storm" was my selection for the colors that matched shirt, pants and shoes.

It was appropriate for the day.

HANG 'EM HIGH

"I concede," Cherie said in defeat. "I've had six days to think about it and I finally concede."

"Are you conceding because ten of us voted for life or are you conceding for your own reasons?" Wings asked.

"I think all of you got me thinking that I should look at my vote more carefully," Cherie said. "Personally, I think she did it maliciously and planned it which we all agreed on. The problem I'm having is all the things we couldn't see. For instance, we weren't allowed to see 349.001, she said numerically, but we were allowed to hear that it was some sort of diary by Allen. We don't know what it said. The other thing that bothers me is the motive. The prosecution said it was done for money but we couldn't find that to be true."

"We don't know the real motive," Victoria volunteered. "We only know she beat him to death."

"That bothers me," she reiterated. "It also bothers me that we don't know where a quarter of a million dollars is. Did it ever exist?" she asked.

"The only person that says it exists is Allen Flores," Parker said. "We know his word isn't worth the paper it's printed on."

"I think Stan knows a lot more than he's letting on to," Doc said.

"I agree with that. He only remembers what is helpful to him."

"I think the mother not coming in to speak in her daughter's defense speaks volumes. There are secrets in there that we'll never know," Althea said.

"Why don't we vote again?" Jeebs offered. "It sounds like we're all the same page and I'd rather not be here until next July."

All of us agreed that we were ready and the six days off had done a lot of good in allowing the question of life or death to ferment in our minds. Cherie passed around a basket and we each dropped in our votes.

One person voted for death while the rest of us voted for life. Sighs of discontent could be heard.

"Let's just submit that and see what the Judge says,' Jeebs said.

"He's just going to send us back here," I offered.

"I voted for death," Butthead volunteered.

"If it's okay with you, can I ask why?" Cherie asked.

"I don't think she was abused and I don't think it had anything to do with her killing him," he said.

"Okay," Cherie said in agreement. "Are your feet firmly planted in the ground? Can we still talk about it?"

"We could talk about it," Butthead acquiesced. "I'm just not making the connection and willing to hear more about it."

More sighs of frustration could be heard and Cherie reacted by going over to the bookshelf where we had the rubber spiny balls and Silly Putty. She gathered them off the shelf and put them in the center of the table.

"Folks, we are almost at the end of the line and we've been here before. Play with the Silly Putty and keep your hands busy. Let the process work itself out, and if Butthead needs to see or hear from us, then he has that right. This is a difficult decision and we need to be fair to everyone involved. We need to try and not be a hung jury if at all possible."

"I don't want to put another jury through this," Annie said. "I think it's only right to try to come to an agreement we can all live with. If it means a couple more days then count me in."

"I appreciate it," Butthead said.

"You don't have to agree on the abuse," Parker said to Butthead. "We all got there in our own way and you don't have to have the same reasons I do."

"Can I ask what reasons you have?" Butthead asked.

"Primarily, it's because the prosecution case didn't hold water when it came to motive. I'm also unclear as to what exactly happened that night. The prosecution should have painted a better picture."

"I agree," Butthead said.

Doc was making a Silly Putty hammer with her hands. I gave her a dirty look.

She mouthed back that she was sorry.

"Consider looking at this like computer code," Parker said. "If you create a code, all the symbols must be in the correct place for the code to work. If this case were like coding for computers, you would get a faulty program because the base root is missing pieces."

"It's not the same thing," Butthead said.

"It kind of is the same thing. How can we put someone to death if we don't understand exactly what happened? We know it was supposed to be a gun used and then it wasn't. We have a witness who was standing two feet from her and he doesn't know what happened. We also have a creep who says he predicted the murder but we can't trust a word he says. All we have is victim and a bunch of spotty questions as to what really happened. I don't think we're excusing her by giving her a life sentence."

"I hear you but I'm not sold, yet" Butthead said.

"That's fine," Cherie interjected. "Let's just talk about the case and let everyone think about their decision."

She had a great handle on things in the jury room. She knew that we could not force Butthead to come to a decision and we had to treat the matter delicately. The best we could do was to talk and discuss without pressuring him. The last thing anyone wanted to do was to get him more firmly planted in his decision.

The conversation flowed as we spent the afternoon looking at the case and our experience. Much of the reason that many of us could not vote for death, were the blank holes in the case. It begged for a smoking gun and we could not find it. The question of spending money was at the top of the list making the prosecution case somewhat weak because it only raised a shadow of a doubt in why she had committed the murder.

We ran the case in circles on the jury room table while many of us squeezed Silly Putty into funny shapes after already having made our decision. Each of the eleven of us had reached our decision in our own way and I'm sure, when compared, the reasoning would be different to each.

We had balanced mitigating circumstances against aggravating circumstances and the scale leaned toward mitigating factors with the most powerful being that of the fate of her children. Maybe we wished that the decision had been easier, or maybe we thought of Dale and the awful way in which he had died. Perhaps we thought that after the filtration process of the court system, what was left was murky enough to go against death.

All of us agreed that there was going to be no happy ending for anyone. The best we could do was to find as pure a justice as we could after reviewing the facts and shady characters involved.

It occurred to me that there could be no good ending in a murder trial. There could only be lessons.

And as long as we didn't hang, I think justice would be served.

DAY 40

THE OTHER SIDE

My 'Peeps' sat on the stone bench in the smoking area of the courthouse. As usual, except for the one day court was canceled, Annie, Doc and Althea sat smoking cigarettes as I walked up. Their painted toenails and crossed legs were lined up in unison. Puffs of smoke wafted in the air headed toward the outdoor seating of 'Change of Venue' across the courtyard.

"What's up with all the people here?" I asked as I lit a cigarette. There were a lot of people hustling about, much more than normal.

"Didn't you hear?" Althea asked. Peace symbol earrings adorned her ears.

"No," I answered.

"They're doing jury selection for the Debra Milke trial."

"Who's that?" I asked. I had stayed away from the news until the

387

completion of the trial.

"She used to be on death row. They let her out because there was no record of her confession. The detective who said there was a confession has some issues."

"Apparently," I said. I sounded like Stan Cook. "Who did she kill?"

"She had a dude take her son to the desert under the ruse he was meeting Santa Claus at Christmas time and had him shot in the head," Doc said with disgust in her voice.

"Glad we're not on that one," I said taking a puff of my cigarette.

A short time later, we all met in the jury room. Cherie got things started right away with a polling of the jury. We each held our breath as we decided a polling of raised hands would work instead of using sheets of paper.

We looked around as hands were raised. Cherie tallied the votes on the Dry Erase board and we were relieved to see that our votes had fallen in unison.

All twelve of us voted for life in prison instead of death.

There was an immense amount of relief as Cherie completed the jury verdict form.

We rang for Sydney, submitted the form and she told us for the last time, it would take forty-five minutes for the court to assemble. Our task was finished except for the final step of telling the court formally.

The room was filled with small talk as Cherie began rolling up the many lists that had adorned the walls during deliberation. We put our jury notebooks in order on the bookshelf. I thought it such a shame that all of our notes would be incinerated.

I looked around the jury room knowing these were our last few minutes in there while the court scurried to assemble. I looked at each of the jurors that I had bonded with during the good and bad times of deliberation and knew I would miss each of them and our experience immensely. We were forever united in a decision that had come from a road of ugliness and discontent.

I would miss Ted, the Unabomber, and his carefree attitude. I remembered what it was like to be twenty-five and thought of the road ahead of him.

Doc would not be forgotten. It had taken me months to learn that she was a doctor and she never showed the air of superiority that usually accompanies being a doctor. She had been the strongest supporter of Dale and would never let us forget the cruel way in which he had died.

Wings had come to be one of my favorite jurors and I would love to be on any plane that had her as an attendant. She was strong and firm in her moral beliefs and I could tell she was a great mother. It still made me laugh that she had hit her husband with a telephone book and how critical an experience that had been during deliberations.

She told me to quit smoking. I promised her I would.

Parker folded his tablet closed with the Spiderman cover. It had taken me the longest time to come to know him. He had been quiet for much of the deliberations but when he said something, it usually stuck. He was always the man who could say that a piece of evidence could be looked at or not. He was the counterpart to my imagination and was always seated in the facts of the case, regardless of who presented it. I was jealous of his balance but not jealous of his collection of ninety-three pairs of shoes.

Jeebs was putting the toys away on the bookshelf saying they would be valuable for the next jury. He had always had the capability to make me smile no matter the circumstance. I wished him luck in having a child as he and his wife had been trying for seventeen months.

"It's not hard work," he said with a mischievous smile.

I was proud to work with Victoria who had begun as a shy juror, and proud that she had lost over one hundred pounds prior to the trial. One could see her confidence grow every day, as she became part of this special group of people. I would miss the soft glint in her eye and her infectious laugh.

I would never forget Sunny who had the guts to stand up and speak of the abuse she went through with her husband. I remember her saying that thirty-five years ago she had called the police during an intense beating only to be told that the police would not come unless she had filed for divorce. I admired her strength in surviving and moving on. She was content in her retirement by relaxing at the pool everyday working on her tan. I wondered if her kids would make her get another job.

One couldn't think of Sunny without thinking of Annie who was blessed with a family that never gave her peace. She would often joke that she would stay at a local motel just to get some alone time. I think she knew how lucky she was. She was a survivor as well and I would go on an RV trip with her anytime.

I wasn't sure if I would miss Butthead but I knew I would. He was a loud obnoxious individual and I respected his wife for having been married to him for thirty-five years. It showed a lot about her patience and character. I now knew why he introduced himself as 'Butthead' the first time we met and it made me smile.

The person I would miss the most was Cherie. I admired her strength and ability to rein us in when we got off track. I admired her organization and ability to keep an open mind during a highly difficult deliberation process. I admired her ability to look past emotion and at the facts. Most of all, her strength was in her incessant energy and I respected that.

We were called into the jury box for the last time.

Marissa DeVault was seated with her defense team in a packed courtroom. The camera zoomed in on the Judge's assistant who read the decision after receiving the jury verdict form from Cherie.

We sat in silence as the Judge read the form and gave it to his assistant. I looked at Marissa whose face was devoid of emotion.

"We, the jury, duly empanelled by the State of Arizona, do recommend a life sentence for the defendant, Marissa DeVault, on April 30, 2014..."

The defense team asked that we be polled and each of us gave our affirmative response that this was our vote by individual. I looked at Marissa and could detect a tone of relief as she nodded her head.

I never looked at her again knowing that, in all probability; she may very well have deserved the ultimate punishment. But, we could only decide based on what we were given. I wondered what we weren't allowed to see.

In moments, we were thanked by Judge Steinle III and dismissed to the jury room for the final time. We were free to leave unless we wanted to speak with the Judge and attorneys after the case. They would visit us in the jury room.

Cherie was organizing her things and she was visibly upset. Her hands were shaking.

"What's wrong?" I asked.

"I thought we were voting for life in prison. I didn't know that she would be paroled in twenty-five years."

"The Judge might decide she gets life without parole," I said.

"I hope so," she said. "If I had known we were voting for parole, I may have made a different decision."

I understood her dilemma but wasn't sure that it would have made a difference. I am comfortable in saying that we didn't remember this subtle but important difference in our decision.

There was relief in the room as we waited for the court actors to come into the room. There was also excitement in that we might be able to get answers for things still left open. I still had some questions that I would love the answer on.

A short time later, after we had tidied up the jury room for the next jury that was sure to come, the defense team, prosecution team and Judge Steinle III appeared in the jury room. It was amazing how many questions there were. We felt like a paparazzi hounding a famous movie star.

"What was evidence number 349.001?" Parker asked.

Mr. Basta answered saying that it was Allen Flores' diary that he had begun in December, weeks before the attack. It had not been allowed because it was too speculative.

"I wanted to ask about the magic shorts," I said with a raised hand. "I thought we could see how she pulled them off and why Dale ended up on the floor the way he did. There was a shin burn on his legs. Why didn't you go into more detail and do you think that's what happened?"

Michelle Arino, the Assistant District Attorney chose to answer. "We suspect that's what happened but we couldn't prove it."

"Dang," I said. I thought it was a pretty good argument a long time ago.

"Detective Bishop?" Annie asked. "Did you really look for 'Eddie' in California and find that no one was named Eddie in California?" in reference to an abuser Marissa claimed she knew.

Detective Bishop blushed remembering the testimony from near the end of the trial when the prosecution said they had tried to look up Marissa's child sex abuser. "Well," he said, "it was all we had. I called an old friend in the police department and he knew of no sex abusers named Eddie."

"It looked like you were grabbing at straws," Althea commented.

"That was the problem with the case," Mr. Basta volunteered. "No matter what road we went down, we would discover lies, inaccuracies and dead ends. It didn't help that the family was completely dysfunctional."

"What happens to the kids?" Sunny asked with concern.

Mr. Tavasoli grappled that question for a moment. "I believe they are going to be okay. CPS, or an organization similar to it, monitors their safety. They live up north and seem to be doing very well."

"That's good," Sunny commented.

"What about Stan and Allen?" Ted asked. "What happens to them?"

"They did what they were supposed to do. We didn't have enough to file charges on either of them even though we know they were implicitly involved."

"So, they're free to do what they want?" Ted asked.

"Yes," Mr. Basta answered. "Unless they get in trouble again, they won't be hearing from us."

"What are the chances that Marissa will get life in prison with no parole?" Cherie asked.

Mr. Basta answered. "Usually, cases like this end up as twenty-years before first parole hearing. It doesn't mean that she'll get out on it, though."

"I wish somebody had been clearer on this prior to deliberation. It bothers me that she gets parole. If I had known that, maybe we would have voted differently," Cherie said.

"I'm sorry the system works that way, too," Mr. Basta answered reassuringly. "I still think you all did an exemplary job."

"What club was Marissa stripping at?" Jeebs asked.

"Do you want to go there?" Mr. Basta answered smiling.

"No, I'm serious. Was it Cheetah's?"

"It was a place called Knockers. You can get the address from me when we finish," Mr. Basta said jokingly.

Annie raised her hand and directed her attention toward Mr. Basta. "What happens to the insurance money?"

"The insurance money is with the court and will eventually go to the kids. Marissa won't see any of it."

"Thank God," Victoria volunteered.

"Speaking of money," I interjected, "why didn't we see where she spent it? Why didn't we see her bank accounts?"

"They couldn't be released due to privacy concerns and we couldn't get hold of her bank records. She had a couple cars but we could not find them. We're sure she got money from Allen but we had a hard time with that piece," Mr. Basta said.

"That's why we couldn't find on the pecuniary segment of the trial," I offered.

Mr. Basta nodded his head. He understood.

"How come you never used the gavel?" Ted asked Judge Steinle.

The Judge laughed. "I have a loud enough voice that I don't need the gavel."

Mr. Tavasoli looked at us and asked if those who had lost their jobs were okay.

I responded, "I'm now the best employee they have," I said, smiling.

"Me, too," Althea said.

"It's surprising what a little phone call from me can do," Judge Steinle III volunteered.

"We had an investigator ready to go to your place of work and shake things up," Detective Bishop said.

I was happy it hadn't gone that far.

"How come Marissa was drawing pictures during the trial?" I asked Andrew Clemency who usually sat next to her during court.

The mitigation specialist, Pamela Mudryj, spoke up. "We had to! She kept asking questions and making comments during testimony and we had to give her something to do. We didn't want her making her situation worse."

"Oh, good," I said. "It looked like disdain for the process. I was wondering why you weren't stopping her."

We were asking questions and jurors were slipping out of the room one by one. We were able to shake hands as they disappeared into the annals of the courthouse and stepped into the hot afternoon sun, decision made and commitment complete.

I had a burning question and finally asked when the questions slowed to a pause.

"This has been a truly educating and amazing experience," I said. "May I write a book about this, especially if it puts the court system in a good light?"

"Absolutely," Judge Steinle III answered. "You are free to speak or write about anything in the trial. If it teaches lawyers how to behave, then I'm all for it," he said with a laugh.

I was relieved and excited at the same because this is why I wanted to be on the trial. Courtrooms are about secrets. Lawyers carry secrets as well as judges. The defendant always has a secret and I was no different. I think I got a couple funny looks from fellow jurors.

I couldn't tell anyone of the project I had endeavored upon. I couldn't tell them because it may have biased them. What if they wanted to be a big star in my book? What if they didn't reveal their true feelings thinking that I would record them? Would it have been fair to the defendant and her right to a fair and unbiased trial? Would it have been fair to the victim and his family?

I watched a couple more jurors leave as Sydney checked that they left their notebooks and she took their juror badges.

This piece had been written to see how much I might change by the end of the trial, and because I hoped something good could be found in something as awful and cruel as Dale's death. I wrote it to discover what I would probably never see again, what it looked like through the eyes of a juror. I was pretty sure that after a trial like this, I would never be selected as a juror again. I knew too much.

I had changed in imperceptible ways to the common eye. Something had changed in my soul. I realized that what I thought in the beginning was not the same as I thought now. I saw what child abuse was and how the trial connected it to my own life through this experience. I realized that as a child, I did what I could to protect myself and my brothers and sisters. I learned that what I had done was not wrong. I also learned that people make mistakes, and sometimes those mistakes are taken to their grave.

I learned that we must forgive ourselves and we must forgive our parents. No one is perfect and there is no handbook on how to raise children. We make mistakes, we forgive and we move on to grow.

I felt a sense of strength and rehabilitation. It was if my soul had been cleaned and was ready to be bared to the world. I would walk with my head high and be grateful for every day I had on this earth.

"One more question," Jeebs asked while we were getting up to follow the other jurors out. "Where did that bump come from on your forehead?" he asked of Mr. Basta.

He laughed touching the bump over his left eye on his forehead. "I was hit by the chrome bumper of a '73 Cadillac when I was seven years old" he said.

"Did you get any brain damage from that?"

"I hope not," Mr. Basta said.

I thought it ironic that the only person with apparent head damage aside from Dale had been the prosecutor in this event.

The remainder of us hugged each other in the lobby of the courthouse and stepped into the afternoon sun. We felt free and content having shed the burden that had overwhelmed our minds over the prior three or four months.

Justice is whatever is left over after the filtration of evidence.

I paused to smoke a final cigarette in the courtyard overlooking the "Change of Venue". I saw jurors scurrying about with their laminated numbers in hand. They were rookies and I wished I could give them advice.

I would tell them to show up on time every day with an expectation to work. I would suggest that they dress appropriately given the decisions they were about to make. I would tell them that their job was to listen, follow directions and make decisions strictly within the confines of the law. I would tell them that they will be taking a journey with the victim and their hearts will be ripped out as they searched for the correct answer called justice.

Then again, I could leave them to decide as they wish because we couldn't talk to each other about what we were doing anyway.

Lady Justice wears a blindfold for a reason.

I wished them luck in my mind and walked to my car, dispatched to my life. I would make decisions and I would continue to grow. I was grateful for the experience and stepped out into the world renewed and refreshed, my heart content.

I hoped that Dale looked upon us with favor.

Final sentencing was in three weeks. The story wasn't quite over...

APOCALYPSE NOW

The drive back to the courthouse three weeks later was familiar as if I had driven it the day before. I dressed in my usual Ralph Lauren oxford shirt and complimented it with a blood red Garcia tie named "Van Gogh's Tree." The tie didn't look like a tree but did feel like a Van Gogh. I parked on the street and reached for my juror tag and realized that I had returned it to the court.

The walk from the parking garage was hot. I was grateful that the trial did not start at this time of year or the weather would have been more torturous than our meager juror pay. The walk to the courthouse had me looking for familiar jurors that were on the DeVault trial. I was saddened to see that no others were arriving for sentencing.

I went because I wanted to see this to the end. The only thing that really bothered me in the three weeks of waiting for final verdict was Cherie's feeling that we had somehow missed the mark by giving the Judge the option for twenty-five years with parole. I was on the fence because I believed there was more than one mitigating factor. I didn't believe we had enough for death and this was the only remaining option. It still nagged at me and I hoped this nagging feeling wouldn't stay with me throughout the rest of my life.

I got to the thirteenth floor and was genuinely surprised when I saw Doc, Cherie, Sunny and Wings. We hugged each other warmly in greeting. We knew the depth of our bond that was made in the process of deliberation. Each of us would remain friends until the day we died. The five of us were a little bit closer as defined by the eventual proceeding.

We walked in through the double doors of Judge Steinle's courtroom. Somehow, the five of us gathered toward a pew on the left side behind where the prosecution team normally sat. We were chattering softly between each other in greetings and being updated on each other's whereabouts during our time away when someone leaned over and told us that this side was reserved for the family of the victim.

We apologized and moved ourselves to the defendant's gallery side of the room and noticed a lot of people coming in. The media took the back row of both sides while the family of the prosecution sat on the left side.

The defendant had not been brought into the courtroom but I recognized both sets of attorneys as they filed in toward the front. Media moved about lugging cameras and laptops.

I watched the bustle and looked toward the empty jury box where we had spent so many hours seeing and hearing evidence. I looked behind me and saw someone sitting in the corner. He was sitting in the seat I had been sitting in when I had originally been called for the jury. I always thought he looked like he could have been Dale's brother.

It seemed like I was a different person after this cycle had run its course. I felt different in my soul as if I had been healed of some terrible calamity. I felt fresh, renewed and confident. I felt validated somehow.

It turns out that the man sitting in my seat of many months ago was an attorney who had just moved to Phoenix and wanted to get a feel of our court system.

I looked in the pew in front of me and realized I was looking at the backs of Dale's children, Rhiannon, Diahnon and Khiernan. Seated next to them was an old lady dressed in red. She wore a cap with her sunglasses on the cap. The lady seated next to her was Marissa's mother, Samantha Carlson. I couldn't believe it.

She didn't look like the monster that I had made her out to be in my mind. She looked like she was worried and overworked being a mother to the kids. She didn't look angry but she did look like she carried the weight of everything for a very long time.

"Nana," she said standing over the old lady in red, "you need to take your hat and sunglasses off. It's disrespectful."

All of a sudden, I realized that it was Marissa's grandmother. I couldn't remember from all Marissa's lies if she had been alive or dead and I last thought she was dead. I watched with interest.

"I'm not taking my hat off," she answered in crackly and stubborn voice.

"You have to," Marissa's mother said.

"I'm eighty-eight years old and I don't have to take my hat off for anyone," she responded.

"Nana! Just take the damn hat off now," Marissa's mother demanded.

The old lady pulled her hat off to reveal silver hair with her hair showing baldness and her hair askew. She brushed her hands through her hair and then rubbed her head as if she was shaking sawdust out. She just shook her head.

I turned my attention toward the girls seated in front of me and couldn't help thinking of the torture that we had been through when they had testified in their mother's defense. They were dressed in Easter Sunday type dresses and looked innocent and naïve to the proceedings. They whispered among each other in their ears. I remembered being that age very well and felt only a little of what might follow them for the rest of their lives.

Seated behind them, I made a curious observation. Sitting in front of me was Marissa's oldest daughter, Rhiannon. I could see the brown lace of her dress on her back. I realized that with the three of them next to each other that Rhiannon's body type was different than her two sisters. I thought of her grandmother, mother and her being born from 'one-night stands', and hoped the cycle would end.

I also wondered where all the fathers were in this family. I had only heard of a stepfather named Michael Wright and another, Dan Carlson.

The court silenced somewhat when Marissa was brought in. It was the first time we had seen her wearing stripes in the courtroom, and I felt they were deserving of her. Her hair was tied back but looked as if a stylist had worked on it. It lacked the frizziness that we had been accustomed to knowing she was taking jail showers with hard water.

A bailiff led her to the empty jury box. Our dear Sydney was not there.

Marissa DeVault's chains made noise as they were wrapped around her ankles and adorned her wrists. She sat in a jury seat and suddenly I realized that she was sitting in the very seat that I had occupied for so many months. It was almost as if I wanted to tell someone to get her out of my seat.

The court silenced as we stood for the entrance of Judge Steinle III. It was good to see him again and it's a different perspective seeing him from the gallery as opposed to seeing him from the jury box. In the jury box, he had been almost eye level and now seated in the gallery, he looked larger than life. His commanding voice announced the beginning of the proceeding.

Mr. Eric Basta walked to the podium. He set some papers down and looked at the Judge. "The State would like to present evidence of jailhouse tapes prior to the start of these proceedings. You need to hear these before you make a decision," he said confidently.

The Judge shook his head and took his glasses off. "Counselor, the trial is over. We are only here for the verdict. We are not here to hear more evidence. You should have presented that during the trial. Do you see a jury seated?" he asked.

"No but this is important for this phase," Mr. Basta defended.

I am not an attorney and don't profess to be one but I was completely surprised. Even I knew that new evidence could not be entered. On one hand, I understood that he was scrapping and clawing for the victim but this seemed wildly inappropriate.

"Are you listening, Counselor? I just said no! Now let's move on," he said firmly.

Mr. Basta shook his head and took a breath. "If that is your position, Judge, then we will have to cite you for cause. You have bullied us, and called us unprofessional, and bush league. We are none of the above and will cite for cause," he reiterated.

The Judge put his glasses on as if he were unconcerned. "Let's move on. Do you have any victim impact statements?"

Mr. Basta answered in the affirmative.

Victim impact statements were read aloud by Dale's sister, Mindi and other members of his family. The courtroom was silent and the Judge watched and listened intently to each statement.

Dale was a good man and did not deserve to die in such a manner. The victim's family had suffered terribly.

The defense began bringing up witnesses to help mitigate the judge's eventual decision. It was painful with the introduction of the three girls. They held each other as they went to the podium. Each of us fought off crying as we revisited statements that we heard prior to our final deliberation.

The youngest girl, Diahnon, could only manage to say "I want my mom" as she was led away from the podium in tears, by her other sisters.

Samantha Carlson, the mother of Marissa stepped to the podium and begged the Judge in the best way she could to go lenient on her daughter. "These kids have been through enough. We are barely hanging on. Don't take away their hope. I know she's my daughter and what she did was wrong but you have to think of the kids."

Judge Steinle III nodded and motioned for the next witness.

The mother of Marissa, Samantha Carlson, took Marissa's grandmother and led her to the podium. The grandmother looked at the Judge and then looked down as if she were searching for words. Unlike the other witnesses, she did not have a document prepared. Finally, she spoke.

"I'm eighty-eight years old and I don't have long on this earth. I know that," she said. "The damage has been done. You need to let her out to be with her family. You should let her out now so I can spend my remaining years with her."

The Judge looked at her and said, "Thank you."

The grandmother was walked away from the podium while whispers could be heard in the gallery.

The Judge nodded toward the bailiff and Marissa was escorted from her seat to the podium. She tried to wipe her eyes but couldn't quit reach the side her face due to the constraints of her handcuffs and chains.

I was looking at her and noticing her hair when I realized that it looked like Marissa's top on her jailhouse grays seemed to have a cut in the center by the neck. I could even see the tops of her breasts as she was walked to the podium. It looked like she had tried to make herself look sexy for this final moment of judgment.

The Judge adjusted his microphone, as he was about to speak.

Suddenly, a man's voice could be heard over the silence of the courtroom. It reminded me in its starkness of the time Butthead had spoken to the Judge out loud when he said he could hear them in sidebar. I felt the same kind of shock.

I looked to my left and a thin older man was speaking but I really didn't hear the words. His hair was dark with lots of gray and fell on his shoulders looking scraggly and unkempt. He was thin and frail and nobody seemed to know who it was.

"Please have this person removed from the courtroom," the Judge said to the bailiff as he motioned to the old man.

I heard someone whisper that it was Dan Carlson, Marissa's stepfather that we had heard so much about. Wasn't this the guy who told Marissa he was her father and then said he was her stepfather when she was twelve or fourteen? Wasn't he the man who allegedly sexually abused his stepdaughter?

I noticed that Marissa's mother didn't acknowledge that he existed which spoke volumes.

It was within moments that the grandmother started to speak, which shocked me more than the stepfather. "I'm glad he's dead!" she belted out.

Judge Steinle didn't have to say a word. His eyes looked at the bailiff who then made her way to the grandmother and started escorting her out. The double doors were swinging closed.

The courtroom heard the grandmother scream back to the doors, "You should have shot him with the gun when you had the chance!" The doors closed behind her.

"Does the defendant have anything to say before I reach my verdict?" the Judge asked Marissa.

I was seated in the gallery at such an angle that I could see Marissa's face in profile. I watched intently as she spoke but I didn't listen beyond the first few words.

It just took one second out of all the months spent with this trial to discover something in the defendant that I had not witnessed before. I am the only juror who detected something in that moment that couldn't be seen unless one was at the right angle. I was at the right angle and saw the change.

She had walked to the podium and looked at her daughters with longing and with a mother's love. But, the moment she started to speak, her face twisted into the same face that she had shown the jury during her allocution statement."

It was the face of torturous pain and grief. It was the face that she had shown us and many of us mistook for honesty.

It was an act, just like the 911 calls in the beginning.

How could I have been so naïve? How did I miss it? How did I not realize that she had five years to practice her allocution 'performance'? It was the same face and the same words that she used for the Judge.

I thought of the prosecution referring to her name as DeVault and the defense referring to her as 'DeVwah".

She was in the prime of her manipulation but her act had been exposed.

I understood in those moments why Cherie had been upset. I felt like I had been duped and hoodwinked. She had tricked us in her performance and I knew that I would spend the next forever of my life living with a decision based on an act.

She spoke of wishing she could turn back the tape and of healthier choices she could have made, but I was torturing myself over being tricked.

Her pleas fell flat in the courtroom.

"I have spent many months thinking about this decision. I have seen the evidence and I have seen the behavior over the last five years of this defendant while she has been incarcerated," Judge

Steinle III said with firmness in his voice. "The jury found premeditation as well as exceptional cruelness in this crime. But the children continue to be an issue in this matter and this is the court's concern. What to do about the children is of great concern," he said as looked at the three girls seated in front of me.

The Judge was as concerned about the girls as we had been and I knew that because of that, he would levy a twenty-five year life term with a chance at parole. I knew it but I wasn't happy about it given my observation of her acting abilities.

"It is for the children that we will close this chapter," Judge Steinle III said. "I have watched you manipulate these children into saying whatever you need without regard to their health and safety. I told you that I was adamant that I did not want these children on the stand and you manipulated them into testifying. Well, there will be no more manipulation."

The Judge paused and then continued. "I have seen your behavior and I have no seen no sign of remorse throughout your incarceration without even mentioning the trial. You have no remorse for the cruel act that you committed."

At that moment, I knew the pendulum was swinging the other way. One could have heard a pin drop in the courtroom.

"It is this court's decision that Marissa Suzanne DeVault be sentenced to life in prison and for the cruelness of the crime of which she was convicted of, she shall serve without the possibility of parole."

I fist pumped in my lap not wanting to make a disturbance but I felt that the decision was right on the money. She didn't deserve parole and she was lucky to have not received the death penalty.

The gallery watched as Marissa was unceremoniously fingerprinted at the center of the courtroom. Justice had been served warmly and we saw it with each roll of her fingers.

The hearing closed with the courtroom being generally pleased with the results and very upbeat. I watched Dale's family members on the other side of the courtroom as they hugged each other.

The convicted murderer's mother corralled the girls in front of me. I was surprised that they were not crying at the fact that their mother had been sent away for life. It was as if they had already known what would happen and expected the result. They busied themselves gathering their things and I realized that none of them had ever made an attempt to contact their mother. They had lost their mother the moment that the defendant had bludgeoned a hammer into her husband's head at least five times.

They had a chance to have good lives. The insurance money would be a minor Band-Aid to the therapy that they would need over the years. I hoped they always had someone to love them and hoped they would have great and fruitful lives.

They were victims just as Dale was a victim.

I felt most for his twin sister, Mindi. I watched as she hugged family and friends after the verdict and I wanted to hug her as well. There must be terrible pain in having your biological twin taken from you in such a manner. I respected her strength.

I was waiting while the courtroom began dispersing when a young lady tapped me on the shoulder. I turned around and recognized her as a young lady that I had seen in the gallery during the length of the trial. She had been there every day, sometimes sitting on one side and sometimes sitting on the other. She was sitting in the media row.

"I would love to hear from a juror," she said. "I'm with the show "Trial Diaries" and I was hoping to sit down with you and get your viewpoint," she said.

"It depends," I answered as I shook her hand.

"What does it depend upon?" she asked.

"What did she do with the money?" I asked.

"Funny you should ask that," she answered. "I think she spent it at the casino. If you remember Allen Flores' ledger, there were some loans for her to go to the casino. Now, here's what I think about Travis Tatro..." she said as we walked out the courtroom doors.

I followed behind her and saw folks gathered in the hallway. I wanted to say something to the family but wasn't sure what to say. I suppose my words had been spoken in the deliberation room and really that was all that needed to be said. The Judge had bailed me out of a lifetime of worrying that we might have made the wrong decision and justice had been served in Dale's name.

"Did you say Travis Tatro?" Eric Basta asked as we walked into the hallway.

"We were just getting started on that," I said.

"Let me show you something," he said as he pulled his handcart to a stop. He reached into a file folder that was in something looking like a milk crate, and removed an eight and a half by eleven sheet of paper. It was a picture.

The picture was taken in 2002 and was taken at a Halloween function. Maybe it was a picture from the strip club back in the Reesy cup days.

Travis was dressed all in black and he was dressed as the devil. His eyes were red from the way the camera took the picture. The teeth of his smile glared proudly while Marissa was wrapped around his leg just below his waist. She was wearing a black lace and satin body suit while her reddened eyes looked lovingly up toward the devil. Her mouth was open with her tongue stuck out, while she embraced her future hit man's leg.

It looked prophetically creepy knowing what I knew now. I remembered her smile and how inappropriate it was the first day that I laid eyes on her.

"One more thing," Mr. Basta said as he reached into his bag. "I think you wanted to see this."

He pulled out a packet of papers and handed them to me. It was evidence number 349.001. I couldn't believe it. I read it voraciously with my eyes widening as I went along.

"This is what we were looking for all during deliberations," I said, surprise in my voice. "Why didn't we get to see this?" I asked.

"We couldn't get it admitted. It was too prejudicial," he said calmly. He had still won the case.

Eric gave me an extra copy.

We saw the Judge and the jurors gathered around him as if he were a rock star. We said we would miss his courtroom and sense of humor. He didn't a have a sense of humor in court and he saw the humor in that.

"I'm so glad you gave her that sentence," I said. "We thought we had made the wrong decision for a moment."

"You made the right decision," he said. "I gave her the best decision for all concerned. This closes the book on the trial. Let's face it if we had given her death, it would have been overturned for one reason or another. They don't even make the lethal injection drug anymore. Did you know that seventy percent of all death penalty cases are overturned?"

"Really," Cherie said.

"Did you know that a death penalty case now costs the taxpayer over twenty million dollars?"

"That's ridiculous," Sunny offered.

"This was best for the kids. She can no longer manipulate them. If they want to see her, then they see her on their terms. This was best to protect them."

"I'm glad you did that. I feel like we can sleep at night," Wings said.

"Do you know what the chance is that a life sentence will be overturned?" he asked.

"Fifty percent," I volunteered, having no idea what I was talking about.

"One percent," Judge Steinle III responded.

We shook his hand and felt like we were parting from a father.

People were dispersing quickly when Jen from the Trial Diaries show grabbed me as we headed toward the elevator. She was the only reporter that had been at the trial every day.

I had always guessed she was Monica Lindstrom. She looked like what Monica Lindstrom might look like, I suppose. I had only heard her on the radio and I hadn't heard from her in five months.

"Do you still want to talk about the case?" she asked.

"Can we talk 'off the record'?" I asked her.

"Do you mean just talk?"

"It's been almost five months since I've been able to talk about this case. Let's go get a cup of coffee," I said. "It would be nice to talk with someone about it. Besides, I would like to read this document 'Something Odd Going On'."

I really did feel like a different person when I walked out the courtroom that day. I do not know if it was the repair of a wound I had sustained many years ago in the 1970's. I felt like I could hold my head high even after having been a whistleblower in the 1980's. Something in my heart had changed, and confidence seemed to overshadow all the insecurities held in my heart and soul over the years.

I had done the best I could with fifteen others in a most difficult and heart wrenching case. In a story where no ending could be happy or good, there was only justice to soften the pain. This was the only 'best scenario' possible given the most horrific of circumstances.

In my heart, I knew there were eleven other people who would always be there, bonded by decision and sacrifice. We were bonded by the images of Dale that would be with us to the end of our days. We were bonded by the sacrifice. Mostly, we were bonded in the knowledge that justice had been served and we gave everything of ourselves in that decision.

I knew each of us would be able to sleep at night.

Jen looked at her watch. Then she looked at her iPhone. "I suppose a cup of coffee would be nice," she said.

"I always thought you were Monica Lindstrom," I said. She laughed and laughed even more when I suggested the Change of Venue.

We took the elevators down and made our way to a Starbucks and sat at a patio table in the shadow of justice, that of the thirteen-story Superior Court building. We sipped coffee and shared a hundred stories and observations. We were able to laugh and I recognized that as something that I had almost forgotten in the prior five months.

Words and speculation flowed from me like a river. Guesses were made and answers searched for in those three hours. Murder is a strange thing to have in common.

I read the document, 'Something Odd Going On', one more time.

"Do you think Allen Flores was a co-conspirator?" Jen asked me.

I thought about it for a moment. "I think his crime was in not reporting what he thought was going to happen. He knew that Dale was going to be killed and did nothing about it. I think Allen's world was a manifestation of Marissa's lies and he didn't know if she was coming or going."

"It would only have been speculation, anyway" Jen said.

I was proud to have been a juror in the greatest justice system in the world where justice happens more often than we give it credit for. I was proud that the victim was able to speak as best as we could find. I was comforted that the family and friends of Dale Harrell might have something to hold on to. I knew that this verdict was right and just.

Part of me will always be happy that we did not sentence someone to death. I would not want to know the life of a convicted murderer as it went through the process of death, only to be regurgitated in court over and over again.

The children will know some peace in that this sentence brings a closure that the death penalty cannot provide. The death penalty raises this murder from the dead repeatedly while life in prison simply closes the door, this murderer never to walk the streets again.

Justice gave its best to say, "The brain-damage stops here."

There is a cement engraving that spans the length of the Jury Commissioner's Building. Its carving reads, "The first duty of society is justice." Its truth is there for all to see.

This experience has made me realize that the jury is the cornerstone of justice and thousands of us do it every day, in secret.

I reached into my briefcase and pulled out my manuscript and slid it over to Jen. "This is what I really think happened...."

I am proud to have been the 13th Juror.

EPILOGUE

Dear Dale,

I wanted to write you to say that I am so sorry for your death and the way you died. You did not deserve to leave this world in such a manner. I will think of you every day for the rest of my life.

I want you to know that you stood with us every day throughout the trial. Doc especially spoke for you and the justice that you deserved.

I know very little about you except that you stood five-foot-seven and weighed one hundred and fifty five pounds. I saw pictures of you in Lake Havasu with your girls and saw your black curly hair in the sun. You looked happy. Nobody could find bad words about you and the way you lived your life. I am so sorry that your life was cut short because of the woman you had married.

I imagine in my dreams that you and I meet somewhere in Arizona. We go into a dusty little bar and you order a Budweiser with a shot of Tequila. I would get a non-alcoholic Beck's beer, and share a drink with you. You are casual and friendly.

We would watch the football draft for the upcoming season and I would see your interest piqued when the Arizona Cardinals made their selection. I thought I remembered seeing some Cardinals paraphernalia in the room where you were attacked.

At some point, I would lean over and tell you that we did everything we could to get the justice you deserved, as you were the reason that twelve strangers had come together to make a decision. I would tell you that it was the best decision we could make with the evidence in front of us.

"I know," you would say lifting a Budweiser to your mouth. "I know."

I would ask you how you could have put up with your wife's antics for all those years. "Why didn't you leave her?" I would press.

You would look at me and then fiddle with the label on the bottle. "The kids," you would answer.

I think I would understand.

You would grab the car keys from your pocket and I would follow you out to your black Jeep. You would unlock the door and climb in.

I would stand there, not knowing what to say.

"You did your best," you would say shutting the door. You would accelerate the engine and drop it into drive.

I watch you as you drive away, your truck spitting gravel in my direction. Your lights disappear into the night becoming red pinpricks against the starlit sky.

I watch as a pillow of dust floats across the parking lot and into the desert night.

"You were a good man and a good father," I would think. "Your children love you."

I thought of Marissa and the life we had spared. One day, her children would come to her wanting to know the truth. They wouldn't want to hear the truth of the court. They would want to hear the truth from the mother who had brutally killed their father.

I thought that Dale would want the same thing.

The truth is what they deserved.

I will miss you, Dale, and everything that I learned from you.

Godspeed

Your friend,

Juror #13

THE END.

NATIONAL DOMESTIC VIOLENCE HOTLINE: 1-800-799-SAFE (7233)

NATIONAL CHILD ABUSE HOTLINE: 1-800-4-A-CHILD (1 800-422-4453)

Twitter: The 13th Juror MD

Facebook: Paul Sanders

The13thJurorMD.com

Also by Paul Sanders:

- "Why Not Kill Her: A Juror's Perspective – The Jodi Arias Death Penalty Retrial"
- "Banquet of Consequences: A Juror's Plight – The Carnation Murders Trial of Michele Anderson"
- "Secret of a Juror: Voir Dire - The Domestic Violence Query"

Coming TBD:

- "Beyond the Pale: Rogue Juror – The Carnation Murders Trial of Joseph McEnroe"

Made in the USA
Coppell, TX
17 August 2022

81609964R00233